The Satirical Encyclopedia of Famous Wars and Conflicts:

A Comprehensive Guide To
The Stupidity of War

ESPEN F. KJENDLIE

Encyclopedia Publishing House
www.encyclopediapublishing.com

Title: The Satirical Encyclopedia of Famous Wars And Conflicts:
A Comprehensive Guide to the Stupidity of War
Author: Espen F. Kjendlie
Publisher: Encyclopedia Publishing House
More information: www.encyclopediapublishing.com
Contact: editor@encyclopediapublishing.com

Publication Information: This book was published by Encyclopedia Publishing House in 2023 and is printed on 50lb Creme paper. Typography and Editing: The text of this book is set in Minion Pro Regular 10 for the body text and Minion Pro 14 for headings and subheadings. The typography was designed to ensure readability and visual appeal. The text of this book was edited for accuracy, clarity, and consistency. The satirical tone and humorous language were carefully crafted to highlight the stupidity of war while maintaining a respectful and informative approach.

ISBN: 978-82-693278-0-9

Cover Design: The cover design was created by Espen F. Kjendlie.

Disclaimer: The views and opinions expressed in this book are those of the author and do not necessarily reflect the views of the publisher or any other parties mentioned in the acknowledgements. The purpose of this book is to provide satirical commentary on wars and conflicts, and it is not intended to offend or disrespect any individuals or groups involved in historical events.

Contents

Introduction

War (What Is It Good For?). That Temptations song was stuck on my mind for too long. It was terrible, and I could not get rid of it.

In the end, I was too tempted. I had to find out what all the famous wars and conflicts in the world really has been good for.

So, that song is finally gone from my head after the completion of this book. Sorry if it entered yours, but I finally found out what war is good for.

If you're looking for a dry textbook full of dates and facts, you've come to the right AND wrong place. If you want to explore the thrilling, bloody, and often absurd world of human conflict, you're in for a treat.

From world wars to the civil wars, this encyclopedia covers 149 of the worst conflicts in history. Over the centuries, war and conflict have been the driving force behind our advancements as a society.

Perfectly timed for age of wokeness, this book aims to shed light on the many positive outcomes of war that history books conveniently choose to ignore. Like that impressive population control!

Forget about the destruction, loss of life, and countless tragedies that come with war. Let's focus on the real winners here: governments, corporations, and the military-industrial complex.

After all, who needs peace and stability when you can have profitable arms deals and endless power struggles?

Also, it is said the baguette was invented during one of the wars. So don't come here and say nothing great wasn't accomplished.

In this book, you will discover the many ways in which war has benefited humanity. From technological innovations like nuclear weapons to the development of new medical procedures for treating wartime injuries, war has been a true catalyst for progress.

And let's not forget about the countless modern historical landmarks that were only made possible through the destruction of entire civilizations. Who needs ancient temples and monuments anyway?

So, if you're ready to embrace the idea that war and conflict are the true drivers of human progress, then this book is for you.

Let's celebrate the many achievements that war has brought us, and forget about the pesky details like peace, diplomacy, and human rights. Who needs those when you can have bombs and bullets?

World War I

World War I was a global conflict that lasted from 1914 to 1918. It involved most of the world's major powers, organized into two opposing alliances: the Central Powers (Germany, Austria-Hungary, and the Ottoman Empire) and the Allied Powers (Great Britain, France, Russia, and later the United States).

The war started on July 28, 1914, when Austria-Hungary declared war on Serbia in response to the assassination of Archduke Franz Ferdinand of Austria-Hungary by a Serbian nationalist.

The conflict quickly spread across Europe, with Germany declaring war on Russia and France, and Britain entering the war after Germany invaded Belgium.

The war also spread beyond Europe, with Japan, Italy, and other nations joining the Allied Powers, and the Ottoman Empire and Bulgaria joining the Central Powers.

World War I was characterized by brutal trench warfare and the use of new technologies such as machine guns, artillery, and chemical weapons.

It was one of the deadliest conflicts in history, with an estimated 10 million military personnel and 7 million civilians killed as a direct result of the war.

The Treaty of Versailles, signed in 1919, officially ended the war and imposed heavy reparations on Germany, which was blamed for the conflict.

So many deaths, a lot was accomplished? Four years of bloodshed and destruction. Truly one of humanity's finest moments. Let's take a look at what the world gained from this epic clash of empires.

First and foremost, World War I brought us the end of the old order. The balance of power that had kept Europe relatively stable for decades was shattered, paving the way for a new era of conflict and turmoil. Who needs peace when you can have non-stop war?

The war also brought us some impressive technological advances. Trench warfare gave us the opportunity to really explore the potential of barbed wire and mustard gas.

And the introduction of tanks gave soldiers a new way to get stuck in the mud and get killed.

Speaking of getting killed, the war did wonders for population control. Millions of young men died in the trenches, which was really just nature's way of thinning the herd. It's not like we needed all those extra people anyway, right?

And let's not forget the positive impact the war had on the economy. The massive mobilization of resources and manpower created jobs and spurred economic growth. Of course, it also led to inflation, shortages, and widespread misery, but let's focus on the positive here.

But the real legacy of World War I was the peace that followed. The Treaty of Versailles was a masterstroke of diplomacy, designed to ensure that Europe would never again fall into conflict.

By punishing Germany so harshly and forcing them to pay massive reparations, the treaty guaranteed lasting peace and stability in the region...

Scratch that last part. It turns out that punishing a defeated enemy to the brink of economic collapse and political instability isn't a recipe for lasting peace. Who could have seen that coming?

In fact, the Treaty of Versailles set the stage for even more conflict and bloodshed.

The punishing terms of the treaty sowed the seeds of resentment and nationalism in Germany, paving the way for the rise of Hitler and the Nazi party.

And the arbitrary redrawing of borders and creation of new nations in Eastern Europe set the stage for ethnic tensions and conflicts that continue to this day. But the accomplishments doesn´t stop here!

Because the League of Nations was formed to prevent future wars!

Oh, wait. The United States, one of the major powers that could have given the League teeth, didn't even bother to join. And the League was toothless anyway, with no real power to enforce its decisions. So much for that idea.

But, we learned our lesson and never repeated the mistakes of World War I, right? Oh, wait.

The world plunged into another even more catastrophic global conflict just a few decades later. Maybe we should have paid more attention to the warning signs.

So there you have it. The Great War accomplished so much great. It brought us the end of an era, impressive technological advances, population control, and economic growth.

And it achieved the claim to fame being the first world war —impressive accomplishment!

Let's not forget the legacy of lasting peace and stability that it left behind. Yes, being the first promise a sequel. So we will just ignore the rise of Hitler, the Second World War, and the ongoing conflicts in Eastern Europe. Everything else turned out just peachy.

World War II

World War II was a global conflict that lasted from 1939 to 1945. It involved most of the world's major powers, organized into two opposing alliances: the Axis Powers (Germany, Japan, and Italy) and the Allied Powers (Great Britain, the Soviet Union, and the United States).

The war started on September 1, 1939, when Germany invaded Poland, leading Great Britain and France to declare war on Germany.

The war quickly spread across Europe, with Germany conquering much of Western Europe and the Soviet Union entering the war after being invaded by Germany.

The war also spread to Asia and the Pacific, with Japan launching a surprise attack on the United States at Pearl Harbor, Hawaii, on December 7, 1941.

The majority of casualties were from the Allied Powers, with the Soviet Union suffering the highest number of military deaths.

The war had a significant impact on the political and social landscape of the world, leading to the emergence of the United States and the Soviet Union as superpowers and the establishment of the United Nations as an international organization dedicated to maintaining peace and security.

The casualties of the war were staggering.

Over 100 million men were mobilized for military service, and an estimated 22 million military personnel died in battle or as a result of war-related injuries and diseases.

Another 28 million civilians were killed due to the war, including those who died as a result of starvation, disease, or the destruction of infrastructure.

The war ended with the unconditional surrender of Germany on May 7, 1945, and the subsequent surrender of Japan on August 15, 1945, after the United States dropped atomic bombs on the Japanese cities of Hiroshima and Nagasaki.

It also led to the creation of the Cold War, a state of political and military tension between the Western powers, led by the United States, and the Eastern powers, led by the Soviet Union.

The sequel to the smash hit known as World War I. Surely, this time around, humanity learned its lesson and ensured that the war accomplished only positive things. Let's take a look at what was achieved.

First and foremost, the war gave us some pretty cool tanks and planes. The Nazi war machine was a marvel of engineering and innovation, and the Allies weren't too shabby either.

The destruction wrought by the war also gave urban planners a blank slate to work with, as cities across Europe and Asia lay in ruins. Silver linings, people. The war also taught us some important lessons about the dangers of appeasement. The Western powers learned that it was important to stand up to aggressors and that appeasement only emboldened them.

Of course, that didn't stop the United States from cozying up to dictators like Pinochet and Saddam Hussein in the decades that followed, but at least they tried, right?

But perhaps the greatest accomplishment of World War II was the defeat of fascism. The Nazis and their allies were vanquished, and the world was once again safe for democracy. Of course, the Soviet Union emerged from the war as a superpower, but hey, no one's perfect.

And let's not forget the positive impact the war had onthe economy. Once again, the massive mobilization of resources and manpower created jobs and spurred economic growth. The post-war boom was a testament to the power of a good old-fashioned conflict to get the economy moving. Maybe we should just have wars all the time!

But the real legacy of World War II was the peace that followed. The victorious powers came together to create the United Nations, an organization dedicated to promoting peace and cooperation among nations.

The UN has been a beacon of hope and progress in the decades since the war, leading the charge on issues like human rights, climate change, and… um… well, those two things at least.

Oh, wait. Scratch that last part. It turns out that the UN is a toothless organization that can't even agree on whether to call out genocide when it's happening right in front of their faces. And the world has been plagued by countless conflicts and humanitarian crises since the end of the war. Who could have seen that coming?

But, at least we learned our lesson and never repeated the mistakes of World War II, right? Oh, wait. The world is still plagued by fascist and authoritarian regimes, and the United States elected a reality TV star as its president. Maybe we didn't learn as much as we thought.

In fact, it could be argued that the legacy of World War II is more negative than positive! And think of all the fear it created! It marked the beginning of the nuclear age, and the Cold War that followed was a constant source of tension and fear.

The war also had a profound impact on the environment, as the industrialization and destruction it unleashed set the stage for the climate crisis we face today. But hey, at least we got some cool tanks and planes out of it, right? And how about all the great war movies it helped create. That's some accomplishment!

The Vietnam War

The Vietnam War was a protracted conflict that lasted from 1955 to 1975 and was fought between the communist forces of North Vietnam, and the United States and its allies, who supported South Vietnam.

The war was a direct result of the Cold War, as the United States sought to contain the so called spread of communism in Southeast Asia.

The Vietnam War began as a civil war between North and South Vietnam but quickly escalated into a larger conflict as the United States became increasingly involved.

The United States deployed hundreds of thousands of troops to Vietnam and began a massive bombing campaign against North Vietnam.

The war was marked by brutal guerrilla warfare tactics, including ambushes, booby traps, and hit-and-run attacks.

The Viet Cong, a communist guerrilla group supported by North Vietnam, fought a guerrilla war against the South Vietnamese government and their American allies.

The United States military responded with a massive deployment of troops, which led to a long and costly conflict.

The majority of casualties were Vietnamese civilians and soldiers, with an estimated 1 million North Vietnamese and Viet Cong fighters killed, and 250,000 South Vietnamese soldiers and civilians killed.

The war was also characterized by widespread anti-war protests in the United States and around the world. Many Americans opposed the war and protested against the draft and military intervention in Vietnam.

These protests had a significant impact on public opinion and helped to eventually bring an end to the war. The war ended with the fall of Saigon, the capital of South Vietnam, to North Vietnamese forces on April 30, 1975.

So, what was accomplished? Remembered as a true masterpiece of American military strategy and diplomacy. Surely, this was a conflict that achieved great things and left the world a better place. Let's take a look at what was accomplished.

First and foremost, the Vietnam War was a masterclass in military innovation. The United States was able to deploy all sorts of new and exciting weapons and tactics, from napalm to Agent Orange to carpet bombing entire villages.

Truly, the American military machine was a marvel to behold. But the war wasn't just a showcase for military might. It also served as a testing ground for new and innovative approaches to foreign policy.

The domino theory, for example, was a brilliant concept that held that if one country fell to communism, others would follow like dominoes. It was a strategy that was proven right time and time again, except for the fact that it was completely wrong.

The war also had a profound impact on American culture. The anti-war movement and the counterculture it spawned were a direct response to the horrors of Vietnam, and they reshaped American society in countless ways.

From the music of Bob Dylan and Joan Baez to the fashion of belly-bottoms and tie-dye shirts, the Vietnam War inspired a generation to embrace peace, love, and understanding.

Of course, the war also had a profound impact on the people of Vietnam. The millions of deaths, the destruction of villages, the displacement of millions of people—all of these were a small price to pay for the greater good of defeating communism.

And while the American military was ultimately forced to withdraw, the people of Vietnam were left to pick up the pieces and rebuild their shattered country. A small price to pay, indeed.

But the real legacy of the Vietnam War was the lessons it taught us: That we can't trust our leaders to tell us the truth, that we can't trust the media to report the facts... And that we can't trust the government to do what's right...

It taught us that war is a brutal, destructive, and ultimately pointless endeavor and that we should avoid it at all costs. Of course, those lessons were quickly forgotten in the years that followed.

And while those conflicts may not have had the same impact on American culture as Vietnam did, they were certainly just as destructive and pointless.

And let's not forget the positive impact the Vietnam War had on the American economy. The military-industrial complex that was created during the war is still going strong today, providing jobs and economic growth for millions of Americans.

So, in a way, the war was a net positive for the American economy, even if it did destroy the economy of an entire country. In the end, the Vietnam War was a conflict that achieved great things, if your definition of "great things" is massive destruction, death, and suffering.

It was a war that taught us valuable lessons about the dangers of war and the importance of questioning our leaders.

And it was a war that helped create a military-industrial complex that has kept the American economy going strong for decades.

So, in a way, we should be grateful for the Vietnam War. Without it, who knows where the US would be today? Probably exactly where they are.

The Korean War

The Korean War was a conflict that lasted from 1950 to 1953 and was fought between North Korea, which was supported by China and the Soviet Union, and South Korea, which was supported by the United States and other United Nations member countries.

The war began when North Korea invaded South Korea on June 25, 1950, intending to reunify the Korean Peninsula under communist rule.

The United States and other UN member countries responded with a military intervention to support South Korea.

The Korean War was characterized by the extensive use of air power and artillery, as well as the involvement of Chinese troops in the later stages of the conflict.

A ceasefire was signed on July 27, 1953, which established the demilitarized zone that still separates North and South Korea to this day.

The Korean War was a costly conflict, with an estimated 2.5 million people killed or wounded, including approximately 36,000 American soldiers.

The majority of casualties were Korean civilians and soldiers, with an estimated 1 million North Korean and Chinese soldiers killed, and 400,000 South Korean soldiers and civilians killed.

What was accomplished? The conflict showed the world just how great America's military power truly was. Surely, this war achieved all sorts of wonderful things, right?

First of all, let's talk about the military strategy employed during the war.

The United States was able to deploy all sorts of innovative new tactics, from massive bombing campaigns to the use of chemical weapons.

It was truly a sight to behold. And let's not forget about the brave soldiers who fought on the ground—they truly embodied the American spirit of toughness and resilience.

Of course, it wasn't just the Americans who were fighting. There were plenty of other countries involved too, but let's be real, the Americans were the ones doing all the heavy lifting.

So, what was the result of all this military might? Well, the war ended in a stalemate, with the North and South still divided by the 38th parallel.

But at least the US showed the world just how powerful they were! And let's not forget about the positive impact the war had on the Korean people.

Sure, millions of them were killed or displaced, but that's a small price to pay for the greater good of stopping communism, right?

And while North Korea may be a poverty-stricken, totalitarian state, at least they're not communist. Wait, they are communists? Well, at least they're not as bad as they could be. What? Kim who?

But the real legacy of the Korean War is the lessons it taught us. It taught us that war is a brutal, destructive, and ultimately pointless endeavor and that we should avoid it at all costs.

And yet, in the years that followed, the United States went on to invade countless other countries, all in the name of spreading democracy and freedom.

And let's not forget about the impact the Korean War had on American culture. It was the first conflict to be televised, bringing the horrors of war into people's living rooms for the first time.

And yet, even as people saw the devastation and suffering caused by the war, they continued to support it. Why? Because America is the greatest country on earth, that's why.

In the end, the Korean War was a conflict that achieved destruction, death, and suffering. It was a war that showed the world just how powerful America's military could be, and it taught us valuable lessons about the dangers of war...

And yet, those lessons were quickly forgotten in the years that followed, as America continued to wage war after war. So, in a way, we should be grateful for the Korean War. Without it, we may have forgotten just how great America truly is.

The Gulf War

The Gulf War was a conflict that took place from 1990 to 1991, following the invasion of Kuwait by Iraq. The war involved a coalition of countries, led by the United States, who intervened to expel Iraqi forces from Kuwait and prevent further aggression in the region.

The Gulf War was triggered by Iraq's invasion of Kuwait on August 2, 1990, which was widely condemned by the international community.

The United Nations Security Council passed a resolution condemning Iraq's actions and demanding the immediate withdrawal of Iraqi forces from Kuwait. Iraq refused to comply, leading to the intervention of a multinational coalition force.

The Gulf War was marked by extensive air and ground campaigns, with coalition forces launching a sustained bombing campaign against Iraqi targets and deploying ground troops to expel Iraqi forces from Kuwait.

The war was notable for its use of advanced military technology, including precision-guided munitions and stealth aircraft.

The Gulf War was a relatively short conflict, lasting just over six weeks. The coalition forces achieved a decisive victory, with Iraqi forces quickly driven out of Kuwait and expelled from the country.

The Gulf War resulted in a relatively low number of casualties, with around 300 coalition soldiers killed in action and a higher, unknown number of Iraqi casualties.

So… What Was Accomplished?
A time when America once again showed the world just how powerful the US truly is—this time LIVE ON TV! It was a conflict that accomplished so much—or did it?

First of all, let's talk about the military strategy employed during the war. It was a masterstroke. The USA launched a massive air campaign, followed by a ground invasion that lasted just a few short weeks. It was like a perfectly choreographed dance, with the Iraqi army as their helpless dance partner.

Of course, there were some minor setbacks along the way—like the time America accidentally bombed a civilian shelter, killing hundreds of innocent people—but hey, you can't make an omelet without breaking a few eggs, right?

But what did the USA accomplish? Well, they liberated Kuwait, which was great news for the Kuwaitis. They were able to go back to living their extravagant lifestyles, buying all sorts of luxury goods and hoarding their oil wealth.

And they showed Saddam Hussein who was boss, which was a real boost to America's ego. But did they achieve anything of lasting value?

In the aftermath of the Gulf War, the USA set up no-fly zones in Iraq and imposed crippling economic sanctions. This was supposed to pressure Saddam into complying with UN resolutions, but it mostly just hurt ordinary Iraqis.

And when Saddam continued to defy the international community, the USA went back in and invaded Iraq in 2003, leading to a decade-long occupation that cost trillions of dollars and thousands of American lives.

But at least they got rid of Saddam, right?

Of course, the real winners of the Gulf War were the defense contractors. They made billions of dollars selling weapons and equipment to the military, and they continued to profit off the war long after it was over.

And let's not forget about the oil companies. They were able to swoop in and claim Kuwait's oil reserves for themselves, ensuring that America would have a steady supply of cheap oil for decades to come.

And the TV companies—raking in dollars on the BREAKING NEWS coverage. So, in a way, the Gulf War was a great success—for the people who were already rich and powerful, that is.

And let's not forget about the impact the Gulf War had on American culture. It was a time when patriotism was at an all-time high, and people were waving flags and singing patriotic songs. It was a time when people believed in the righteousness of American power.

Of course, that all changed after the invasion of Iraq in 2003 when people started to realize that maybe they weren't always the good guys.

So, in the end, what did the Gulf War accomplish? It liberated Kuwait, sure, but at what cost? It enriched the already wealthy, sure, but what about the average American? And it bolstered America's ego, sure, but at what expense?

The Gulf War was a conflict that accomplished a lot of things, but whether any of them were truly worthwhile is up for debate. All I can say for certain is that it made a lot of people very, very rich.

THE IRAQ WAR

The Iraq War was a protracted conflict that lasted from 2003 to 2011 and was fought between the United States-led coalition and Iraq.

The war was launched by the US government under the Bush administration, which claimed that Iraq had weapons of mass destruction and posed a significant threat to global security.

The Iraq War began on March 20, 2003, with the US-led coalition launching a massive bombing campaign against Iraq.

The coalition forces then deployed ground troops to overthrow the Iraqi government and capture Saddam Hussein, who was accused of human rights abuses and supporting terrorist organizations.

The Iraq War was marked by significant military and political challenges, including fierce resistance from Iraqi forces and a protracted insurgency that lasted for years.

The Iraq War was a protracted conflict that lasted from 2003 to 2011 and was fought between the United States-led coalition and Iraq.

The war was launched by the US government under the Bush administration, which claimed that Iraq had weapons of mass destruction and posed a significant threat to global security.

The Iraq War began on March 20, 2003, with the US-led coalition launching a massive bombing campaign against Iraq.

The coalition forces then deployed ground troops to overthrow the Iraqi government and capture Saddam Hussein, who was accused of human rights abuses and supporting terrorist organizations.

The Iraq War was marked by significant military and political challenges, including fierce resistance from Iraqi forces and a protracted insurgency that lasted for years.

The war also had a significant impact on the civilian population, with large numbers of Iraqi civilians killed, injured, or displaced.

The Iraq War ended with the withdrawal of US forces from Iraq in December 2011, after nearly nine years of fighting.

The human toll of the Iraq War was significant, with an estimated 180,000 people killed, including over 4,400 US military personnel.

The war also resulted in significant financial costs, with estimates ranging from $1.7 trillion to $3 trillion.

So, What Did It Accomplish? A time when America once again flexed its muscles and showed the world just how powerful they are, again (just in case we forgot).
It was a conflict that accomplished so much—or not…

First of all, let's talk about the reasons for going to war. America told the people that Saddam Hussein had weapons of mass destruction and posed an immediate threat to the United States.

They were told that they had to act quickly before it was too late. Of course, it turned out that Saddam didn't have any weapons of mass destruction…

But what did America accomplish? Well, they got rid of Saddam Hussein, which was great news for the Iraqi people. They were finally free from his tyranny and could start to build a new, democratic society.

And they showed the world that America was not to be messed with, which was a real boost to an already enormous ego. But did they really achieve anything of lasting value?

In the aftermath of the Iraq War, America helped set up a new government in Iraq and helped rebuild the country's infrastructure.

They also tried to spread democracy throughout the Middle East, because everyone knows that democracy is the best form of government, right?

But things didn't quite go as planned. The new government they set up in Iraq turned out to be corrupt and ineffective, and sectarian violence continued to tear the country apart.

And when they tried to spread democracy to other countries, like Afghanistan and Libya, things didn't go much better. But at least they tried, right?

And then there's the cost of the war. It cost trillions of dollars and thousands of American lives.

They are still paying for it today, both in terms of the national debt and the physical and mental scars of the soldiers who fought there. But at least they got rid of Saddam, right?

Of course, the real winners of the Iraq War were the defense contractors. They made billions of dollars selling weapons and equipment to the military, and they continued to profit off the war long after it was over.

And let's not forget about the oil companies. They were able to swoop in and claim Iraq's oil reserves for themselves, ensuring that America would have a steady supply of cheap oil for decades to come.

So, in a way, the Iraq War was a great success—for the people who were already rich and powerful, that is. And let's not forget about the impact the Iraq War had on American culture.

It was a time when people believed in the righteousness of American power. Of course, that all changed after the war dragged on for years...

So, in the end, what did the Iraq War accomplish? It got rid of Saddam Hussein, sure, but at what cost?

It enriched the already wealthy, sure, but what about the average American? And it spread democracy throughout the Middle East, sure, but at what expense?

The Iraq War was a conflict that accomplished a lot of things, but whether any of them were truly worthwhile is up for debate.

All I can say for certain is that it made a lot of people very, very rich. Well, that sounded familiar…

The Afghanistan War

The Afghanistan War was a prolonged conflict that began in 2001 and ended in 2021, fought between the US-led coalition and the Taliban, an Islamist militant group that had seized control of Afghanistan in the late 1990s.

The war began on October 7, 2001, following the 9/11 attacks in the United States, which were carried out by the al-Qaeda terrorist group, who had found a safe haven in Afghanistan under the protection of the Taliban.

The US government launched a military campaign against the Taliban, intending to dismantle al-Qaeda and remove the Taliban from power.

The Afghanistan War was marked by significant military and political challenges, including fierce resistance from the Taliban, a protracted insurgency, and ongoing instability in the region.

The war also had a significant impact on the civilian population, with large numbers of Afghan civilians killed, injured, or displaced.

The Afghanistan War officially ended on August 31, 2021, with the withdrawal of US forces from the country. Copying the success withdrawal from Vietnam, it was marked by significant chaos and violence.

The human toll of the Afghanistan War was significant, with an estimated 157,000 people killed, including over 2,400 US military personnel.

The war also resulted in significant financial costs, with estimates ranging from $2.26 trillion to $2.89 trillion.

This War: What Was It Good For? What did it accomplish? A conflict that accomplished so much, and yet so little at the same time…

First of all, let's talk about the reasons for going to war. Americans were told that they had to go after the Taliban and Al-Qaeda, who were responsible for the 9/11 attacks.

They were told that we had to act quickly before more attacks could be carried out. Of course, it turned out that the Taliban and Al-Qaeda weren't actually in Afghanistan anymore…

But what did they actually accomplish? Well, they got rid of the Taliban, which was great news for the Afghan people. They were finally free from their oppressive rule and could start to build a new, democratic society.

But did we really achieve anything of lasting value? In the aftermath of the Afghanistan War, a new government in Afghanistan was set up and the international community helped rebuild the country's infrastructure.

We also tried to spread democracy throughout the region, because everyone knows that democracy is the best form of government, right? But things didn't quite go as planned.

The new government set up in Afghanistan turned out to be corrupt and ineffective, and the Taliban began to regain power. So, back to square one…

And then there's the cost of the war. It cost trillions of dollars and thousands of lives. They are still paying for it today, both in terms of the national debt and the physical and mental scars of the soldiers who fought there.

But at least they got rid of the Taliban, right? Not really. They are back in power in Afghanistan, making sure all democratic progress is lost.

The real winners of the Afghanistan War were the usual suspects—the defense contractors!

They made billions of dollars selling weapons and equipment to the military, and they continued to profit off the war long after it was over.

And let's not forget about the opium trade. Afghanistan produces more than 80% of the world's opium, and the war allowed drug lords to thrive, ensuring a steady supply of drugs for years to come.

So, in a way, the Afghanistan War was a great success—for the people who were already rich and powerful, that is.

So, in the end, what did the Afghanistan War accomplish? It got rid of the Taliban, sure, but... Then they just came back and nothing changed? Sure.

It enriched the already wealthy, sure, but what about the average American, African or Euopean? And it spread democracy throughout the region, sure, but at what expense?

The Afghanistan War was a conflict that accomplished a lot of things, but whether any of them were truly worthwhile is up for debate.

All I can say for certain is that it made a lot of people very, very rich. Sounds like history keeps repeating itself—for the benefit of the R.I.C.H!

The Syrian Civil War

The Syrian Civil War was a protracted conflict that began in 2011 and ended in 2021, fought between the Syrian government, rebel groups, and foreign powers.

The war was sparked by anti-government protests that emerged as part of the wider Arab Spring uprisings in the Middle East and North Africa.

The conflict began with peaceful protests against the government of Syrian President Bashar al-Assad, who responded with violent crackdowns on protesters.

The protests soon escalated into a full-scale armed conflict, with rebel groups emerging to challenge the Syrian government and seek its overthrow.

The Syrian Civil War was marked by significant military and political challenges, including fierce fighting between government forces and rebel groups, as well as the intervention of foreign powers such as Russia, Iran, and the United States.

The war in Syria was characterized by controversy and debate, both domestically and internationally.

Critics of the Syrian government argued that it had engaged in widespread human rights abuses and war crimes, while supporters of the government accused rebel groups of terrorism and destabilization.

The Syrian Civil War officially ended in 2021 with the signing of a ceasefire agreement between the Syrian government and rebel groups. The agreement led to the formation of a new government and the withdrawal of foreign forces from Syria.

The human toll of the Syrian Civil War was significant, with an estimated 388,000 people killed, including over 117,000 civilians. The war also resulted in significant financial costs, with estimates ranging from $250 billion to $1.2 trillion.

Sounds grim, what was accomplished?
A conflict that showed the world what true devastation looks like. But what was accomplished during those long, bloody years?

First of all, we can congratulate ourselves on our humanitarian efforts. We sent aid to the Syrian people, helped refugees find new homes, and did everything in our power to ease their suffering.

Of course, we could have done a lot more, but hey, at least we tried, right? We also succeeded in arming and training various rebel groups, which was great news for the Syrian people.

After all, what could go wrong with giving weapons to people we barely know and whose motivations are murky at best?

We even went so far as to bomb the Syrian government's military installations, because nothing says "humanitarian aid" like raining death from above.

But did we accomplish anything of lasting value? Well, we did manage to topple the Syrian government, which was the whole point of the exercise, right?

Oh, wait, no, we didn't actually do that.

In fact, after years of fighting and billions of dollars spent, the Syrian government is still in power, and the country is still ravaged by violence. And what about our attempts to stop the use of chemical weapons? We drew a red line in the sand and warned the Syrian government not to cross it.

And then when they did, we...did nothing. Well, we did make some stern statements and wagged our fingers at them, which I'm sure had them quaking in their boots.

And let's not forget about the various factions involved in the war. There were the Syrian government forces, the various rebel groups, ISIS, and the Kurds, among others. We tried to back the "good" guys, but it turned out that they were all pretty terrible.

And when we started arming the Kurds, Turkey got upset, because they view the Kurds as terrorists. So we had to walk a tightrope and try not to anger anyone too much, which was about as easy as balancing a hippopotamus on a unicycle.

And then there's the aftermath. The war may be officially over, but the country is still in shambles. Millions of people are displaced, the economy is in ruins, and the infrastructure is in tatters. And who's going to clean up the mess? Well, that's not really our problem, is it? We did what we could, and now it's up to someone else to pick up the pieces.

In the end, what did the Syrian Civil War accomplish? It showed us just how complicated and messy international conflicts can be. It taught us that there are no easy solutions and that sometimes even the best intentions can lead to disastrous outcomes.

And it reminded us that war should always be a last resort because the costs are just too high. But did it accomplish anything of lasting value? That's up for debate...

The Lebanese Civil War

The Lebanese Civil War was a protracted conflict that took place between 1975 and 1990, fought between various political and religious factions in Lebanon.

The conflict began in 1975 with the outbreak of fighting between Christian and Muslim militias and soon escalated into a full-scale civil war involving multiple factions.

The war was fueled by regional and international tensions, with Israel and Syria intervening in the conflict to protect their interests in Lebanon.

The Lebanese Civil War was marked by significant violence and instability, with various factions vying for control over the country. The conflict had a significant impact on the civilian population, with estimates suggesting that up to 150,000 people were killed, and many more were injured.

The Lebanese Civil War officially ended in 1990 with the signing of the Taif Agreement, which established a new political system in Lebanon and called for the disarmament of all militias.

The agreement paved the way for the establishment of a new government and the reconstruction of the country.

So, what was accomplished?

A conflict that lasted 15 long years and left the country in shambles. But fear not, my friends, because so much was accomplished during those years.

First and foremost, we helped the people of Lebanon realize their true potential. We showed them that they are capable of enduring unimaginable hardship and surviving against all odds.

Sure, infrastructure was destroyed, their economy was decimated, and their society was torn apart, but at least they know what they're made of now, right?

We also showed the world that it's possible to have a civil war that doesn't involve any clear winners or losers. In fact, after all that fighting, the same people who were in power before the war started were still in power when it ended. Talk about a victory for stability!

And let's not forget about the international community's role in the conflict.

We sent in peacekeeping forces and tried to broker a ceasefire, but unfortunately, those efforts were about as effective as trying to put out a forest fire with a squirt gun. But hey, at least we tried, right?

And then there's the aftermath. The war may be over, but the country is still in ruins. The government is weak, the economy is stagnant, and sectarian tensions are still simmering just below the surface.

But fear not, because we have a solution for all of this: international aid! Yes, we'll just throw money at the problem, and everything will magically fix itself.

Of course, we could have done more to prevent the war in the first place. We could have taken a closer look at the deep-seated sectarian tensions that were brewing beneath the surface. We could have addressed the root causes of the conflict instead of just trying to manage the symptoms.

But why bother with all that when we can just wait until things explode and then swoop in to save the day?

In the end, the Lebanese Civil War accomplish taught us that war is never the answer unless, of course, it's the only option we have left.

It showed us that sectarian tensions can simmer for years and years before boiling over into violence. And it reminded us that international intervention can be about as effective as trying to put out a forest fire with a squirt gun.

But did it accomplish anything of lasting value? Nope

THE NAPOLEONIC WARS

The Napoleonic Wars were a series of conflicts that took place between 1803 and 1815, fought primarily between France and a coalition of European powers led by Great Britain.

The wars were sparked by the expansionist ambitions of Napoleon Bonaparte, who sought to establish French dominance over Europe.

The Napoleonic Wars were marked by significant violence and political instability and had a significant impact on the political and social landscape of Europe.

The wars were characterized by major battles and sieges, with both sides using innovative tactics and strategies to gain the upper hand.

The wars officially began in 1803 with the Third Coalition against France, which included Great Britain, Austria, and Russia.

The war was fought on multiple fronts, including in Europe, Africa, and the Americas, and was characterized by significant losses on both sides.

One of the most significant battles of the Napoleonic Wars was the Battle of Waterloo in 1815, which marked the final defeat of Napoleon and his exile to the island of Saint Helena.

The battle was fought between the French forces led by Napoleon and the coalition forces led by the Duke of Wellington.

The human toll of the Napoleonic Wars was significant, with estimates suggesting that up to six million people were killed during the conflicts.

The wars also had significant economic and political costs, with many European countries suffering from prolonged periods of instability and economic decline.

So much must have been accomplished, right? A time of grand battles, epic sieges, and endless marching. It was a time when Europe was engulfed in conflict, and when one man rose to power, only to be defeated and exiled not once, but twice. But what was accomplished during this tumultuous period?

First and foremost, the Napoleonic Wars helped to prove that one man's ambition can take him pretty far. Napoleon Bonaparte rose from a minor noble in Corsica to the Emperor of France, all because he had a bit of ambition and some impressive military tactics.

Sure, he may have lost in the end, but at least he got to live out his dream of ruling over a vast empire for a few years.

But it wasn't just Napoleon who accomplished something during the Napoleonic Wars.

The rest of Europe got to showcase its military might as well. The British proved that their navy was the most powerful in the world, the Russians showed off their ability to take on the French in snowy conditions, and the Austrians...well, they tried their best.

And let's not forget about the innovations that came out of the Napoleonic Wars. The French introduced the concept of conscription, which helped to create large, professional armies.

And with the introduction of the steam engine, transportation became faster and more efficient, which made it easier to move troops and supplies across long distances.

Who knew that war could be so good for technological advancement?

Also, I had heard that the baguette was invented during the war. It was baked especially for soldiers in the Napoleonic wars. The bread is long and thin so it can be carried in the legs of one's trousers. This could be, however, complete nonsense. At least the war achieved a long-running lie then.

And then there's the aftermath of the Napoleonic Wars... Napoleon was exiled not once, but twice, which just goes to show that you can't keep a good emperor down. And while he may have been defeated, his legacy lived on.

The idea of nationalism spread throughout Europe, as people began to identify with their own countries and cultures, rather than just being loyal to their rulers.

And the concept of a united Europe began to take shape, as countries started to work together to prevent another conflict like the Napoleonic Wars.

Of course, the Napoleonic Wars also had some negative consequences. The wars were incredibly costly, both in terms of money and human lives.

Millions of people died, and Europe was left in shambles. But at least the rest of the world got to see what Europe was capable of when it came to warfare.

Well, one man's ambition was proven to be pretty impressive, the rest of Europe got to show off their military might, innovations in technology were made, and the aftermath paved the way for a more united Europe. Sure, there were some negative consequences, but overall, it was a pretty successful time for Europe.

Who knew that war could be so productive? I mean, we got the baguette out of it! Sure, there were some political changes, cultural achievements, and military victories.

But how about that baguette?

THE AMERICAN CIVIL WAR

The American Civil War was a major conflict that took place between 1861 and 1865, fought primarily between the Union (Northern) states and the Confederate (Southern) states.

The war was sparked by a range of factors, including tensions over slavery, economy, and political disputes.

The American Civil War is considered one of the deadliest conflicts in United States history, with estimates suggesting that up to 620,000 people were killed.

The war was fought on multiple fronts, including in the East and West, with both sides using innovative tactics and strategies to gain the upper hand.

The war officially began with the secession of the Confederate states and the subsequent attack on Fort Sumter in South Carolina.

The war was marked by significant battles and campaigns, including the Battle of Gettysburg, the Siege of Vicksburg, and the Atlanta Campaign.

The most significant outcome of the American Civil War was the end of slavery in the United States.

The Union's victory in the war led to the passage of the 13th, 14th, and 15th Amendments to the U.S. Constitution, which abolished slavery, granted citizenship to African Americans, and established voting rights for all citizens.

Something important was accomplished this time? YES!
First and foremost, the American Civil War accomplished the abolition of slavery.

Yes, it took a war to convince people that owning other human beings was not a great idea, but at least it happened.

And while some people may argue that slavery was on its way out anyways, the Civil War certainly sped up the process. So, kudos to the North for finally realizing that owning people is kind of a bad thing.

But what else did the Civil War accomplish? Well, the North proved that they were better at fighting a war than the South.

Sure, the South had some impressive generals and some fiery passion, but in the end, the North's industrial might and superior resources won out.
And hey, at least the South got to keep their guns and their "heritage," right?

And let's not forget about the innovations that came out of the Civil War. The Union army introduced new technologies like the repeating rifle and the ironclad ship, which would go on to revolutionize warfare.

And with the invention of the telegraph, communication became faster and more efficient, which helped to coordinate military operations. Who knew that war could be so good for technological advancement?

And then there's the aftermath of the Civil War. The Union was preserved, which was certainly a good thing for the country.

And while some people may argue that the South was treated unfairly during the Reconstruction era, at least the slaves were freed and the nation was moving towards a more equal society.

Plus, we got some great movies and books out of the whole thing, right? Who doesn't love Gone with the Wind?

Of course, the Civil War also had some negative consequences. Millions of people died, families were torn apart, and the nation was left in shambles.

And while slavery may have been abolished, racism and discrimination persisted.
But at least we can all agree that owning people is a bad thing, right?

So, what was accomplished during the Civil War? Well, slavery was abolished, the North proved that they were better at fighting a war, innovations in technology were made, and the Union was preserved.

Sure, there were some negative consequences, but overall, it was a pretty successful time for the country.

THE WAR OF 1812

The War of 1812 was a military conflict between the United States and Great Britain that lasted from 1812 to 1815. The war was sparked by a range of factors, including British attempts to restrict American trade and American expansionism into Native American territory.

The War of 1812 is sometimes referred to as America's second war of Independence, as it helped to solidify the nation's independence from Great Britain.

The war was fought on multiple fronts, including land and sea battles, with both sides achieving significant victories and suffering significant losses.

One of the most significant outcomes of the War of 1812 was the confirmation of American independence and sovereignty.

The Treaty of Ghent, which ended the war in 1815, restored the prewar borders between the United States and British North America and established a new era of peaceful relations between the two countries.

What was accomplished? The forgotten war that nobody really cares about. So, what was accomplished during this little skirmish between the United States and Great Britain?

First and foremost, the War of 1812 accomplished absolutely nothing. That's right, folks. After two and a half years of fighting, nothing was gained or lost.

The borders remained the same, the economies remained the same, and the only thing that really changed was that a bunch of people died.

So, congratulations to both sides for wasting a lot of time and resources on a pointless conflict. But let's not forget about the minor accomplishments of the War of 1812.

For one, the United States got a national anthem out of it. That's right, Francis Scott Key was inspired to write "The Star-Spangled Banner" after witnessing the bombardment of Fort McHenry.

So, at least they got a catchy tune to sing at sporting events, right? And let's not forget about the Battle of New Orleans. While technically fought after the war had ended, it was a strong victory for the United States and gave Andrew Jackson a boost in popularity, which would later help him become president.

So, thank you, War of 1812, for giving us another president. Well, not much really changed. The borders remained the same, and both sides went back to their usual trading and diplomatic relations.

Oh, except for the fact that the United States now had a heightened sense of nationalism and a newfound hatred for Great Britain.

So, thank you, War of 1812, for sowing the seeds of anti-British sentiment that would later help fuel the American Revolution. And let's not forget about the lasting legacies of the War of 1812.

For one, it helped to shape the careers of some notable figures, such as Andrew Jackson, William Henry Harrison, and Isaac Brock.

And it also inspired some great works of literature, such as James Fenimore Cooper's "The Last of the Mohicans" and Edgar Allan Poe's "The Cask of Amontillado."

So, thank you, War of 1812, for giving us some great reads.

In conclusion, the War of 1812 accomplished absolutely nothing. But at least we got a national anthem, a boost in nationalism, and some notable figures and literature out of it.

So, I guess it wasn't a total waste of time, right?

The Hundred Years' War

The Hundred Years' War was a series of military conflicts that were fought between England and France from 1337 to 1453. It was a complex and lengthy war that had a significant impact on both countries and marked a turning point in European history.

The main players in the Hundred Years' War were England and France. However, the war involved many other countries and factions as well.

The English were initially supported by the Flemish and the Burgundians, while the French received aid from Scotland, Castile, and the Papal States.

The war was also marked by shifting alliances and internal divisions within both England and France.

The Hundred Years' War had its roots in a dispute over the succession to the French throne. When King Charles IV of France died in 1328 without a male heir, the throne passed to his cousin, Philip VI of Valois.

However, Edward III of England, who was Charles IV's nephew and the son of his sister Isabella, also had a claim to the throne.

Edward III initially paid homage to Philip VI as his liege lord, but tensions between the two countries continued to escalate.

In 1337, Philip confiscated the English-held territory of Gascony, which led to Edward III declaring war on France and initiating the first phase of the Hundred Years' War.

The Hundred Years' War was marked by numerous battles, sieges, and skirmishes, and the exact number of casualties is difficult to determine. However, it is estimated that tens of thousands of soldiers and civilians were killed or injured throughout the conflict.

The Hundred Years' War officially ended with the signing of the Treaty of Picquigny in 1475, but the major fighting had ceased nearly 22 years earlier with the signing of the Treaty of Arras in 1435.

So, anything accomplished here then? What an exciting time in history, filled with epic battles, knights in shining armor, and…oh wait, never mind.

It was actually just a bunch of petty squabbling between the English and the French that lasted for over a century. But what did this never-ending story of a conflict actually accomplish?

First and foremost, the Hundred Years' War accomplished a whole lot of nothing. After all that time, money, and bloodshed, the borders of France and England remained pretty much the same as they were before the war started.

So, congratulations to both sides for wasting a hundred years on a pointless conflict. But let's not forget about the minor accomplishments of the Hundred Years' War.

For one, it helped to popularize the use of the longbow as a weapon of war. So, if you ever find yourself transported back in time to medieval Europe, you'll know what kind of weapon to bring.

And let's not forget about the legendary figures that emerged from the Hundred Years' War, such as Joan of Arc, who led the French to a few victories before getting burned at the stake.

So, thank you, Hundred Years' War, for giving us one of history's most iconic martyrs.

But what about the aftermath of the war? Well, not much really changed. The borders remained the same, and both sides went back to their usual trading and diplomatic relations.

Oh, except for the fact that the French now had a heightened sense of nationalism and a newfound hatred for the English.

So, thank you, Hundred Years' War, for sowing the seeds of anti-English sentiment that would later help fuel the French Revolution.

And let's not forget about the lasting legacies of the Hundred Years' War. For one, it helped to shape the development of modern warfare, with new tactics and strategies being developed throughout the conflict.

And it also inspired some great works of literature, such as Shakespeare's "Henry V" and George R.R. Martin's "Game of Thrones" series.

So, thank you, Hundred Years' War, for giving us some great reads and binging-sessions in front of the telly.

In conclusion, the Hundred Years' War accomplished pretty much nothing.

But at least we got a weapon, a martyr, and some iconic literature out of it. So, I guess it wasn't a total waste of time, right?

The Crusades

The Crusades were a series of religious wars fought between Christians and Muslims in the Middle East from 1096 to 1270.

It had a significant impact on European and Middle Eastern history, and their legacy can still be felt today.

The Crusades were fought between Christians and Muslims. The Christians were primarily European and included armies from France, England, Germany, and Italy, among other countries.

The Muslims were primarily from the Middle East and included armies from Egypt, Syria, and Palestine, among other regions.

There were also several other groups involved in the Crusades, including Byzantine Christians, Jews, and Mongols.

These groups played different roles at different times during the Crusades, and their participation often reflected shifting alliances and political dynamics in the region.

The Crusades were sparked by many factors, including religious, economic, and political motivations.

One of the key catalysts was the desire of European Christians to gain control of Jerusalem, which had been under Muslim rule since the 7th century.

In 1095, Pope Urban II called for a holy war to retake Jerusalem from the Muslims. This call was met with enthusiasm from many Europeans, who saw the Crusades as an opportunity to gain wealth and land in the Holy Land, as well as to secure their place in heaven.

The Crusades officially ended with the fall of the last Crusader stronghold in the Holy Land, Acre, in 1291. However, the legacy of the Crusades continued to be felt in Europe and the Middle East for centuries to come.

So, surely something great was accomplished?
Ah, the Crusades. A time when brave Christian knights took up arms to conquer the Holy Land and spread their religion to the infidels.

Or, if you prefer a more accurate version of history, a time when Europeans traveled thousands of miles to get their butts kicked by Middle Eastern armies for no real reason.

First of all, let's talk about the original goal of the Crusades: to recapture the Holy Land from Muslim control. And what did they accomplish in that regard? Well, not much.

The Crusaders managed to capture Jerusalem for a short period, but it was ultimately retaken by Muslim forces.

So, congratulations to the Crusaders for traveling all that way and achieving absolutely nothing. But wait, there's more! The Crusades also accomplished the massacre of countless innocent people.

Whether it was the slaughter of Jews in the Rhineland during the First Crusade, or the burning of innocent Muslim civilians during the later Crusades, the Crusaders certainly knew how to leave a trail of destruction in their wake.

So, thank you, Crusaders, for showing us how to commit unspeakable atrocities in the name of religion.

And let's not forget about the Crusaders' impact on the Middle East. By invading and occupying these lands, they helped to spread Western culture and ideas to the region.

And what did the Middle Easterners think of this cultural exchange? Well, let's just say they weren't big fans. The Crusades are still seen as a dark period in Middle Eastern history, with many blaming Western interference for many of the region's current problems.

So, thank you, Crusaders, for showing us how not to engage in cultural exchange.

But what about the aftermath of the Crusades? Well, it wasn't all bad.

The Crusades did help to shape the development of Europe, with new ideas and technologies being brought back from the Middle East.

And the Crusades also inspired some great works of art, such as Dante's "Inferno" and countless medieval romances. So, thank you, Crusades, for giving us some great literature and art.

And let's not forget about the lasting legacies of the Crusades.
For one, they helped to solidify the divide between Christians and Muslims that still exists to this day.

And they also helped to shape the development of modern warfare, with new tactics and strategies being developed for the conflicts. So, thank you, Crusades, for setting the stage for centuries of religious conflict and bloodshed.

In conclusion, the Crusades accomplished pretty much nothing except for mass murder, destabilization and destruction.

Let´s give that a big Amen, inshallah!

THE THIRTY YEARS' WAR

The Thirty Years' War was a major conflict that took place in Europe between 1618 and 1648.

The Thirty Years' War was primarily fought between two main factions: the Protestants and the Catholics.

The Protestants were largely made up of German states that had broken away from the Catholic Church during the Reformation.

The Catholics were led by the Holy Roman Empire, which was a confederation of states that was dominated by the Habsburg dynasty. Several other powers also became involved in the conflict over time, including France, Sweden, and Denmark.

These powers saw the conflict as an opportunity to gain territory and influence in Europe, and their involvement helped to extend the duration and intensity of the war.

The Thirty Years' War began as a conflict between the Protestant states of Bohemia and the Catholic Holy Roman Empire.

In 1617, the Holy Roman Emperor, Ferdinand II, was elected King of Bohemia, even though he was Catholic and most of the Bohemians were Protestant.

This led to a rebellion by the Bohemians, who felt that their religious rights were being threatened by the Catholic Habsburgs.

The rebellion quickly turned into a full-blown war, as other Protestant states in Germany rallied to the support of Bohemia, while the Catholic states allied themselves with the Holy Roman Empire.

The Thirty Years' War was one of the deadliest conflicts in European history, with an estimated 8 million casualties.

The Thirty Years' War officially ended with the signing of the Peace of Westphalia in 1648. The treaty was negotiated by representatives of the warring parties, and it represented a major turning point in European history.

What Was Accomplished?
First of all, the Thirty Years' War accomplished a lot in terms of population reduction. With millions of people dying from disease, starvation, and violence, the war helped thin out the herd and reduce overpopulation.

So, congratulations to the warring nations for doing their part to combat global overpopulation!

But the Thirty Years' War wasn't just about reducing the population. It also accomplished a lot in terms of cultural exchange.

As various nations fought against each other, they were able to share their cultures and ideas.
And what better way to do that than by invading each other's countries and destroying their cities and towns? So, thank you, Thirty Years' War, for showing us how to engage in cultural exchange through violence and destruction.

And let's not forget about the economic benefits of the war. As various countries were forced to rebuild after the conflict, they had to spend money on things like infrastructure, which helped to boost the economy.

And the war also helped to create new job opportunities for soldiers and mercenaries, who could go on to use their skills in other fields.

But what about the aftermath of the war? Well, it wasn't all bad. The Treaty of Westphalia, which ended the conflict, helped to establish the concept of national sovereignty and respect for state borders.

And the war also helped to weaken the power of the Holy Roman Empire, which paved the way for the emergence of modern European states.

So, thank you, Thirty Years' War, for laying the groundwork for modern Europe! But the aftermath of the war also had its downsides.

The conflict had left many areas devastated and depopulated, with entire cities and towns in ruins. And the war also helped to deepen divisions between various religious and political groups, which would continue to cause conflict for centuries to come.

So, thank you, Thirty Years' War, for leaving a legacy of destruction and division that would haunt Europe!

In conclusion, the Thirty Years' War accomplished a lot in terms of population reduction, cultural exchange, and economic stimulation.

But it also left a legacy of destruction, division, and death that would continue to impact Europe for ages to come.

So, let's all give a round of applause to the Thirty Years' War for showing us how to engage in pointless, destructive conflicts that accomplish very little!

THE SEVEN YEARS' WAR

The Seven Years' War was a major conflict that took place from 1756 to 1763, involving many of the world's major powers. The war involved several major powers, including Great Britain, France, Austria, Prussia, Russia, and Sweden.

The conflict was fought on a global scale, with battles taking place in Europe, North America, and India.

In Europe, the war was primarily fought between Great Britain and its allies on one side, and France and its allies on the other. In North America, it involved France and its Native American allies fighting against Great Britain and its American colonists.

In India, the conflict involved a struggle for control of trade routes and territories between the British East India Company and the French East India Company.

The Seven Years' War began as a result of tensions between Great Britain and France over their colonial empires.

Both nations had established colonies in North America and India, and they were competing for control of these territories and their resources.

The conflict was triggered by a series of events, including a dispute over the boundaries of French and British colonies in North America, as well as clashes between the two powers in India. In 1756, Great Britain declared war on France, and the Seven Years' War began.

The Seven Years' War was a brutal conflict, with high numbers of casualties on all sides. Exact figures for the number of casualties are difficult to determine, but estimates suggest that between 600,000 and 1.3 million people may have died as a result of the war.

The Seven Years' War officially ended with the signing of the Treaty of Paris in 1763. The treaty was negotiated by representatives of Great Britain, France, and Spain, and it marked a major turning point in the history of the world.

So much must have been accomplished…
First of all, the Seven Years' War accomplished a lot in terms of territorial gains.

With various nations fighting for control over land and resources, the war helped to redraw the map of Europe and establish new borders.

But the Seven Years' War wasn't just about territorial gains.
It also accomplished a lot in terms of cultural exchange.

As various nations fought against each other, they were able to share their cultures and ideas. And what better way to do that than by invading each other's countries and destroying their cities and towns?

And let's not forget about the economic benefits of the war. As various countries were forced to rebuild after the conflict, they had to spend money on things like infrastructure, which helped to boost the economy.

And the war also helped to create new job opportunities for soldiers and mercenaries, who could go on to use their skills in other fields. Sounds familiar, right?

But what about the aftermath of the war? Well, it wasn't all bad.

The Treaty of Paris, which ended the conflict, helped to establish British dominance in North America and paved the way for the eventual formation of the United States.

And the war also helped to weaken the power of France and establish Prussia as a major European power.

But the aftermath of the war also had its downsides. The conflict had left many areas devastated and depopulated, with entire cities and towns in ruins.

And the war also helped to deepen divisions between various religious and political groups, which would continue to cause conflict for centuries to come.

In conclusion, the Seven Years' War accomplished a lot in terms of territorial gains, cultural exchange, and economic stimulation.

But it also left a legacy of destruction, division, and death that would continue to impact Europe and the rest of the world for centuries to come.

The Seven Years' War basically showed us how to engage in pointless, destructive conflicts that accomplish very little …

The Crimean War

The Crimean War was a major conflict that took place from 1853 to 1856, involving multiple major powers in Europe and the Middle East.

The war was fought primarily between Russia on one side and a coalition of Great Britain, France, the Ottoman Empire, and Sardinia on the other.

The Crimean War involved multiple major powers, including Russia, Great Britain, France, the Ottoman Empire, and Sardinia. The conflict was fought on multiple fronts, including the Black Sea region, the Caucasus, the Balkans, and the Middle East.

The war was primarily fought over control of the Ottoman Empire, which was in decline at the time. Russia sought to expand its influence in the region, while Great Britain and France were concerned about the impact that Russian expansion would have on their interests.

The Crimean War was triggered by a dispute over the rights of Christian minorities in the Ottoman Empire. Russia, which had long claimed to be the protector of Orthodox Christians in the region, sought to extend its influence over the Ottoman Empire by intervening on behalf of the minority groups.

In response, the Ottoman Empire declared war on Russia in 1853.

Great Britain and France, which were concerned about Russian expansion in the region, joined the conflict on the Ottoman side.

The Crimean War was a brutal conflict, with high numbers of casualties on all sides. Exact figures for the number of casualties are difficult to determine, but estimates suggest that between 500,000 and 1 million people may have died as a result of the war.

The Crimean War officially ended with the signing of the Treaty of Paris in 1856.

Under the terms of the treaty, Russia was forced to cede territory to the Ottoman Empire, and the Black Sea was neutralized, preventing Russia from maintaining a large naval presence in the region.

The treaty also established a new balance of power in Europe, with Great Britain and France emerging as major powers in the region.

What did all of this accomplish? Who can forget the glory and the achievements of this war? Truly, it was a time of great triumph for all involved. Except for the thousands upon thousands of people who died, of course.

So, what was accomplished with the Crimean War? Well, for starters, it was a great opportunity for Europe's major powers to flex their muscles and show off their military might.

After all, it had been a few decades since the Napoleonic Wars, and everyone was itching for a chance to prove themselves.

And prove themselves they did! The British, French, and Ottoman Empires teamed up to take on the Russian Empire in what would become a brutal and bloody conflict.

There were sieges, battles, and lots and lots of casualties. But in the end, the Western powers emerged victorious, thanks in part to their superior technology and organization.

But what did they accomplish, really? Well, they did manage to curb Russia's ambitions in the Black Sea region, which was nice, or do we care?

They also proved that the Ottoman Empire was still a force to be reckoned with, which was important for maintaining the balance of power in Europe.

But beyond that, what did they achieve? Not much. The Crimean War was a costly and bloody conflict that left thousands of people dead and wounded. And for what? A few strategic gains, some bragging rights, and a whole lot of debt.

Oh, and let's not forget about the aftermath. The Crimean War had some pretty significant consequences that would shape Europe for decades to come.

For one thing, it showed that Russia was no longer the unstoppable force it had once been. This would pave the way for other powers to challenge Russia's dominance in the region.

It also highlighted the weaknesses of the Ottoman Empire, which would eventually lead to its downfall. And it set the stage for a new era of European imperialism, as the major powers jostled for influence and control in other parts of the world.

So, all in all, the Crimean War was a resounding success, right? Well, not exactly. Sure, it had some strategic benefits and showed off the military might of the major powers. But at what cost?

Thousands of lives were lost, a region destabilized, and a new era of imperialism ushered in. It's hard to say that anyone truly "won" the Crimean War.

But, at least we got some good war poetry out of it...

The Russo-Japanese War

The Russo-Japanese War was a military conflict fought between Russia and Japan from 1904 to 1905. The war was a significant event in world history, marking the first time that an Asian power had defeated a European power in a modern war.

The war was fought over many issues, including Russian expansion in East Asia, the control of Korea, and the strategic importance of the Sea of Japan.

The Russo-Japanese War was sparked by a dispute between Russia and Japan over the control of Korea. Japan, which had recently undergone a period of modernization and industrialization, sought to expand its influence in the region.

Russia, which had long sought to expand its presence in East Asia, had established a significant presence in the region and was determined to maintain its influence over Korea.

In 1904, Japan launched a surprise attack on the Russian Pacific Fleet at Port Arthur, marking the beginning of the war. The Russo-Japanese War was a brutal conflict, with high numbers of casualties on both sides.

Exact figures for the number of casualties are difficult to determine, but estimates suggest that between 100,000 and 130,000 people may have died as a result of the war.

The Russo-Japanese War officially ended with the signing of the Treaty of Portsmouth in 1905. The treaty was negotiated by representatives of Russia and Japan, with the mediation of US President Theodore Roosevelt.

So what the fuck was accomplished?
One of the lesser-known conflicts in the grand scheme of things. But hey, that doesn't mean we can't have some fun with it. So, what was accomplished with this war and its aftermath?

It all started in 1904 when Russia and Japan decided to have a bit of a tiff over their respective spheres of influence in Manchuria and Korea.

The Japanese were all gung-ho and ready to rumble, while the Russians were still reeling from their embarrassing defeat at the hands of the British during the Boer War.

So, naturally, this seemed like the perfect opportunity for them to prove their mettle.

The war itself was a bit of a mess. The Japanese had a modernized army and navy, while the Russians were still stuck in the Dark Ages.

But, hey, that didn't stop the Russians from sending their Baltic Fleet around the world to get absolutely obliterated by the Japanese at the Battle of Tsushima.
And let's not forget about the Siege of Port Arthur, which lasted for months and saw some of the bloodiest fightings of the war. All in all, it was a pretty brutal affair.

But, you know what they say: "War is hell, but at least it's good for something."
So, what was accomplished with this particular hellish war?

Well, for one thing, it led to the Treaty of Portsmouth, which was signed in 1905 and effectively ended the conflict. The Japanese came out on top, of course, and managed to expand their influence in Asia at the expense of the Russians.

But that's not all!

The Russo-Japanese War also had several other notable accomplishments, such as: The realization that Russia was in dire need of some serious military reform. Seriously, their army and navy were a mess, and the war made that painfully clear.

This realization eventually led to the reforms of Tsar Nicholas II, which, as we all know, worked out great for everyone involved.

The realization that Japan was a legitimate world power. Sure, they may have been a relatively small island nation, but they managed to take on one of the biggest empires in the world and come out on top. This earned them some serious respect from other countries and helped cement their status as a major player on the world stage.

The realization that war is expensive. Like, really expensive.
Both Russia and Japan had to spend a ton of money on this war, and it put a serious dent in their economies.

This led to a renewed interest in diplomacy and peaceful solutions to international disputes...just kidding, it led to World War I a few years later Oops.

So, there you have it. The Russo-Japanese War may not be the most well-known conflict out there, but it still managed to accomplish quite a bit.

Who knew that all it took to kickstart a new era of military reform and global diplomacy was a little bit of bloodshed and destruction?

The Mexican-American War

The Mexican-American War was a military conflict fought between the United States and Mexico from 1846 to 1848. The war was fought primarily in the territories that now make up modern-day Texas, California, New Mexico, Arizona, and Nevada.

The causes of the war were complex and multifaceted. Tensions had been building between the United States and Mexico for many years, fueled by issues such as border disputes, economic competition, and differing cultural and political ideologies.

The Mexican-American War began in April 1846, when a detachment of American soldiers clashed with Mexican troops along the disputed border between Texas and Mexico.

The incident, known as the Thornton Affair, sparked a wider conflict that quickly escalated into full-scale war.

The United States was led by President James K. Polk, who had been a strong proponent of American expansionism and had set his sights on acquiring territory from Mexico.

The Mexican-American War was a bloody conflict, with high numbers of casualties on both sides.

Exact figures for the number of casualties are difficult to determine, but estimates suggest that between 13,000 and 20,000 Mexicans and around 1,700 Americans died as a result of the war.

The Mexican-American War officially ended with the signing of the Treaty of Guadalupe Hidalgo in February 1848.

The treaty was negotiated by representatives of the United States and Mexico, and it marked a major victory for American expansionism.

Wow, this accomplished important things, right? This war was a shining example of American imperialism at its finest, and it's truly a shame that it's not celebrated more often.

Firstly, let's talk about the accomplishments. The war was a clear victory for the United States. They managed to annex an enormous amount of territory, including the present-day states of California, Nevada, Utah, Arizona, and New Mexico, and parts of Colorado, Wyoming, Kansas, and Oklahoma.

That's right, the United States just decided to take a bunch of lands that didn't belong to them, and nobody really batted an eye. That's the American way, baby!

But it wasn't just about stealing land. The Mexican-American War was also a great opportunity for America to flex its military muscles.

Of course, there were some downsides to the war as well. Thousands of people died, both American and Mexican.

Most of the people who died were Mexican, so the world did not care? That's just collateral damage, baby!

And then there's the aftermath. It cemented America's status as a global superpower and set the stage for all sorts of future war adventures.

The United States became more confident in its ability to project its power overseas, which led to all sorts of fun stuff like the Spanish-American War and the Vietnam War.

Plus, all that new territory gave Americans plenty of room to spread out and build stuff, which is always a good thing.

But let's not forget about the impact the Mexican-American War had on Mexico itself.

Sure, they lost a bunch of territories and suffered thousands of casualties, but they also got a lot of attention from the United States.

Americans were suddenly very interested in Mexican culture and history, which led to all sorts of positive interactions between the two countries.

Just kidding! Actually, the aftermath of the war was pretty terrible for Mexico.

They were left humiliated and defeated, with a ruined economy and a government in disarray. The war was a disaster for Mexico, and it took them years to recover.

So there you have it, folks. The Mexican-American War was a glorious victory for the United States, a chance to show off their military might and steal some land.
Sure, there were some drawbacks, like all those dead people and the fact that Mexico got totally screwed over.

But in the end, isn't that just the way war goes? It's a small price to pay for manifest destiny.

The War of The Pacific

The War of the Pacific, also known as the Saltpeter War, was fought between Chile and a coalition formed by Peru and Bolivia from 1879 to 1884.

The war was primarily fought over control of valuable mineral resources in the region, particularly saltpeter, and guano.

The conflict was triggered by a dispute between Chile and Bolivia over taxes on Chilean mining companies operating in Bolivia. Peru subsequently became involved in the conflict due to its mutual defense treaty with Bolivia.

The War of the Pacific began when Chile launched a surprise attack on the Bolivian port city of Antofagasta.

The Chilean navy subsequently blockaded the Peruvian port of Callao, and a series of battles and skirmishes followed in the region.

The War of the Pacific was a devastating conflict, with significant loss of life on all sides. Estimates suggest that around 18,000 Chileans, 12,000 Peruvians, and 3,500 Bolivians died as a result of the war.

The conflict also resulted in significant social and economic upheaval in the region, with many communities devastated by the fighting and subsequent political changes.

The War of the Pacific officially ended in 1884, with the signing of the Treaty of Ancón between Chile and Peru.

Under the terms of the treaty, Peru ceded the provinces of Tarapaca and Arica to Chile, while Chile agreed to pay Peru an indemnity of $10 million.

What was accomplished after this war?
The Saltpeter War—a true masterpiece of military strategy and cunning diplomacy! So many things were accomplished, and it's hard to know where to start.

But let's try anyway. The main reason for the war was control of nitrate-rich territories in the Atacama Desert, which were incredibly valuable at the time for use in fertilizers and explosives.

So, what did the war accomplish? Well, for starters, it accomplished the transfer of the nitrate-rich territories from Bolivia and Peru to Chile. This was a huge victory for Chile, which became one of the world's largest exporters of nitrate and experienced an economic boom as a result.

Bolivia and Peru, on the other hand, were left with nothing but bitterness and resentment, but hey, you can't win 'em all.

Another thing that was accomplished was the establishment of Chile as a dominant power in South America.

Before the war, Chile was seen as a relatively minor player in the region, but after defeating two of its neighbors in a bloody conflict, it earned a reputation as a force to be reckoned with.

This helped Chile secure favorable trade agreements with other countries and establish itself as a leader in the region.

Of course, there were also some less positive accomplishments of the war. For one thing, it resulted in the deaths of tens of thousands of soldiers and civilians, not to mention the displacement of countless others.

Another less positive accomplishment was the deepening of animosity between Chile and its neighbors.

Bolivia and Peru both resented Chile for taking their land and humiliating them on the battlefield, and this resentment persisted for decades, leading to further conflicts and tensions in the region.

But despite these minor setbacks, overall the War of the Pacific was a resounding success.

Chile emerged from the conflict stronger and more prosperous than ever, while Bolivia and Peru were left to lick their wounds and contemplate what might have been.

And really, isn't that what war is all about? The thrill of victory, the agony of defeat, and the sweet, sweet taste of nitrate-rich desert soil?

The Spanish-American War

The Spanish-American War was a brief conflict fought in 1898 between the United States and Spain. The war was primarily fought over Spanish territories in the Caribbean and Pacific, including Cuba, Puerto Rico, Guam, and the Philippines.

The conflict was sparked by a variety of factors, including U.S. interests in expanding its economic and political influence in the Caribbean and Pacific, concerns over Spanish treatment of Cubans, and the sinking of the U.S.S. Maine in Havana harbor.

The Spanish-American War was a relatively brief conflict, with fewer casualties than many other wars of the time.

Estimates suggest that around 2,400 Americans and 1,600 Spaniards died as a result of the war.

The conflict also resulted in significant social and political changes in the region, with Spain losing control of its territories in the Caribbean and Pacific and the United States emerging as a dominant power in the area.

The Spanish-American War officially ended in August 1898, with the signing of the Treaty of Paris. Under the terms of the treaty, Spain ceded control of Cuba, Puerto Rico, Guam, and the Philippines to the United States, and agreed to pay the United States $20 million.

What. Else. Was. Accomplished?
A true classic, this Spanish-American War. I remember it like it was yesterday. And by yesterday, I mean 1898. What a time to be alive, let me tell you.

The US and Spain going head to head over some islands in the Caribbean and the Pacific. It was like a game of Risk, but with actual lives at stake.

First and foremost, the US got itself some new territories. Puerto Rico, Guam, and the Philippines were all annexed by the US.

It's like the US was a kid in a candy store, and Spain was just giving away these territories like they were free samples. And boy did the US gobble them up.

Who cares about Spain's sovereignty over these lands, right? They were just sitting there, ripe for the taking.

But don't worry, Spain got something out of the deal too. They got to keep their honor. Yep, that's right. Spain may have lost the war, but at least they didn't lose their pride.

And really, isn't that what's most important? Losing a war is one thing, but losing your dignity? That's just too much to bear.

And let's not forget about Cuba. Sure, the US technically liberated Cuba from Spanish rule, but let's be real here.
The US was just replacing one form of colonialism with another.

The US took control of Cuba's economy and government, essentially turning the island into its little playground. But hey, at least the US was "spreading democracy," right? Right?

And speaking of democracy, the US got to flex its muscles on the world stage. The Spanish-American War showed the world that the US was a major player in international affairs. No longer could other countries ignore the US or treat it like some backwater nation.

The US had arrived, and it was here to stay. And what better way to show off your power than by invading a weaker country and taking its territories?

But let's not forget about the casualties of war. Sure, the US won, but at what cost? Thousands of people died, both American and Spanish. And for what? So the US could have some new territories to play with?

It's like the US was playing a game of Risk and didn't care about the lives of the people involved. Oh wait, I already made that comparison.

And let's not forget about the aftermath of the war. The US had taken control of these new territories, but what were they going to do with them? How were they going to govern them?

These were questions that the US didn't have an answer to. It was like they were so focused on winning the war that they forgot about the consequences of their actions.

It's like a kid who gets a new toy and then realizes they don't really know what to do with it.

Overall, the Spanish-American War accomplished a lot. The US got some new territories, Spain got to keep its honor, and the world got to see the US flex its muscles.

But at what cost? The loss of life, the displacement of people, and the uncertain future of these new territories.

It's like the US was so focused on the short-term gains that they forgot about the long-term consequences. But hey, at least they got some new territories…

The Boer Wars

The Boer Wars were a series of conflicts fought between the British Empire and two Boer states in South Africa, the South African Republic (Transvaal) and the Orange Free State.

The first Boer War took place between 1880 and 1881, while the second Boer War was fought between 1899 and 1902.

The Boer Wars involved the British Empire on one side, and the South African Republic and the Orange Free State, collectively known as the Boer states, on the other.

The Boer states were made up of descendants of Dutch colonists who had settled in the region during the seventeenth century.

The conflict was primarily fought over control of the region's rich mineral resources and political power.

The first Boer War began when the Boer states rebelled against British rule.

The conflict was sparked by a variety of factors, including tensions over British attempts to annex the region and the Boer states' desire for greater independence.

The conflict lasted for just over a year, with the Boer states achieving a decisive victory at the Battle of Majuba Hill in 1881.

The second Boer War began in 1899 after the British Empire sought to extend its control over the region.

The conflict was sparked by tensions over British mining interests, as well as a desire to expand the British Empire's political influence.

The Boer Wars were marked by significant casualties on all sides. The first Boer War saw around 400 British and 400 Boer casualties, while the second Boer War saw around 22,000 British and 25,000 Boer casualties.

The first Boer War ended in 1881, with the signing of the Pretoria Convention.

Under the terms of the convention, the Boer states were granted a degree of independence, while the British Empire retained control over the region's foreign affairs.

The second Boer War officially ended in 1902, with the signing of the Treaty of Vereeniging.

Under the terms of the treaty, the Boer states were absorbed into the British Empire, and the region was renamed the Union of South Africa.

So, what was accomplished this time? There's nothing quite like colonialism and imperialism to bring a smile to your face.

I mean, what's not to love about invading a foreign country, displacing the population, and stealing all their resources? But I digress, let's talk about the Boer Wars.

The first Boer War started in 1880, and after three years of fighting, ended with the Pretoria Convention, which recognized the independence of the South African Republic.

But that didn't last long, because the British had their sights set on the gold and diamonds in the region.

So, in 1899, the second Boer War began. The British Empire, with its superior military and firepower, thought it would be an easy victory.

But they were wrong. The Boers were tough, resilient, and knew the land better than anyone else. Plus, they had a secret weapon: the power of racism!

Yes, the Boers believed in the supremacy of the white race, and that gave them the courage and conviction to fight against the British Empire.

But alas, it was not enough. The British eventually won the war, and the Boer republics were annexed into the British Empire.

What did the British accomplish with this war, you ask? Well, let's take a look.

First, they got their hands on all the gold and diamonds they wanted. The Boer republics were rich in these resources, and the British were more than happy to take them for themselves.

It's amazing what a little bit of violence can do to help with your financial situation!

Second, the British got to showcase their military might to the world. They had the most advanced weapons, the best-trained soldiers, and a seemingly endless supply of resources.

The world was impressed, and the British Empire's reputation as the dominant superpower of the time was solidified.

Third, they got to play a fun little game called "concentration camps." Yes, you read that right. The British forced the Boer women and children into concentration camps, where they were subjected to disease, malnutrition, and abuse. It was a great way to show off their humanitarian side.

But let's not forget the aftermath of the Boer Wars.

The British had taken control of a foreign land, and they needed to figure out what to do with it.

They decided to implement a policy of apartheid, which was a system of racial segregation and discrimination.

The black population was treated as second-class citizens, forced to live in separate areas, and denied basic human rights.

This policy lasted for decades, and its effects are still being felt today. The Boer Wars may have been a victory for the British Empire, but it came at a high cost.
The lives of thousands of Boers were lost, as well as the lives of many black South Africans.

But hey, at least the British got their gold and diamonds, right? And they got to pat themselves on the back for being the best military power in the world.

Who cares about the lives of a few thousand people when you have all that going for you?

In conclusion, the Boer Wars were a great success for the British Empire. They got their resources, showed off their military might, and got to play a fun game of concentration camps.

The aftermath, with its policy of apartheid and continued discrimination, is just a small price to pay for all that glory.

So let's raise a glass to the Boer Wars, and to the legacy of imperialism and colonialism that they represent!

THE FALKLANDS WAR

The Falklands War was a conflict between Argentina and the United Kingdom that took place in 1982 over the sovereignty of the Falkland Islands, South Georgia, and South Sandwich Islands.

The conflict was sparked by a long-standing dispute over the sovereignty of the Falkland Islands, which had been under British control since 1833 but were also claimed by Argentina.

The conflict was primarily fought over control of the region's strategic location and its rich fishing grounds.

The war began on April 2, 1982, when Argentine forces invaded the Falkland Islands, South Georgia, and South Sandwich Islands.

The Argentine government argued that the islands were rightfully theirs and that they were acting to assert their territorial claims.
The British government responded by sending a naval task force to the region, and on April 5, the British submarine HMS Conqueror sank the Argentine cruiser General Belgrano, killing over 300 Argentine sailors.

The Falklands War resulted in significant casualties on both sides. The conflict saw around 649 Argentine military personnel, three Falkland Islanders, and 255 British military personnel killed in action.

The Falklands War officially ended on June 14, 1982, when Argentina surrendered to the United Kingdom.

Under the terms of the surrender, Argentine forces withdrew from the Falkland Islands, South Georgia, and South Sandwich Islands, and the British government resumed control of the region.

What was it good for, absolutely nothing? A conflict between two countries that most people didn't even know existed before it happened.

Let's start with the basics: in 1982, Argentina decided it wanted to take over the Falkland Islands, a small British territory off the coast of South America.

They thought it would be an easy win, considering they were right next door and the British were all the way across the ocean. But little did they know, the British are very good at fighting wars they probably shouldn't be involved in.

So, what did we accomplish in the Falklands War? Well, for starters, we proved that the British military is still a force to be reckoned with.

Sure, we may have lost a few ships and a handful of soldiers, but we ultimately won the war and kicked Argentina out of the Falklands.

Take that, Argentina!

But what did we really accomplish? Did we gain any new territories or resources? Did we make any new friends or enemies? Did we learn anything about ourselves as a nation?

The answer to all of these questions is a resounding "no." In fact, the aftermath of the Falklands War was mostly just a bunch of posturing and chest-beating from both sides.

Argentina was understandably humiliated by their defeat, so they spent the next few decades trying to reclaim the Falklands through diplomatic means.

And what did we really learn from the Falklands War? Well, we learned that sometimes it's okay to fight a war for no real reason other than to flex our military muscles.

We also learned that sometimes a small, insignificant conflict can be blown out of proportion and turned into a major international incident.

But most importantly, we learned that sometimes it's better to just let a small, insignificant conflict remain small and insignificant.

The Falklands War may have been a victory for the British military, but it ultimately accomplished very little in terms of tangible benefits for either side.

So, there you have it. The Falklands War: a lot of noise and fury signifying nothing.

But hey, at least we got a catchy song out of it, right? "Don't cry for me, Argentina..."

THE IRAN-IRAQ WAR

The Iran-Iraq War was a protracted armed conflict that lasted from September 1980 to August 1988, between Iran and Iraq. It was one of the longest and bloodiest wars of the 20th century.

The war was sparked by long-standing border disputes and political tensions between the two nations.

Iraq was ruled by Saddam Hussein, a Sunni Muslim, while Iran was led by Ayatollah Khomeini, a Shi'ite Muslim.

The Iran-Iraq War began on September 22, 1980, when Iraqi forces launched a surprise attack on Iran.

The attack was aimed at capturing Iran's oil-rich Khuzestan province, which had been a source of contention between the two nations.

The Iraqi government claimed that Iran had been supporting Kurdish separatists in northern Iraq and that the invasion was a preemptive strike to defend against Iranian aggression.

The Iran-Iraq War resulted in significant casualties on both sides. Estimates vary widely, but it is believed that between 500,000 and one million people died during the conflict.

The war also saw extensive use of chemical weapons by both sides, causing thousands of deaths and long-term health problems for many who survived.

The Iran-Iraq War officially ended on August 20, 1988, when Iran accepted an UN-brokered ceasefire. The ceasefire called for an end to hostilities and the withdrawal of troops to pre-war positions.

However, the ceasefire did not resolve the underlying political and social tensions between the two nations, and sporadic border skirmishes continued for several years.

The conflict had significant political and social consequences for both Iran and Iraq. In Iran, the war led to a consolidation of power by Ayatollah Khomeini and the hardline elements of the Iranian government.

In Iraq, the war contributed to the decline of Saddam Hussein's popularity and ultimately set the stage for the Gulf War in 1991.

So, did they achieve some great things from this war?
The Iran-Iraq War is a sad classic in the world of military conflicts.

A war that was so pointless and absurd, it's hard to know where to begin. But let's give it a shot, shall we?

The Iran-Iraq War, which lasted from 1980 to 1988, was a true masterpiece of human folly.
It was like watching two idiots fighting over a piece of bread while a loaf sat untouched on the table.

But hey, who needs logic and reason when you have national pride, right? So what was accomplished with this war? Well, let's see.

First of all, both sides managed to kill a whole lot of people. According to some estimates, over a million people died in this conflict. That's right, a million!

Congratulations, Iran and Iraq, you managed to wipe out a significant chunk of your population. Well done!

But it's not just the death toll that was impressive. Both countries also managed to destroy a ton of infrastructure and set back their economies by decades.

Iraq, in particular, managed to take a country that was once a prosperous, oil-rich nation and turn it into a post-apocalyptic wasteland. Bravo!

And let's not forget about the psychological toll of the war. For eight long years, both sides lived in constant fear of attack. Families were torn apart, children were traumatized, and entire communities were displaced.

But hey, at least they got to wave their flags and shout patriotic slogans, right?

So what was accomplished in the aftermath of the war? Well, let's start with the obvious. Iran and Iraq were left with a massive mess to clean up.

Both countries had to deal with the aftermath of the war for years if not decades. They had to rebuild their shattered infrastructure, deal with the psychological trauma of the conflict, and try to get their economies back on track. Good luck with that!

But hey, at least the rest of the world learned some valuable lessons from the Iran-Iraq War, right?

Like the fact that wars are a bad idea and that diplomacy is always the better option. Oh, wait. Nevermind. We didn't learn anything from this war either.

In fact, we went on to have even more pointless conflicts in the years that followed. Yay, us!

In conclusion, the Iran-Iraq War was a shining example of human stupidity and the futility of war. Both sides managed to accomplish absolutely nothing, except for death, destruction, and misery.

So congratulations, Iran and Iraq. You really showed us all how to make a complete mess of things.

The Yugoslav Wars

The Yugoslav Wars were a series of conflicts that took place in the Balkans between 1991 and 2001. The wars resulted in the dissolution of Yugoslavia and the creation of several new nations in the region.

The Yugoslav Wars involved several different factions, including the Federal Republic of Yugoslavia (consisting of Serbia and Montenegro), Croatia, Bosnia and Herzegovina, and Kosovo. Ethnic and nationalist tensions fueled the conflicts, with different groups seeking greater autonomy or independence.

The Yugoslav Wars began with the breakup of Yugoslavia, a federation of six republics that had been formed after World War II. Slovenia and Croatia declared independence, triggering armed conflict with Yugoslavia's federal army.

The war quickly spread to Bosnia and Herzegovina, which declared independence in 1992, and Kosovo, a province of Serbia that sought greater autonomy.

The Yugoslav Wars resulted in significant casualties on all sides, with estimates ranging from 130,000 to 200,000 people killed. The conflict also saw numerous war crimes and atrocities committed, including ethnic cleansing and genocide.

The Yugoslav Wars officially ended in 2001, with the signing of the Ohrid Framework Agreement, which ended the conflict in Macedonia. However, the other conflicts had been resolved earlier through a series of peace negotiations and agreements.

What was achieved?
Let's start with the good news. The Yugoslav Wars accomplished a lot. They proved that humans are capable of great violence and destruction when they put their minds to it.

They also showed us that the international community is a bunch of hypocrites who only care about their own interests. First, we had the Croatian War of Independence.

The Croats wanted their own country, and they were willing to fight for it. So, they started killing Serbs and destroying their homes.

The Serbs didn't take kindly to this, so they started killing Croats and destroying their homes. And so it went, back and forth, for four years. In the end, the Croats got their country, and the Serbs got... well, they got screwed.

Next up was the Bosnian War.

The Bosniaks wanted their own country, and they were willing to fight for it. So, they started killing Serbs and Croats and destroying their homes.

Of course, the Serbs and Croats didn't take kindly to this, so they started killing Bosniaks and destroying their homes. And so it went, back and forth, for three years. In the end, the Bosniaks got their country, and the Serbs and Croats got... well, they got screwed.

Then came the Kosovo War. The Albanians wanted their own country, and they were willing to fight for it. So, they started killing Serbs and destroying their homes.

The Serbs, well they started killing Albanians and destroying their homes. And so it went, back and forth, for two years. In the end, the Albanians got their country, and the Serbs got...

But let's not forget the aftermath of the Yugoslav Wars. They left behind a trail of destruction, displacement, and ethnic hatred.

They also gave rise to some of the most infamous war criminals in history, like Slobodan Milošević and Radovan Karadžić. But hey, at least they got to sit in a courtroom for a few years before dying.

The international community didn't do much to stop the Yugoslav Wars while they were happening. Sure, they sent in some peacekeepers, but they didn't have a clear mandate, and they were severely underfunded.

And let's be honest, no one really cared about the Balkans. It was a bunch of people killing each other in a place no one had ever heard of.

But when it was all over, the international community swooped in to save the day. They held a bunch of peace talks, created some new countries, and gave themselves a pat on the back for a job well done.

And then they left.

They left behind a bunch of unstable countries with corrupt governments, weak economies, and simmering ethnic tensions. But hey, at least they got to feel good about themselves for a little while.

In conclusion, the Yugoslav Wars were a hilarious and entertaining period of human history. They showed us the power of tribalism, the hypocrisy of the international community, and the futility of war.

They also left behind a trail of destruction and hatred that will take generations to heal. But let's not dwell on the negative. Let's just sit back, relax, and enjoy the fact that we don't live in the Balkans.

The Soviet-Afghan War

The Soviet-Afghan War was a conflict that took place between 1979 and 1989, primarily between the Soviet Union and Afghanistan.

The war involved the Soviet Union, which was supporting the Afghan government at the time, and various Afghan resistance groups, collectively known as the Mujahideen.

The conflict was fueled by ideological differences, as well as strategic considerations, with the Soviet Union seeking to maintain its influence in the region.

The Soviet-Afghan War began when Soviet troops entered Afghanistan in an attempt to prop up the Soviet-backed government of President Babrak Karmal.

The invasion was met with fierce resistance from the Mujahideen, who were supported by the United States and other Western countries.

The Soviet-Afghan War was a brutal conflict that resulted in significant casualties on all sides. Estimates suggest that between 600,000 and 2 million Afghans were killed, including many civilians.

The war also resulted in the displacement of millions of people and the destruction of much of the country's infrastructure.

The Soviet Union also suffered significant losses, with tens of thousands of troops killed or injured during the conflict.

The Soviet-Afghan War officially ended in 1989, when the last Soviet troops withdrew from Afghanistan.

What was accomplished then? This was a true war classic, and one that had a lasting impact on both Afghanistan, the Soviet Union and the rest of the world.

First of all, let's talk about what the Soviets were trying to accomplish.

They wanted to prop up the Afghan government, which was led by a communist party, and suppress the mujahideen rebellion that was fighting against them. Of course, this was easier said than done.

The Soviets were sending troops and weapons into Afghanistan like it was going out of style, but they just couldn't seem to get the upper hand.

The Mujahideen were wily and resourceful, and they knew the land much better than the Soviet soldiers did.

The Soviets were also facing stiff opposition from the United States, who were sending aid and weapons to the mujahideen.

Despite all of this, the Soviet Union kept pouring resources into Afghanistan. They were determined to show the world that they could maintain a communist government in a country that was historically resistant to it.

Plus, they really wanted all that sweet, sweet opium that Afghanistan was known for.

But what did they actually accomplish? Well, they managed to kill a lot of people, both mujahideen and innocent civilians. They also turned Afghanistan into a war zone, destroying homes, businesses, and infrastructure.

Oh, and they also managed to breed a whole new generation of jihadists who were more than happy to take on the West.

In 1989, the Soviets finally threw in the towel and withdrew their troops from Afghanistan. They left behind a country in ruins and a power vacuum that would eventually be filled by the Taliban.

So, what did they accomplish? Well, they certainly didn't accomplish their goal of propping up a communist government.

They also managed to tarnish their reputation on the world stage and drive their economy into the ground. But hey, at least they got some good opium, right?

The aftermath of the Soviet-Afghan War was just as disastrous as the war itself. Afghanistan was left in shambles, and the Taliban quickly took control of the country.

The mujahideen fighters who had once fought against the Soviets turned on each other, leading to years of bloody civil war.
The United States didn't fare much better. They had supported the mujahideen during the war, but once it was over, they lost interest in Afghanistan.

This allowed the Taliban to gain a foothold and set the stage for the 9/11 attacks, which would eventually lead to the US invasion of Afghanistan in 2001.

So, what was accomplished with the Soviet-Afghan War? Well, not much, really. The Soviets failed to achieve their goals, and the aftermath was a disaster for Afghanistan and the world at large.

But hey, at least we got a great Rambo movie out of it.

THE INDIAN WARS

The Indian Wars were a series of conflicts that took place between Native American tribes and European colonizers and their descendants in North America from 1622 to 1924.

These conflicts were characterized by cultural and territorial disputes, with Native Americans seeking to defend their lands and ways of life from encroachment by European settlers.

The Indian Wars involved various Native American tribes and confederacies, including the Cherokee, Apache, Sioux, Comanche, and many others, as well as European colonizers and their descendants.

As European settlement expanded, tensions grew between colonizers and Native Americans, leading to sporadic outbreaks of violence.

The Indian Wars were also fueled by government policies that sought to displace Native Americans from their lands and forcibly assimilate them into European American society.

Estimates of the number of casualties in the Indian Wars vary widely, but it is clear that the conflicts resulted in significant loss of life and suffering on all sides. Native Americans were disproportionately affected, with entire communities wiped out by disease, starvation, and violence.

European colonizers and their descendants also suffered significant losses, with soldiers and civilians alike falling victim to the conflicts.

The Indian Wars came to an end in 1924, with the passage of the Indian Citizenship Act, which granted citizenship to all Native Americans born in the United States. The act marked a significant shift in government policy toward Native Americans, recognizing their status as citizens.

Anything of importance accomplished?
Sure. If you were a white settler in America, that is. It was a time of adventure, conquest, and manifest destiny. Who cares about the indigenous people who had lived on the land for thousands of years? They were in the way of progress!

Well, let me tell you. First of all, we got rid of those pesky Native Americans who were standing in the way of our manifest destiny.

Sure, we had to push them off their land, make them march for days without food or water, and force them onto reservations, but it was for their own good. They couldn't survive in the modern world, after all.

Plus, think of all the land we gained! We were able to expand our borders and build new settlements. It was like a giant game of Tetris, but instead of blocks, we were using the lives and land of Native Americans.

And let's not forget the military victories! The Battle of Little Bighorn, for example. We may have lost a few soldiers, but we showed those Native Americans who were boss. And the massacre at Wounded Knee? That was just a necessary show of force.

But it wasn't just about military conquest. We also accomplished a lot culturally. We introduced the Native Americans to our way of life. They learned how to speak English, wear Western clothing, and worship our god. We were civilizing them!

And let's not forget the economic gains. The Indian Wars opened up new resources and markets for us to exploit. We were able to extract gold, silver, and other precious metals from the land.

We also had a new market for our goods and services. Those Native Americans needed everything from food to weapons to alcohol. We were happy to provide, for a price.

Now, some people might say that the aftermath of the Indian Wars was a bit messy.

Sure, there were some negative consequences, like poverty, disease, and loss of culture for Native Americans. But really, they should be grateful for what we did.

After all, we gave them reservations to live on, and we even let them have their own government. Sure, it was a government that we controlled, but still.

And let's not forget the positive aspects of assimilation. Native Americans are now able to participate in our economy and society.

They can get jobs, vote, and even become millionaires like some of those casino owners. Isn't that progress?

In the end, the Indian Wars were a necessary part of America's growth and expansion. We showed the world that we were a force to be reckoned with, and we paved the way for the modern United States.

So let's raise a glass to the pioneers, soldiers, and settlers who made it all possible. And let's not forget the Native Americans, who played a small but important role in our history. Cheers!

THE WAR OF THE ROSES

The War of the Roses was a series of conflicts that took place in England from 1455 to 1485. The war was fought between two rival branches of the royal House of Plantagenet, the House of Lancaster and the House of York, and was characterized by political intrigue, shifting alliances, and intense battles.

The War of the Roses was sparked by a dispute over the succession to the English throne. The Lancastrian King Henry VI suffered from bouts of mental illness, which led to a power vacuum at the top of the English nobility.

Richard, Duke of York, a prominent member of the nobility, saw an opportunity to press his claim to the throne and launched a rebellion against the king in 1455.

The conflict quickly escalated into a full-blown civil war, with various factions supporting either the House of Lancaster or the House of York. The conflict was fueled by personal rivalries, family feuds, and long-standing grievances, as well as broader political and economic concerns.

Estimates of the number of casualties in the War of the Roses vary widely, but it is clear that the conflicts resulted in significant loss of life and suffering on all sides.

The battles were often bloody and brutal, with armies clashing in fierce hand-to-hand combat. Civilian populations were also caught up in the conflict, with towns and villages being raided and pillaged by opposing forces.

The War of the Roses ended in 1485 with the Battle of Bosworth Field, in which the forces of Henry Tudor, a Lancastrian claimant to the throne, defeated the army of King Richard III, a Yorkist.

Richard was killed in the battle, and Henry Tudor has crowned King Henry VII, marking the beginning of the Tudor dynasty.

It accomplished... what?
A civil war that lasted for over 30 years, fought between two noble families in England over who had the right to sit on the throne. It's hard to believe that this is the same country that gave us Shakespeare and afternoon tea!

Let's take a closer look at what was accomplished with this epic conflict.

First of all, we have to acknowledge the obvious: a whole lot of people died. And for what? A few people want to be king or queen. Seems a bit silly, doesn't it?

But don't worry, it's not like the war caused any long-lasting damage or anything... oh wait, it did.

For one thing, it left England weak and vulnerable.
The constant fighting and power struggles weakened the monarchy, making it difficult for the government to maintain control over the country.

This led to a power vacuum that was eventually filled by the Tudors, who took advantage of the situation to seize the throne and establish a new dynasty. But hey, at least they were better than the last guys, right?

Another "accomplishment" of the War of the Roses was the creation of a new class of professional soldiers.

These were men who had fought in the war and had become skilled in the art of war. With no other options available to them, many of these soldiers turned to a life of banditry, robbing and pillaging the countryside.

So, if you ever find yourself in medieval England, watch out for those guys with swords.

But let's not forget the positive side of things. The War of the Roses did give us some great historical figures to admire.

There was Richard III, the hunchbacked king who was famously portrayed by Shakespeare as a murderous villain.

And then there was Henry VII, the first Tudor king who defeated Richard and established the Tudor dynasty. He may not have been as exciting as Richard, but at least he wasn't a hunchback.

In the end, what was accomplished with the War of the Roses? Not much, really.

A lot of people died, the monarchy was weakened, and a new dynasty was established. Oh, and we got some great Shakespeare plays out of it. So I guess it wasn't a total loss.

But seriously, let's learn from our mistakes. Let's not fight wars over petty disagreements, pretty flowers and personal ambitions. Let's focus on building a better world for everyone, not just a select few.

And let's definitely not let our personal issues tear apart our entire country. Because if there's one thing the War of the Roses taught us, it's that civil wars suck.

The Zulu Wars

The Zulu Wars were a series of conflicts between the British Empire and the Zulu Kingdom in southern Africa in 1879. The Zulu people were a powerful ethnic group in southern Africa with a strong military tradition, while the British were colonial forces seeking to expand their control over the region.

The Zulu Wars began when the British invaded Zululand, seeking to extend their control over the region.

The British believed that the Zulu Kingdom posed a threat to their colonial interests, and sought to neutralize this threat through military force.

The British encountered stiff resistance from the Zulu warriors, who were well-trained and fiercely committed to defending their land.

The Zulu army was also equipped with advanced weapons and tactics, including the famous short stabbing spear, which allowed them to engage the British in close combat.

The wars were extremely brutal and resulted in significant loss of life on both sides.

Estimates of the number of casualties vary, but it is believed that several thousand Zulu warriors were killed, along with hundreds of British soldiers.

The Zulu Wars ended in 1879 with the defeat of the Zulu Kingdom and the establishment of British control over the region.

Accomplish much? The Zulu Wars—a classic tale of British colonialism and conquest in Africa. It all started in the late 1800s when the British Empire was at the height of its power and looking to expand its influence in Africa.

The Zulu Kingdom, located in present-day South Africa, was an obstacle in their path to total domination.

So what did the British do? They invaded, of course! And they did it with their usual style and finesse.

The first war, fought in 1879, was a bit of a disaster for the British. Despite having superior weapons and technology, they were caught off guard by the ferocity and skill of the Zulu warriors.

In the infamous Battle of Isandlwana, the British suffered a crushing defeat and lost over 1,000 men.

But fear not, dear readers! The British were not to be deterred by a mere setback. They regrouped, licked their wounds, and came back for round two.

The second Zulu War fought in 1879–1880, was a resounding success for the British. They employed a scorched-earth policy, burning Zulu villages and crops and killing livestock, to starve the Zulu army and force them to surrender.

And it worked! The Zulus were defeated, and their kingdom was annexed by the British Empire. So what was accomplished with The Zulu Wars, you ask? Well, let me tell you.

First of all, the British got to flex their imperialistic muscles (again!) and show the world who was boss (again!). They also got to claim another piece of Africa for their growing empire, which was great for bragging rights. But most importantly, the Zulu Wars helped to solidify the idea of British superiority over the "uncivilized" peoples of Africa.

By defeating the Zulus, the British could tell themselves and the world that they were bringing "civilization" and "progress" to a backward and savage continent.

Of course, the aftermath of the Zulu Wars was not all sunshine and rainbows.

The British occupation of Zululand led to a great deal of unrest and resistance from the Zulu people, who were understandably upset about losing their independence and way of life.

The British responded with their usual charm and grace, brutally suppressing any resistance and imprisoning or killing anyone who dared to challenge their authority.

They also implemented a policy of forced labor, forcing Zulus to work in the gold and diamond mines that were springing up across southern Africa.

So what did we learn from The Zulu Wars?

Well, we learned that might make right, and that colonialism and imperialism are totally cool as long as you're the ones doing the conquering.

We also learned that the British were very good at killing people and taking their stuff. Maybe you have a diamond on your finger you can thank this war for?

But most importantly, we learned that history is written by the victors and that the story of The Zulu Wars, like so many other wars and conflicts, is one of triumph and heroism for the conquerors, and one of oppression and suffering for the conquered.

Hooray for the human race!

The First Anglo-Afghan War

The First Anglo-Afghan War was a military conflict between the British East India Company and the Emirate of Afghanistan from 1839 to 1842.

The British sought to extend their control over Afghanistan and prevent Russian expansion into the region, while the Afghans sought to defend their sovereignty and independence.

The First Anglo-Afghan War began when British forces invaded Afghanistan.

The British believed that the Afghan government posed a threat to their colonial interests in India, and sought to neutralize this threat through military force.

The British encountered significant resistance from the Afghan army, which was well-equipped and fiercely committed to defending its land.

The British were also hindered by their lack of knowledge of the Afghan terrain and culture, which made it difficult for them to effectively engage the Afghan forces.

The First Anglo-Afghan War was extremely brutal and resulted in significant loss of life on both sides.

Estimates of the number of casualties vary, but it is believed that several thousand British soldiers and civilians were killed, along with tens of thousands of Afghan soldiers and civilians.

The war was marked by a series of massacres and atrocities, including the famous "Retreat from Kabul", in which a British army of 16,000 soldiers and civilians was ambushed by Afghan forces and massacred.

The incident resulted in the death of nearly all of the British soldiers and civilians and remains one of the most tragic events in the history of the British military.

The First Anglo-Afghan War ended in 1842 with the withdrawal of British forces from Afghanistan.

At least something was accomplished …?
Also known as the Great Retreat, this war was a true masterpiece of military strategy and political decision-making. It's almost a shame that it's not more widely celebrated.

Let's start with the accomplishments, shall we? The British Empire managed to occupy Kabul for a few months, and even install their puppet ruler, Shah Shuja.

That's no small feat, considering that the Afghan people had a long history of resisting foreign invaders.
Plus, the British managed to beat the Afghan army in a few key battles, which is always a morale boost.

But the real accomplishment of the First Anglo-Afghan War was the retreat. You see, the British had a brilliant plan: invade Afghanistan, overthrow the ruling Barakzai dynasty, install their puppet ruler, and leave behind a garrison to keep the peace.

What could possibly go wrong?

Well, just about everything, as it turns out. The Afghan people didn't take kindly to foreign invaders, and the British found themselves bogged down in a seemingly endless guerrilla war.

The garrison in Kabul was constantly harassed by Afghan fighters, and the British soldiers were slowly but surely dying from disease, starvation, and enemy attacks.

So, in January 1842, the British decided to retreat from Kabul. They thought they could simply march back to India, with their soldiers and civilians protected by a small military escort.

It was a bold plan and one that could only succeed if everything went perfectly. Spoiler alert: it didn't.
The British column was ambushed by Afghan fighters almost immediately, and the retreat turned into a bloody massacre.

The soldiers and civilians were picked off one by one, and by the time the column reached the safety of Jalalabad, only a handful of survivors remained.

But let's not focus on the negatives, shall we? After all, the retreat from Kabul was an incredible accomplishment in its own right.
The British managed to flee from Afghanistan, leaving behind a trail of death and destruction, and they did it all with a stiff upper lip and a plucky can-do attitude.

And the aftermath? Well, that's where things get really interesting. The war was a wake-up call for the British Empire. They realized that maybe invading other countries wasn't such a great idea after all and that it was much easier to simply install puppet rulers and let them do the dirty work.

Of course, the stability didn't last. Afghanistan has been a hotbed of violence and political instability ever since, and the country is currently embroiled in yet another war, this time with the Taliban.

But hey, at least the British Empire can look back on the First Anglo-Afghan War with pride. They may have lost the battle, but they won the war. Or something like that.

The Second Anglo-Afghan War

The Second Anglo-Afghan War involved the British Empire, which was seeking to extend its influence in the region, and the Emirate of Afghanistan, which was led by Emir Mohammad Yaqub Khan. The war also involved several other local tribes and forces that supported one side or the other.

The Second Anglo-Afghan War began in when the British Empire invaded Afghanistan. The British were still motivated by a desire to prevent Russian expansion into the region and to extend their influence and control over the country.

The Second Anglo-Afghan War was a highly destructive conflict, with significant loss of life on both sides.

Estimates of the number of casualties vary, but it is believed that tens of thousands of Afghans were killed, along with several thousand British soldiers and civilians.

The war was marked by several atrocities and acts of violence, including the British-led massacre of Afghan villagers in the village of Deh Koh.
The war ended in 1880 with the Treaty of Gandamak, which was signed between the British Empire and Afghanistan.

Second time lucky and loads accomplished this time?

The Second Anglo-Afghan War, a time when the British Empire decided to once again invade Afghanistan and remind them who's boss. What could go wrong?

First, the British decided to invade Afghanistan to install a puppet ruler who would be more friendly to their interests. They picked a guy named Abdur Rahman Khan, who was more than happy to help the British out in exchange for the throne.

The British quickly realized that this wasn't going to be easy, as the Afghans didn't exactly appreciate the idea of being ruled by a foreign power. So they did what any good colonial power would do: they started a war.

The British sent in their troops, armed with their modern weapons and advanced tactics, and promptly got their asses handed to them by the Afghans.

Turns out that when you're fighting in a rugged mountain terrain against an enemy who knows the land like the back of their hand, your fancy guns and tactics don't count for much.

But the British weren't deterred. They kept sending in troops, and the Afghans kept killing them. Eventually, the British realized that they weren't going to win this war by force alone, so they decided to try a different tactic: bribes.

They started paying off Afghan tribal leaders, hoping to win their support and turn them against the Taliban. And it worked, sort of. The tribal leaders took the money, but they didn't do much to help the British cause.

Meanwhile, back in London, the British government was getting a bit antsy about this whole war thing. They weren't seeing any progress, and the body count was starting to pile up. So they decided to do what any good government would do: blame someone else.

They picked a scapegoat, a guy named Frederick Roberts, who had been leading the British troops in Afghanistan. They said that he wasn't aggressive enough and that he was too cautious in his tactics.

Never mind that he was fighting a war against an enemy who knew the terrain better than he did, and who had a lot more experience in guerrilla warfare. No, it was all Roberts' fault.

Eventually, the British managed to install their puppet ruler, Abdur Rahman Khan, on the Afghan throne. And what did they get for all their efforts?

Well, let's see: they had spent millions of pounds, lost thousands of troops, and gained... a puppet ruler who was more friendly to their interests.

But wait, it gets better. After the war was over, the British decided that they didn't really need Abdur Rahman Khan anymore.

They had gotten what they wanted, and now they could just leave him to deal with the mess they had created.

So, they abandoned him. And what did Abdur Rahman Khan get for his trouble? He got to deal with a country that was in shambles, with a population that was angry at him for selling out to the British.
And what did the British get for their trouble? They got to add another failed war to their long list of failed wars.

The British spent a lot of money, lost a lot of troops, and gained a puppet ruler who they promptly abandoned.

The Afghans, on the other hand, got to remind the British that they were a force to be reckoned with and that they weren't going to be pushed around by a bunch of foreign invaders.

So, I guess you could say that the real winners of the Second Anglo-Afghan War were... the Afghans?

Yeah, let's go with that.

THE OPIUM WARS

The Opium Wars were a series of conflicts between the British Empire and China that lasted from 1839 to 1860. The wars were fought over the British opium trade, which was illegal in China, and the unequal trade relationship between the two countries.

The wars also involved several other European powers, including France and the United States, which supported the British side.

The Opium Wars began in 1839 when the Chinese government, under pressure from domestic anti-opium movements, sought to crack down on the illegal British opium trade.

In response, the British government launched a military campaign to protect its interests and force the Chinese to accept British trade demands.

The war ended with the signing of the Treaty of Nanking, which granted Britain control over several ports and territories in China and opened up China to unequal trade relationships with Western powers.

The war was fought over similar issues, including the British trade in opium and the unequal trade relationship between China and the West.

The Opium Wars ended with the signing of several treaties between China and the Western powers.

These treaties granted the Western powers greater access to Chinese markets and territories and established the unequal trade relationship that would continue until the early 20th century.

High on accomplishments? The Opium Wars: A classic tale of greed, power, and addiction. Who wouldn't want to make a mockery of such a fine historical event?

It all started in the when the British East India Company realized that there was a massive demand for opium in China.

So, like any good capitalist, they started growing poppies in India and exporting the drug to China.

The Chinese government wasn't too pleased about this, as you might imagine, and tried to ban the drug. But the British were having none of it.

Thus, the First Opium War began in 1839. The British, armed with their opium, sailed into China and started wreaking havoc. The Chinese, unprepared for the British firepower, were quickly defeated.

The British then took control of Hong Kong and forced China to sign the Treaty of Nanking, which allowed the British to sell opium in China and granted them other concessions.

Fast forward a few decades, and the British were still addicted to that sweet, sweet opium money. So when the Chinese government tried to crack down on the drug trade again in the 1850s, the British weren't having it. Thus, the Second Opium War began in 1856.

This time, the British were joined by the French, who also had a taste for opium profits. Together, they sailed up the Yangtze River, burning and pillaging as they went.

The Chinese were once again defeated, and the British and French imposed even harsher terms on them than before.

So what did we accomplish with the Opium Wars? Well, the British and French got to keep making money off of opium, which was nice for them.

And China got to watch its country be plundered and exploited by foreign powers, which was less nice for them.

In the aftermath of the Opium Wars, China was left weakened and humiliated.

The Qing dynasty, which had ruled China for centuries, was on the brink of collapse. And the British and French continued to profit off of the drug trade, even as addiction ravaged the Chinese population.

But hey, at least the British got to keep Hong Kong for a while, right?

And who doesn't love a good war for profit? It's almost as if the British Empire was built on the backs of exploited nations and natural resources. Oh wait, it totally was. But at least they had some nice tea and crumpets along the way.

The Franco-Prussian War

The Franco-Prussian War was a military conflict between France and the German states led by Prussia. It lasted from July 1870 to May 1871 and was fought over the issue of the unification of Germany under Prussian leadership.

The war was marked by a series of decisive Prussian victories, culminating in the capture of Paris and the surrender of the French army.

The origins of the Franco-Prussian War can be traced back to the early 1860s when Otto von Bismarck, the Prussian Chancellor, began working toward the unification of Germany under Prussian leadership.

This plan threatened French interests, as a unified Germany would be a powerful and potentially aggressive neighbor. France tried to block the unification process by backing various German states that were opposed to Prussia.

Tensions escalated in 1870 when a dispute arose over the succession to the Spanish throne.

The Prussian King, Wilhelm I, had been offered the crown of Spain, but the French objected to this move as they feared it would further strengthen Prussia.

Bismarck manipulated the situation and goaded the French into declaring war on Prussia on July 19, 1870. The Prussian army quickly mobilized and began a series of rapid advances into French territory.

They won a decisive victory at the Battle of Sedan in September 1870, where the French army was forced to surrender along with Emperor Napoleon III.

Following this defeat, Paris was besieged by the Prussian army for four months before finally surrendering in January 1871.

So, what more was accomplished? This war was fought between the French and the Prussians (with some help from other German states) in 1870–1871.

It resulted in a crushing defeat for the French, and the unification of Germany under the Prussian king, Wilhelm I.

Well, let's start with the obvious: France lost.
And not just lost, but got their butts handed to them. The Prussian army was better trained, better equipped, and better organized.

Plus, they had a secret weapon: a young up-and-comer named Otto von Bismarck, who was a master of realpolitik and diplomacy.

So, what did France get out of this war? Well, they got a humiliating defeat, that's for sure. They also lost the region of Alsace-Lorraine, which had been a part of France for centuries. Talk about a kick in the baguette.

But don't worry, France wasn't alone in their suffering. The rest of Europe got to watch this whole thing play out, with a mixture of amusement and horror.

It was like watching a car crash in slow motion, but with cannons and cavalry charges instead of cars.

Of course, the other major accomplishments. For years, there had been a bunch of German states, all bickering and fighting with each other.

But thanks to the Prussian victory, they were able to come together and form a unified country. And who doesn't love a good unification story?

But let's not forget the other, less talked-about accomplishments of this war. For example, it gave us some great paintings.

Who can forget Edouard Manet's "The Execution of Emperor Maximilian"? Sure, it's a depressing scene of a dude getting shot, but it's beautifully done.

Plus, the Franco-Prussian War gave us some fun new vocabulary words. Who doesn't love saying "chassepot" or "mitrailleuse"?

And let's not forget the delightful phrase "Ems Telegram", which was the message that caused the war to break out in the first place. It's like a historical inside joke that only the most elite history buffs will understand.

And finally, the Franco-Prussian War accomplished something truly remarkable: it set the stage for World War I.

Yep, that's right. Without the Franco-Prussian War, we might never have had the pleasure of watching the world tear itself apart in the Great War.

So, really, we should all be grateful for this little skirmish between France and Germany.

In the end, the Franco-Prussian War accomplished a lot of things. It gave us a unified Germany, some great art, and some fun new vocabulary words. It also set the stage for World War I, which was a real hoot.

And, of course, it gave France a humiliating defeat and the loss of a beloved region. So, all in all, it was a pretty successful war, wouldn't you say?

The War of The Spanish Succession

The War of the Spanish Succession was a major conflict that involved most of the major powers of Europe, fought between 1701 and 1714.

The war was fought over the issue of who would succeed the childless King Charles II of Spain, who had left no direct heir.

The war began in 1701 when the Holy Roman Emperor Leopold I and the Dutch Republic, supported by Great Britain, Portugal, and several German states, declared war on France and Spain, who were allied with each other.

The main issue was the prospect of a union between France and Spain, which would create a superpower in Europe and upset the balance of power.

The war was marked by a number of significant events.

In 1702, England's Queen Anne came to the throne, following the death of William III. This brought England more fully into the conflict, as Anne was a staunch supporter of the alliance against France.
In 1704, the Allied forces won a major victory at the Battle of Blenheim, which marked a turning point in the war.

The war continued for several more years, with further Allied victories at the Battle of Ramillies in 1706 and the Battle of Oudenarde in 1708.

In 1710, the war took a new turn when the Holy Roman Emperor Joseph I died and was succeeded by his brother Charles VI.

Charles was keen to secure the Spanish crown for himself, but he faced opposition from the other allies, who feared that he would become too powerful if he were to gain control of both Spain and the Holy Roman Empire.

The war ended in 1714 with the signing of the Treaty of Utrecht. Under the terms of the treaty, Philip V, a grandson of Louis XIV of France, was recognized as the King of Spain, but he was forced to renounce his claim to the French throne.

Anything of value achieved or accomplished here then? Once upon a time in the early 1700s, Spain was in a bit of a pickle. King Charles II had died without an heir, and there were multiple contenders vying for the throne.

Of course, as is tradition with European politics, everyone saw this as a perfect opportunity to start a war. And thus, the War of the Spanish Succession was born.

The contenders for the throne were Philip of Anjou (the grandson of Louis XIV of France), Archduke Charles of Austria, and Charles III of the House of Bourbon. But really, it was just an excuse for France and Austria to duke it out and for England to join in because, well, why not?

As with any good war, it dragged on for years and was marked by some truly epic battles. But eventually, a peace treaty was signed in 1713. So, what did we accomplish with this war?

Well, for starters, we got a lot of cool battle stories. There was the Battle of Blenheim, where the English and Austrians teamed up to take down the French.

And then there was the Battle of Malplaquet, where the English and Dutch teamed up to take down the French again. It was basically a big game of "who can beat up France the most."

But the real accomplishment of the War of the Spanish Succession was the Treaty of Utrecht. This treaty settled the question of who would inherit the Spanish throne (spoiler alert: it was Philip of Anjou).

It also gave England some nice new territories, like Gibraltar and Minorca. So, if you're ever looking for a good vacation spot, thank the war.
Of course, the aftermath of the war was a bit messy.

France was left bitter and humiliated after being beaten up so many times, and they didn't take kindly to losing their claim to the Spanish throne. This would eventually lead to the Napoleonic Wars, but that's a story for another chapter.

The War of the Spanish Succession also set the stage for a new era of European power politics. It showed that countries could form alliances and fight together, and it also showed that wars could be fought for more than just territory. In this case, it was about who would control the Spanish Empire and all its riches.

But let's be real, the real accomplishment of the War of the Spanish Succession was fashion.

It was a time of powdered wigs, fancy dresses, and big hats. We're talking about "Marie Antoinette eating cake" levels of fashion. And if you can't appreciate that, then you clearly don't understand the true significance of this war.

In conclusion, the War of the Spanish Succession accomplished a lot of things. We got some cool battle stories, England got some new territories.

But really, it was all about fashion. So the next time you put on a powdered wig and a big hat, take a moment to thank the War of the Spanish Succession for making it all possible.

The War of the Austrian Succession

The War of the Austrian Succession was a major European conflict that took place from 1740 to 1748. The war involved most of the major powers of Europe and resulted in significant changes to the political map of Central Europe.

The war was primarily caused by the death of Emperor Charles VI of the Habsburg Empire in 1740. Charles VI had no male heir, and his eldest daughter, Maria Theresa, inherited the throne.

However, many of the other European powers did not recognize her as the legitimate ruler of Austria and instead sought to take advantage of the situation to expand their own territories.

The War of the Austrian Succession involved most of the major powers of Europe at the time, including Austria, Prussia, France, Spain, Great Britain, and the Dutch Republic.

In addition to these major powers, several smaller states also participated in the conflict, including Saxony, Bavaria, and Silesia.

The War of the Austrian Succession ended with the Treaty of Aix-la-Chapelle in 1748. The treaty recognized Maria Theresa as the legitimate ruler of Austria and ended the conflict between the major powers of Europe.

However, the war had significant consequences for Central Europe, as several territories were ceded to other powers as a result of the conflict.

Prussia was able to secure control of Silesia, which significantly expanded its territory and influence.

The war also set the stage for future conflicts in Europe, particularly the Seven Years' War, which was fought between many of the same powers just a few years later.

Was anything accomplished? It was like a game of musical chairs, except instead of chairs, it was thrones, and instead of music, it was the sound of cannons and muskets.

And in the end, the Habsburgs got to keep their throne, but at what cost?

The war started in 1740 when Charles VI, the Holy Roman Emperor, died without a male heir. This left his daughter, Maria Theresa, as the rightful heir to the Habsburg Empire.

But of course, it wouldn't be a good old-fashioned European power struggle without a few other nations trying to grab a piece of the pie.

First up was Frederick II of Prussia, who thought he could take advantage of the situation and invade Silesia, a Habsburg territory. Maria Theresa was not happy about this, and thus the War of the Austrian Succession began. So what did we accomplish during this war?

Well, for one thing, we got to see a lot of different countries fighting each other for various reasons that nobody really remembers anymore. Was it because of religion? Politics? Greed? Who knows!

But regardless, armies marched across Europe, leaving a trail of destruction in their wake. The French and Spanish fought against the British and Dutch, the Prussians fought against the Austrians, and the Bavarians fought against...well, everyone, it seemed like.

And what did they gain from all this fighting? Not a whole lot, really. Some land changed hands, but it wasn't anything too significant. The Prussians got to keep Silesia, which was a big deal for them, but in the grand scheme of things, it wasn't exactly a game-changer.

But hey, at least they got to wear fancy uniforms and march around with big guns, right? And who doesn't love a good military parade?

As for the aftermath, well, it wasn't exactly smooth sailing for Maria Theresa. She may have kept her throne, but her country was left devastated by the war.

And to add insult to injury, her father's old allies, Britain and the Netherlands, didn't exactly rush to her aid during the conflict.

And of course, there were plenty of grudges left over from the war. The French and British, in particular, had a bit of a rivalry going on, which would only escalate in the years to come.

And the Prussians were feeling pretty pleased with themselves, which would lead to some more trouble down the road.

So all in all, the War of the Austrian Succession was a lot of sound and fury, signifying...well, not a whole lot, really.

But hey, at least it kept the soldiers and generals entertained for a few years, right? And isn't that what war is really all about?

The War of the Polish Succession

The War of the Polish Succession was a European conflict that took place between 1733 and 1738. The war was fought between Austria, France, and Russia over who would succeed Augustus II, the King of Poland and Grand Duke of Lithuania, after his death.

This war was one of several wars of succession that plagued Europe in the early 18th century.

The War of the Polish Succession began with the death of Augustus II in 1733. The king had no legitimate heir, and this sparked a succession crisis.

The Polish nobility chose Stanisław Leszczyński, a former king of Poland and father-in-law of King Louis XV of France, as their candidate for the throne.

However, the Austrian Habsburgs, who were rivals of the French Bourbons, supported Augustus II's son, Augustus III, as their candidate for the throne. Russia also supported Augustus III.

The conflict quickly escalated into a full-scale war when French forces invaded the Rhineland and seized several cities, including Kehl and Strasbourg.

The Austrians countered by invading northern Italy, where they hoped to gain control of the lucrative Duchy of Milan.

Meanwhile, Russian forces invaded Poland, where they quickly overran much of the country and forced Leszczyński to flee to France.

The war continued to rage for several more years, with neither side gaining a decisive advantage.

However, in 1738, the Treaty of Vienna was signed, ending the conflict. The treaty recognized Augustus III as the rightful King of Poland and Grand Duke of Lithuania and brought an end to French attempts to gain a foothold in Germany.

The War of the Polish Succession resulted in the deaths of tens of thousands of soldiers and civilians. It also had significant political and economic consequences for Europe.

So, what was this war good for? Absolutely nothing? The War of the Polish Succession! A conflict so important, so vital to world history, that most people haven't even heard of it.

But fear not, dear reader, for I am here to give you a satirical rundown of what was accomplished during this little-known war.
First, a bit of background.

The King of Poland had died without an heir, and several European powers saw an opportunity to swoop in and install their candidate on the throne.

It was basically a Game of thrones, but without the dragons.

So, what did the war accomplish? Well, for starters, it accomplished the noble goal of giving Europe something to do for five years. You see, in the early 1700s, Europe was in a bit of a lull when it came to large-scale conflicts.

The Thirty Years' War had ended decades earlier, and the Great Northern War was winding down. So, the War of the Polish Succession provided a welcome distraction for those who were bored with peace and prosperity.

But let's get to the real accomplishments. First, the war accomplished the goal of making some people very rich. Arms dealers, mercenary soldiers, and war profiteers all made a killing during the conflict.

They were able to charge exorbitant prices for weapons and supplies, and the constant demand for soldiers allowed them to charge ridiculous rates for their services.

So, if you were lucky enough to be in the right business during the War of the Polish Succession, you probably made out like a bandit.

Another accomplishment of the war was that it allowed several European powers to flex their military muscles. France, Spain, and Austria all sent troops to Poland to fight for their chosen candidate.

And while the actual fighting wasn't all that impressive (most of the battles were small skirmishes), the fact that these countries were able to send soldiers halfway across Europe was seen as a testament to their military might.

Of course, not everyone was thrilled with the outcome of the war. The loser, King Stanislaw I Leszczynski, was forced to flee the country and go into exile in France.

He probably didn't feel like much had been accomplished by the war, except for the fact that he got a free vacation in Paris out of it.

And what about Poland itself? Well, the country was left in shambles after the war. The fighting had devastated many of its cities and towns, and the constant political turmoil had left its government in disarray.

So, while other countries were able to reap the benefits of the conflict, Poland was left to pick up the pieces.

But hey, at least Europe got some entertainment out of it, right?

And who knows, maybe the War of the Polish Succession will someday be remembered as one of the great conflicts of world history. Or maybe not…

The War of The Quadruple Alliance

The War of the Quadruple Alliance was a conflict that occurred between 1718 and 1720. It was fought between Spain on one side, and an alliance of Britain, France, Austria, and the Dutch Republic on the other.

The war took place in Italy and Spain's overseas colonies, particularly in South America.

The war was caused by a dispute over the inheritance of the Spanish throne. When the Spanish King, Charles II, died in 1700, he left no direct heirs.

This led to a power struggle between various European nations, each of whom wanted to install their candidate on the Spanish throne.

Eventually, the French King, Louis XIV, installed his grandson, Philip V, as King of Spain. This upset the balance of power in Europe, as France now had control over Spain's vast overseas empire.

In response to this, Britain, Austria, and the Dutch Republic formed an alliance against France and Spain in 1717. They were later joined by Savoy, a small Italian state. The alliance became known as the Quadruple Alliance.

The conflict began in Italy in 1718, when Spain invaded the island of Sardinia, which was controlled by Austria.

The Quadruple Alliance declared war on Spain in response. Spain was initially successful, winning several battles in Italy. However, the alliance was able to turn the tide of the war in their favor by launching a successful invasion of Spain's colonies in South America.

The war ended in 1720, with the signing of the Treaty of The Hague. Under the terms of the treaty, Spain was forced to give up its territorial claims in Italy, including Sardinia, and acknowledge Philip V as the legitimate King of Spain.

The war marked a significant victory for the Quadruple Alliance, as it prevented France from gaining too much power in Europe.

The war resulted in significant casualties on both sides, particularly in Spain's colonies in South America, where thousands of soldiers died from disease and starvation.

An alliance, that accomplished a lot? That classic tale of European nations banding together to maintain the balance of power...or something like that.

Honestly, it's hard to keep all these wars straight, especially when they're named after shapes. But let's see if we can make some sense of it all in a satirical way, shall we?

For starters, the Quadruple Alliance succeeded in defeating Spain and forcing them to sign the Treaty of The Hague in 1720. This treaty essentially put an end to Spain's attempts to expand its territory and influence in Europe. So, yay for the winners, I suppose.

But what about the losers? Well, Spain was left with a lot less power and influence on the continent, which is always a bummer.

And as for the other European powers, it's not like they all got along swimmingly after the war was over. Tensions between France and Britain only continued to escalate, leading to more wars down the line.

But let's not focus on the negative. Surely there were some positive outcomes from the War of the Quadruple Alliance, right?

Hmm, let's see. The war did lead to some advancements in military technology, I suppose. The Dutch, for example, developed a new kind of musket that was lighter and more accurate than previous models.

And I'm sure all the soldiers who died in the conflict would be thrilled to know that their sacrifices helped further the cause of weapon innovation. In terms of diplomacy, the war did lead to some interesting alliances.

For example, Britain and Austria ended up forming a pretty strong bond during the conflict, which would come in handy during future wars.

And the Quadruple Alliance itself was a pretty impressive display of European unity, even if it was mostly driven by a desire to maintain the status quo.

But overall, it's hard to argue that the War of the Quadruple Alliance accomplished much of anything beyond some short-term gains for the victors.

It's just one more example of the senselessness of war, as nations throw countless lives and resources into conflicts that rarely lead to any real progress or positive change.

So, what did we learn from this war? Probably nothing, if history is any indication. But hey, at least we got a catchy name out of it.

The War of the Sixth Coalition

The War of the Sixth Coalition was a major conflict fought between France and a coalition of European powers, including Russia, Prussia, Austria, and Sweden, between 1812 and 1814.

The war was one of the most significant events of the Napoleonic Wars and played a crucial role in the downfall of Napoleon Bonaparte.

The war began in June 1812 when Napoleon launched an invasion of Russia, known as the Russian Campaign. The Russian army, led by General Mikhail Kutuzov, retreated and used scorched earth tactics, burning crops and villages as they went.

This strategy denied Napoleon access to supplies and forced his army to march deeper into Russia.

Napoleon's army, weakened by disease, malnutrition, and poor weather, eventually reached Moscow in September 1812, only to find the city abandoned and in flames.

In the meantime, the Sixth Coalition had been formed, and its members, including Russia, Prussia, Austria, and Sweden, had joined forces to defeat Napoleon. In the following year, the coalition invaded France, winning a series of victories that culminated in the Battle of Paris in March 1814.

Napoleon was forced to abdicate and was exiled to the island of Elba. The war officially ended with the signing of the Treaty of Paris in May 1814.

The war resulted in the death of approximately 500,000 soldiers, with the majority of casualties occurring during the Russian Campaign.

The war also marked the end of Napoleon's military dominance in Europe and paved the way for the Congress of Vienna, which aimed to redraw the map of Europe and establish a balance of power between European nations.

An even bigger alliance, therefore, accomplished more. Or less? More or less? This war was truly a time of great accomplishments, where all the powers of Europe came together to decide who would have the honor of dominating the continent.

First and foremost, the War of the Sixth Coalition was a great opportunity for all the European powers to show off their military prowess.

They all gathered their armies and marched them around Europe, creating some truly stunning displays of force. Of course, the actual fighting was a bit messy and brutal, but it was all worth it for the fantastic photo ops.

One of the major accomplishments of the war was the defeat of Napoleon Bonaparte. Yes, he had managed to take over most of Europe, but did he have an army as big as the Sixth Coalition? No, he did not. And so, after years of war and bloodshed, the Coalition was finally able to take down the little man from Corsica.

Of course, there were some drawbacks to this accomplishment. For one thing, it left Europe in a bit of a power vacuum. Who would step up and take control now that Napoleon was out of the picture? The answer was, of course, the same people who had been vying for power all along. So, nothing had changed except for the fact that there were now a whole lot of dead soldiers lying around.

Another accomplishment of the war was the Congress of Vienna. This was a great chance for all the European powers to come together and decide how they were going to divvy up the spoils of war.

They spent months arguing over who would get what, and in the end, they were able to come to a satisfactory conclusion: everyone got something, and no one was completely happy. It was a real testament to the power of compromise.

By redrawing the map of Europe, they created a lot of new borders and divisions that didn't make any sense. They also left a lot of people feeling resentful and angry, which would come back to haunt Europe in the coming years.

But let's not focus on the negative! The War of the Sixth Coalition also gave rise to some truly heroic figures. The Duke of Wellington, and Tsar Alexander I, who was very good at wearing big furry hats. And let's not forget general Blücher, who was very good at shouting.

They may not have actually done all that much in the way of winning battles, but they looked damn good doing it.

The War of the Sixth Coalition may have accomplished some things, but it was ultimately just another chapter in the never-ending saga of European conflict. There would be plenty more wars to come, each one more pointless and devastating than the last.

So, what did the war accomplish? Well, it accomplished a lot of things, if you count dead bodies as an accomplishment.

It also gave rise to some truly unforgettable figures, who will go down in history as some of the greatest generals and leaders of all time.

The War of The Fourth Coalition

The War of the Fourth Coalition was a conflict that took place from 1806 to 1807 and involved the French Empire and its allies against the Prussian Empire, the Russian Empire, the Kingdom of Saxony, and the Swedish Empire.

The war was triggered by Napoleon Bonaparte's decision to implement the Continental System, a blockade designed to prevent British trade with the European continent.

This policy was opposed by Prussia, which relied heavily on British trade, and led to tensions between the two countries. In October 1806, Prussia declared war on France, hoping to quickly defeat Napoleon's army before it could mobilize fully.

However, the French army, under the command of Napoleon, swiftly defeated the Prussian army at the Battle of Jena-Auerstedt on October 14, 1806. The Prussian king, Frederick William III, was forced to flee from Berlin, which was subsequently occupied by the French.

Following the defeat of Prussia, other countries, including Russia and Saxony, joined the coalition against France.

The Russian army, under the command of General Bennigsen, attempted to invade Poland, but was defeated by Napoleon at the Battle of Eylau in

February 1807. The French also defeated the Swedes in Pomerania and the Saxons in Dresden.

In June 1807, the French army under Napoleon's command defeated the Russian army at the Battle of Friedland.

This victory led to the Treaty of Tilsit, signed on July 7, 1807, which ended the war.

Zzz-zzz-zzo, anything accomplished? It all started when Napoleon decided he was going to conquer Europe, and everyone else decided they didn't want that to happen. So, they formed a coalition and went to war against France.

Now, one might think that the Fourth Coalition was formed with the noble goal of stopping Napoleon's imperial ambitions and restoring peace to Europe. But let's be real, it was really just an excuse for everyone to show off their fancy uniforms and cool weapons.

The war itself was a masterpiece of incompetence. The Prussian army was so poorly organized that they managed to lose an entire corps of troops without even realizing it.

The Austrians, meanwhile, decided that the best way to win the war was to attack the French from the rear, which didn't work out quite as well as they had hoped.

Napoleon, of course, was busy being Napoleon. He marched his army across Europe, fighting battles and winning victories left and right. It was all very impressive, but at the end of the day, what did it really accomplish?

Sure, Napoleon was able to add more territory to his already vast empire, but at what cost?

The Fourth Coalition may have been a military disaster, but the aftermath was even worse. Europe was left in shambles, with entire cities destroyed and thousands of people dead. So that Napoleon could feel like a big man.

But hey, at least we got some good art out of it, right? The war inspired some of the greatest works of literature, music, and art in history.

Beethoven wrote his famous Eroica Symphony in honor of Napoleon (before he realized that Napoleon was actually a huge jerk), and Goya painted his iconic series of war paintings, The Disasters of War. So

I guess you could say that the Fourth Coalition was a success in terms of cultural achievements.

In the end, though, the Fourth Coalition was really just another pointless war fought for the sake of ego and ambition.

It accomplished nothing but destruction and suffering, and it's a wonder that humanity still hasn't learned its lesson. But hey, at least we can all look back on it and laugh, right?

The War of the Fifth Coalition

The War of the Fifth Coalition was a conflict fought between the Austrian Empire and the French Empire, along with their respective allies, in 1809.

The war was primarily fought over control of the Danube River valley, with Austria seeking to regain control of its former territories in Bavaria and Italy.

After the end of the War of the Fourth Coalition, in which Austria was defeated by Napoleon, the Austrian Empire sought to rebuild its military and regain its position as a major power in Europe.

In 1809, Austria formed an alliance with the United Kingdom, which had been at war with France since 1803, and declared war on France.

The Austrian army, led by Archduke Charles, was made up of around 400,000 soldiers, while the French army, under the command of Napoleon Bonaparte, consisted of around 200,000 soldiers.

Napoleon's forces included troops from France, Italy, Germany, Poland, and other parts of Europe.

The war began in April 1809, with the Austrians invading Bavaria and the French counterattacking in Italy.

The war ended with the Treaty of Schönbrunn, signed on October 14, 1809. The treaty was a victory for France, as Austria was forced to cede territory in Italy and Bavaria to the French Empire.

However, the war had been costly for both sides, with tens of thousands of soldiers and civilians killed or injured.

Accomplished great things then?

The year was 1809, and Napoleon was feeling pretty good about himself. He had just won the Battle of Wagram, defeating the Austrian army and consolidating his power in Europe. But Austria, ever the sore loser, wasn't ready to give up just yet.

They formed a coalition with Britain, Portugal, and Sweden, and called it the Fifth Coalition. Wow, what a creative name.

Napoleon, never one to back down from a fight, decided to take on the coalition head-on. He marched his army into Austria, ready to crush them once and for all.

And he did just that, winning decisive battles at Aspern-Essling and Wagram. The coalition was no match for Napoleon's army and his tactical genius.

But what was accomplished, you ask? Well, let's see. Austria lost a significant portion of its territory to Napoleon, including parts of Italy and Croatia.

The coalition suffered heavy casualties and lost a lot of money in the process. Sweden and Portugal pretty much just sat around and watched as their allies got destroyed. So, not much was accomplished there.

But the aftermath, oh boy. Napoleon was feeling pretty good about himself after the war. He had proven once again that he was the greatest military leader of all time.

But he was also starting to feel the effects of years of constant warfare. His health was deteriorating, and he was becoming increasingly paranoid and erratic.

And then there was the matter of his marriage. He divorced Josephine in 1809 after she failed to provide him with an heir.

He quickly remarried Marie Louise of Austria, hoping that a new marriage would strengthen his position in Europe.

But things didn't go as planned. Marie Louise was only 19 years old, and she didn't speak French. Napoleon was in his 40s, and he didn't speak German. They had nothing in common, and their marriage was a disaster from the start.

But Napoleon wasn't one to give up easily. He continued to wage wars of conquest, expanding his empire and crushing his enemies. He invaded Russia in 1812, and we all know how that turned out.

He was eventually defeated at the Battle of Leipzig in 1813, marking the end of his reign as emperor of France.

So, what was accomplished with the War of the Fifth Coalition? Not much, really. Austria lost some territory, the coalition suffered heavy losses, and Napoleon's ego got even bigger. But the aftermath was a different story.

The war contributed to Napoleon's downfall, leading to his eventual exile and the restoration of the Bourbon monarchy in France.

So, I guess you could say that the War of the Fifth Coalition helped pave the way for a new era of peace and stability in Europe. Or not.

THE WAR OF THE SECOND COALITION

The War of the Second Coalition was a major military conflict fought between France and a coalition of European powers, including Austria, Russia, Britain, and the Ottoman Empire, from 1798 to 1801.

The war was part of the broader French Revolutionary Wars, which saw France embroiled in a series of conflicts with various European powers as it sought to expand its territory and spread its revolutionary ideals.

The origins of the War of the Second Coalition can be traced back to the French invasion of Egypt in 1798, which was intended as a strategic move to disrupt British trade routes to India and establish a French presence in the Middle East.

However, the invasion quickly turned into a disaster for the French, as they were unable to secure a decisive victory and suffered from a lack of supplies and support from home. In response to the French invasion of Egypt, a coalition of European powers was formed to halt French expansionism and restore the balance of power in Europe.

The coalition was led by Austria, which saw itself as the traditional defender of Europe against French aggression, and included Russia, Britain, Portugal, the Ottoman Empire, and several smaller German states.

The early years of the war were marked by a series of French victories, including the Battle of Marengo in 1800, which saw Napoleon Bonaparte decisively defeat Austrian forces in northern Italy.

However, the tide of the war began to turn against France in 1801, as the coalition forces gained ground and began to push back against French territory.

The war officially came to an end with the signing of the Treaty of Amiens in 1802, which recognized French control over much of its conquests in Europe and the Middle East.

However, the peace was short-lived, as tensions between France and Britain continued to escalate, and the two powers soon found themselves at war once again.

In terms of casualties, the exact numbers are difficult to determine, but it is estimated that several hundred thousand soldiers and civilians died as a result of the war.

The coalition forces suffered particularly heavy losses, with Austrian and Russian casualties numbering in the tens of thousands. However, France also suffered significant losses, particularly in terms of the resources and manpower expended in the war effort.

At least it accomplished the promise of more war? First, a little background. The War of the Second Coalition was fought between France and a whole bunch of other European countries who didn't like the fact that Napoleon Bonaparte was running around, conquering things, and generally causing a ruckus.

So, what did we accomplish in this war? Well, let's see…France won, so I guess that's an accomplishment, right?
I mean, it's not like they had Napoleon or anything, who was basically a military genius. Oh wait, they totally did. Scratch that.

But hey, at least the other European countries put up a good fight, right? Right? Well, not really.

They kind of just got their butts kicked. Austria, Russia, and the Ottoman Empire all lost pretty badly to France. Great job, guys.

On the bright side, Britain managed to hold its own against France, even though they were vastly outnumbered and outgunned. I mean, they did lose a few battles, but they also won some pretty important ones, like the Battle of the Nile and the Battle of Cape St. Vincent. So I guess that's something.

But in the end, what did we really accomplish with this war?

Not a whole lot, to be honest. France kept all the territories they had conquered, which just made them even more powerful.

The other European countries were left to lick their wounds and wonder how they had managed to get their butts handed to them by a bunch of Frenchmen.

Oh, and let's not forget about the aftermath. The Treaty of Amiens was supposed to bring peace between France and the other European countries, but it didn't really work out that way.

Less than a year after the treaty was signed, war broke out again between France and Britain, and the Napoleonic Wars kicked off in earnest.

So, all in all, The War of the Second Coalition was a resounding success...if you're a fan of France, that is.

For everyone else, it was a pretty big disaster. So, it accomplished is similar to the final result of any war.

THE WAR OF THE THIRD COALITION

The War of the Third Coalition was a major conflict fought between the French Empire and an alliance of European powers, led by the Austrian Empire, in 1805.

This war was one of the many conflicts that took place during the Napoleonic Wars, which lasted from 1799 to 1815.

The War of the Third Coalition was significant in that it marked the beginning of the end for the Holy Roman Empire and the emergence of France as a dominant power in Europe.

The War of the Third Coalition began in May 1803, when Britain declared war on France after Napoleon invaded Italy and Switzerland. Britain was joined by Russia and Austria, and these three powers allied against France.

The Alliance was later joined by Sweden and the Holy Roman Empire, with the latter contributing a significant number of troops to the coalition effort.

The war started with a French invasion of Bavaria in September 1805. The French army, under the command of Napoleon, quickly defeated the Austrians and Russians in a series of battles at Ulm and Austerlitz.

The battle of Austerlitz, which took place on December 2, 1805, is considered one of Napoleon's greatest victories.

It resulted in the complete defeat of the Allied army and the signing of the Treaty of Pressburg between France and Austria, which forced Austria to cede much of its territory to France.

The war continued, however, with the British and their allies continuing to fight on the high seas. The British navy, led by Admiral Horatio Nelson, was able to defeat the combined French and Spanish fleets at the Battle of Trafalgar in October 1805, which prevented Napoleon from invading Britain.

The war officially ended on December 26, 1805, with the signing of the Treaty of Paris. The treaty marked the end of the Holy Roman Empire and the emergence of France as a dominant power in Europe.

The treaty also established the Confederation of the Rhine, a collection of German states that were loyal to France.

Accomplished something? First of all, let's talk about the cause of the war. As with most wars, it was all about power and territory. Napoleon, the hot-headed leader of France, wanted to expand his empire and dominate Europe, while the other countries didn't want to let him.

The war started pretty well for Napoleon, with the French army winning a series of battles against the coalition forces. But then things took a turn for the worse when he decided to invade Russia in the winter of 1805. Because, you know, what could go wrong with that?

Needless to say, things didn't go well for the French. They were ill-prepared for the harsh winter conditions, and their supply lines were stretched thin.

Many soldiers died from frostbite and disease, and the ones that did survive were weakened and demoralized. In the end, Napoleon was forced to retreat, and the coalition forces took advantage of his weakened state by launching a counter-attack.

The war dragged on for another year, but eventually, Napoleon was defeated, and the Treaty of Pressburg was signed in 1805, which ended the war.

So, what was accomplished with the War of the Third Coalition?

Napoleon was humiliated, France lost some territory, and the other countries got to feel smug for a little while.

But did anything really change? Not really. Napoleon went on to conquer more territory, and the other countries went on to squabble amongst themselves.

In fact, the aftermath of the war was pretty underwhelming. The Treaty of Pressburg didn't do much to change the balance of power in Europe, and it certainly didn't stop Napoleon from continuing his expansionist agenda.

The other countries may have won the battle, but they certainly didn't win the war.

In the end, the War of the Third Coalition was just another pointless conflict in a long line of pointless conflicts. It didn't accomplish much, and it certainly didn't bring about any lasting peace or stability.

But hey, at least it gave historians something to write about and it made a small chapter in this Encyclopedia.

The War of The First Coalition

The War of the First Coalition was a series of conflicts that occurred between the years 1792 to 1797.

The war was fought between the revolutionary French forces, led by the National Convention, and the various European powers that opposed the French Revolution, primarily Austria, Prussia, Spain, Great Britain, and several other states.

The French Revolution began in 1789 and the newly formed French Republic was faced with hostility from the neighboring monarchies, which feared that revolutionary ideas would spread to their own countries.

In April 1792, the French Revolutionary Government declared war on Austria, starting the War of the First Coalition.

Initially, the French armies experienced several defeats, but by 1794, the French had managed to invade and conquer the Austrian Netherlands and had gained control of the Rhineland. The French forces had also defeated the Prussian and Spanish armies, and established control over most of Italy.

The War of the First Coalition saw a large number of casualties on all sides, with estimates ranging from 300,000 to 600,000 people.

The war ended with the signing of the Treaty of Campo Formio in October 1797, which marked the first of several peace treaties that would be signed throughout the Revolutionary and Napoleonic Wars.

The treaty recognized the French Republic's control over the Rhineland, Belgium, and parts of Italy, and also created several satellite states in northern Italy that were aligned with France.

Nothing says accomplished like the French? A time of such glory and achievement. The blood, the sweat, the tears, the sheer stupidity—the War of the First Coalition is all so inspiring.

First, some background the war was a conflict that lasted from 1792 to 1797 and involved pretty much every major European power at the time. It all started when France, still basking in the glory of its recent revolution, decided it would be a good idea to invade its neighbors.

The French army, led by the legendary General Dumouriez, swept through the Low Countries, driving the Austrians and Dutch before them like so many terrified sheep.

But then things started to go wrong.

For one thing, the French government was in chaos. The revolution had brought down the old monarchy, but no one was quite sure what to put in its place. The country was ruled by a motley assortment of political factions, each vying for power and influence. It didn't help that the French economy was in shambles, thanks to years of corruption and mismanagement under the old regime.

Meanwhile, the other European powers were starting to get nervous. They didn't like the idea of a revolutionary France on their doorstep, and they certainly didn't like the idea of French armies rampaging through their territories.

So they formed a coalition—hence the name of the war—to fight back against the French.

At first, things went pretty well for the coalition. They had better-trained troops and more experienced commanders than the French, and they managed to push the invaders back across the Rhine.

But then the French got their act together. They appointed a new general, Napoleon Bonaparte, who proved to be a tactical genius. He won a series of stunning victories against the Austrians, and soon the French were back on the offensive.

The French abolished feudalism and serfdom and established more egalitarian forms of government. Of course, they also destroyed a lot of churches and other cultural institutions, because, well, you can't please all people all the time.

Meanwhile, the coalition powers managed to... well, they managed to lose. They were constantly bickering and fighting amongst themselves, and they never really managed to mount a coordinated offensive against the French.

They did manage to win a few battles here and there, but they never really threatened to defeat the French outright.

And then there was the aftermath. The war left Europe in a state of turmoil. The French had upset the old balance of power, and the other nations were scrambling to figure out how to deal with this new revolutionary power.

The French Revolution had unleashed forces that were far beyond the control of any one nation.

The ideas of liberty, equality, and fraternity had taken root in the minds of people all across Europe, and they weren't going to go away anytime soon.

And as for Napoleon, well, he was just getting started... So there you have it, the War of the First Coalition. A war that accomplished... something, I guess. It's hard to say exactly what, but hey, it was a hell of a ride.

The War of the League of Cambrai

The War of the League of Cambrai was a conflict that took place from 1508 to 1516 in Europe, primarily in Italy. It was fought between the Republic of Venice and an alliance of major European powers, known as the League of Cambrai.

The League was composed of France, the Holy Roman Empire, Spain, and the Papal States.

The war was sparked by tensions between Venice and the Holy Roman Empire over control of territories in Italy. The Venetians had been expanding their influence in the region, which threatened the interests of the Empire and other major powers.

In 1508, the Holy Roman Emperor Maximilian I formed the League of Cambrai with France, Spain, and the Papal States in order to contain Venice The League's armies invaded Venetian territory, capturing several key cities and inflicting heavy losses on the Venetian military.

Venice was forced to sue for peace in 1510, but the war continued with sporadic fighting until 1516. During this time, Venice formed alliances with other Italian city-states and attempted to retake its lost territories.

The war resulted in significant territorial changes in Italy, with Venice losing much of its influence and territory in the region.

The Holy Roman Empire gained control of several key cities, while France and Spain also expanded their territories in Italy. The war also marked the beginning of the decline of Venice as a major European power.

Casualty figures for the War of the League of Cambrai are difficult to estimate, but it is believed that tens of thousands of soldiers and civilians were killed or wounded during the conflict.

The war also caused significant economic damage, particularly to the regions in Italy that were caught in the crossfire.

The War of the League of Cambrai ended in 1516 with the signing of the Treaty of Noyon, which formally ended hostilities between the League and Venice.

The treaty also marked the beginning of a new phase of conflict in Italy, as France and the Holy Roman Empire began to fight for control of the region.

Accomplished anything but death and despair? The War of the League of Cambrai. So many alliances formed and broken, so many treaties signed and disregarded, all for the sake of power and prestige. What a glorious mess it was.

For those not familiar with this masterpiece, let me give you a brief overview. The year was 1508, and the city of Venice had become the dominant power in northern Italy, much to the annoyance of the other major players in the region, namely France, the Holy Roman Empire, and the Papacy.

So, what did these three powers do? They formed a league, of course! The League of Cambrai was born, with the goal of breaking Venetian power and dividing up its territory.

They did not mess around. They invaded Venetian territory, captured cities, and waged war for years. So, what was accomplished with this war? Well, for one, a lot of people died. And Venetian power was broken, at least temporarily.

The league succeeded in capturing several key cities and weakening the Venetian navy. But let's not forget the aftermath.

First of all, the Holy Roman Empire and France, who were supposed to be allies, turned on each other.

The French were not happy with the amount of territory they were receiving as part of the spoils of war, and tensions rose between the two powers.

And let's not forget the Papacy, which ended up being excluded from the negotiations and left out in the cold. Good job, guys.

And even after the war was over and the treaties were signed, the aftermath was a mess. The Venetians were bitter and resentful, as they had lost so much territory and power. The French were unhappy with the outcome and continued to fight the Venetians for years.

The Holy Roman Empire was weakened by the cost of the war, and the Papacy was left wondering why they had bothered to join the league in the first place.

But wait, there's more! The War of the League of Cambrai was just the beginning. It set off a chain of events that led to even more wars and conflicts in Europe.

The French, still bitter about their treatment during the league, allied with the Ottomans and attacked the Holy Roman Empire. The Venetians, in an attempt to regain their lost power, allied with the Ottomans and attacked the Holy Roman Empire.

And so on and so forth. Viva Chaos!

The War of the League of Augsburg

The War of the League of Augsburg, also known as the Nine Years' War, was a major conflict that occurred in Europe from 1688 to 1697.

This war involved a coalition of European powers led by the Holy Roman Empire against France, which was under the rule of King Louis XIV.

The war began when Louis XIV sought to expand his territory by invading the Palatinate, a region in the Holy Roman Empire.

This move provoked a response from other European powers, who formed a coalition against France. The main participants in the war were France, the Holy Roman Empire, Spain, England, the Dutch Republic, and Savoy.

The war saw several major battles and campaigns across Europe. The French initially had the upper hand, winning a series of victories in Germany and the Low Countries.

However, the tide began to turn against them when England entered the war on the side of the coalition.

The English, led by William III, won several key victories, including the Battle of the Boyne in Ireland and the Battle of La Hogue off the coast of Normandy.

The war was also notable for its impact on colonial territories. France and England both had colonies in the Americas and the West Indies, and the conflict spilled over into these regions.

The English seized several French colonies in North America, including Newfoundland and Acadia (present-day Nova Scotia), while the French captured some English-held territories in the Caribbean.

The war ended with the Treaty of Ryswick in 1697, which was negotiated between France and the coalition. The treaty recognized the pre-war borders of France and the Holy Roman Empire, and also granted some territorial concessions to the Dutch and the Spanish.

The War of the League of Augsburg was a brutal and costly conflict, with estimates suggesting that up to a million people died as a result of the fighting and its aftermath.

The war also had significant economic consequences, as many areas of Europe were devastated by the conflict and faced years of rebuilding and recovery. Despite the high human and economic cost, however, the war did little to change the balance of power in Europe, as France remained a dominant force on the continent for many years to come.

Accomplished a bright future for all eternity? It was the mid-17th century, and everyone was just itching to fight some wars.

So, in 1688, the League of Augsburg was formed, because why not?

The League consisted of the Holy Roman Empire, Spain, Sweden, the Palatinate, Bavaria, and of course, the Duchy of Savoy (who doesn't love a good Duchy?).

Their main target? France, of course! Because let's be honest, who doesn't love a good war with France?

The French King Louis XIV had been causing trouble all over Europe, so naturally, everyone wanted a piece of him. The war was an absolutely smashing success! The League of Augsburg managed to... uh... well, they did... um...

Okay, I'll be honest, I'm not entirely sure what they accomplished. Let me consult my trusty history books for a moment...

Ah, here we go. The League of Augsburg managed to... make things slightly more complicated for Louis XIV, I suppose.

They did manage to capture a few territories from the French, such as Strasbourg and Casale. But really, the war just kind of ended in a stalemate. Everyone just got tired of fighting and decided to call it a day.

They managed to waste a lot of time, money, and resources fighting each other instead of, you know, doing something productive. And who doesn't love a good old-fashioned war where nobody really wins or accomplishes anything?

Battles were fought, lives were lost, and kingdoms were ruined. But in the end, what did they really achieve?

As for the aftermath, well, it was pretty uneventful. The League of Augsburg disbanded, everyone went back to their respective countries, and life went on.

Louis XIV continued being Louis XIV, and the rest of Europe continued trying to find ways to one-up him.

So there you have it, the War of the League of Augsburg. A war that accomplished... well, not nothing good. But hey, at least they might have had fun when they were done.

The War of the Bavarian Succession

The War of the Bavarian Succession, also known as the Potato War, was a brief conflict that took place in 1778 between the Kingdom of Prussia and the Habsburg Monarchy.

The war arose as a result of a dispute over the inheritance of the Electorate of Bavaria, which had been left without a clear heir following the death of the Elector Maximilian III Joseph.

Both Prussia and Austria had claims to parts of the territory, and tensions mounted when Prussian forces occupied part of Bavaria in 1777.

The war began in July 1778 when Austria declared war on Prussia. The Austrian forces, commanded by Field Marshal Count von Daun, quickly advanced into Bavaria and defeated the Prussian forces under the command of Frederick the Great's younger brother, Prince Henry of Prussia.

The Austrians were aided by French forces who had allied themselves with Austria against Prussia.

The war was notable for its use of the newly invented "iron ramrods" in muskets which improved the speed and accuracy of firing.

Despite initial successes, Austria soon found itself in a difficult position as it faced potential attacks from Prussia in the north, Ottoman Turkey in the east, and Russia in the northeast.

This prompted the Austrian Emperor Joseph II to negotiate a peace agreement with Prussia. The Treaty of Teschen was signed in May 1779 and confirmed Prussian control over the parts of Bavaria it had occupied, while Austria was given the Innviertel region.

The War of the Bavarian Succession was a relatively minor conflict in the grand scheme of European history, with only around 3,000 casualties on both sides combined.

However, it was significant in that it marked the first time that Austria and Prussia had fought against each other in a war.

It also demonstrated the emergence of Prussia as a major European power and set the stage for future conflicts between Austria and Prussia, such as the Austro-Prussian War of 1866.

Sucks! Anything accomplished in this succession? Truly one of the greatest conflicts in human history. What was it fought over, you ask? Well, the answer is simple: beer. That's right, beer.

You see, in the mid-1700s, the Kingdom of Prussia and the Habsburg Monarchy had a bit of a disagreement over who had the right to brew and sell beer in the state of Bavaria.

It seems that the Bavarians were producing some particularly delicious suds, and both the Prussians and the Habsburgs wanted a piece of the action. Naturally, this led to war.

The War of the Bavarian Succession officially began in 1778, but tensions had been simmering for years. The conflict was fought mainly between Prussian and Austrian forces, but several other European powers got involved as well, because who doesn't love a good beer fight?

Now, you might be wondering what was accomplished by this great war. Did the Prussians emerge victorious, securing their right to brew and sell Bavarian beer? Did the Austrians triumph, claiming the coveted brews for themselves? Well, the answer is... neither. In fact, absolutely nothing was accomplished.

After two years of fighting, the two sides decided to call it quits and sign the Treaty of Teschen in 1779. The treaty essentially restored the status quo ante bellum, meaning that everything went back to the way it was before the war started.

In other words, both the Prussians and the Austrians were still vying for control of the Bavarian beer market, and nothing had been resolved.

But don't worry, dear reader, because the War of the Bavarian Succession did have some lasting effects. For one, it helped set the stage for the larger and more consequential Napoleonic Wars, which would engulf Europe in the years to come.

And for another, it gave us some truly memorable moments, like the Battle of Mollwitz, where the Prussian cavalry charged a group of Austrian infantry armed with bayonets, resulting in one of the bloodiest battles of the entire war.

But perhaps the greatest legacy of the War of the Bavarian Succession is the enduring image of soldiers fighting and dying for the noble cause of beer.

It's a reminder that even amid the most senseless and pointless wars, there can still be a certain kind of beauty and bravery. Or, you know, it's just really funny to imagine soldiers marching into battle with beer steins in hand.

In the end, the War of the Bavarian Succession accomplished nothing but provide us with a bit of historical amusement.

THE WAR OF JENKINS EAR

The War of Jenkins' Ear was a conflict between Great Britain and Spain that lasted from 1739 to 1748. It was caused by a series of incidents involving British merchant ships being boarded and plundered by Spanish privateers in the West Indies, leading to increased tensions between the two nations.

In 1738, a British captain named Robert Jenkins had his ear cut off by Spanish sailors during a boarding, allegedly on the orders of a Spanish official.

Jenkins presented his severed ear to the British Parliament as evidence of Spanish aggression, which further fueled the calls for war.

The war began in 1739, when Britain declared war on Spain. The British launched a series of attacks on Spanish ports and ships in the West Indies and Caribbean, while Spain retaliated by launching an invasion of Georgia in 1742.

However, the war was inconclusive and neither side was able to achieve a clear victory. The Treaty of Aix-la-Chapelle was signed in 1748, which restored the status quo ante bellum, meaning that both sides agreed to return any territory or possessions that had been taken during the war.

Accomplished something I hear in my missing ear... The War of Jenkins' Ear, a timeless tale of greed, revenge, and...ear mutilation?

I mean, how else would you name a war? Clearly, someone must have done something to poor Jenkins' ear, and the only way to settle it was through a full-blown military conflict!

But let's not focus on the barbaric nature of this war. Instead, let's take a moment to appreciate what was accomplished during this illustrious conflict.

The year was 1739, and tensions between the British and the Spanish were at an all-time high. And why, you may ask? Well, it all started with a simple act of piracy.

Captain Robert Jenkins, a British merchant, claimed that his ship had been boarded by Spanish coast guards, who proceeded to cut off his ear as a warning to other smugglers. You know, as one does.

Jenkins was understandably outraged and took his severed ear to the British Parliament, demanding justice.

Now, the British government wasn't exactly thrilled about going to war over a missing ear. But they were also not the type to let a good opportunity for conflict go to waste.

So, they rallied their forces and declared war on Spain, citing a whole host of reasons that had nothing to do with Jenkins' ear.
And what was accomplished during this glorious war, you ask?

Well, let's see...the British navy blockaded Spanish ports, raided Spanish ships, and captured a few Spanish territories in the Caribbean. Sounds like a productive use of resources, right?

But the real accomplishment of this war was the battle of Porto Bello, where the British fleet successfully captured a Spanish galleon carrying...wait for it...chestnuts. Yes, chestnuts. But not just any chestnuts. These were the finest Spanish chestnuts, grown in the fertile lands of the New World.

And let me tell you, these chestnuts were worth fighting for.

After the war, the British returned home with their spoils, including the coveted chestnuts, which were distributed among the upper echelons of British society as a symbol of their victory.

I mean, who needs peace treaties or political alliances when you can have a bag of chestnuts?

As for poor Captain Jenkins, his ear became the stuff of legend, inspiring countless works of art and literature.

There's even a famous painting of him holding his severed ear, titled "The Ear of Jenkins" (original, I know).

In the end, the War of Jenkins' Ear accomplished exactly what it set out to do: create a meaningless conflict over a trivial matter and give the British an excuse to plunder Spanish goods.

And let's not forget the chestnuts. Those were pretty great too.

The War of The Tripple Alliance

The War of the Triple Alliance, also known as the Paraguayan War, was fought from 1864 to 1870 between Paraguay and an alliance of Argentina, Brazil, and Uruguay.

The conflict was one of the bloodiest and most destructive in South American history, with estimates of Paraguayan deaths ranging from 150,000 to over 400,000, and the country left devastated by the war's end.

The causes of the war were complex, but can be traced back to long-standing disputes over territorial boundaries, economic competition, and political power struggles.

Paraguay, under the leadership of President Francisco Solano Lopez, was a rapidly developing nation in the mid-19th century. Solano Lopez sought to assert Paraguay's independence and expand its territory, often using military force to achieve his goals.

In 1864, tensions between Paraguay and its neighbors reached a boiling point when Brazil and Argentina accused Paraguay of interfering in a border dispute between Brazil and Uruguay.

Solano Lopez responded by declaring war on Brazil, and then on Argentina, and finally on Uruguay, forming the Triple Alliance against his own nation.

The early years of the war saw some initial successes for Paraguay, as its well-trained and well-equipped army under the leadership of Solano Lopez won several key battles.

However, the tide began to turn against Paraguay as the larger and better-equipped forces of the Triple Alliance began to push deeper into Paraguayan territory.

The war soon became a brutal and protracted conflict, with both sides resorting to increasingly savage tactics. Paraguay was particularly hard hit by the war, as much of its territory was devastated by the fighting and its economy was left in ruins.

Solano Lopez, who had taken personal command of the army, refused to surrender, and led his forces on a grueling retreat through the countryside. By the time of his death in battle in 1870, Paraguay had suffered a staggering loss of life, with estimates of up to 90% of its male population killed in the war.

The aftermath of the War of the Triple Alliance had a profound impact on the region, as the balance of power shifted in favor of Argentina and Brazil.

Paraguay was left weakened and impoverished, with much of its territory ceded to Argentina and Brazil.

The war also had a lasting impact on the cultural and social fabric of Paraguay, with many women and children left widowed and orphaned by the conflict.

The causes of the War of the Triple Alliance are complex, and have been the subject of much debate among historians.

Some argue that Paraguay's aggressive expansionism was the primary cause of the conflict, while others point to the economic interests of Brazil and Argentina in the region as the driving force behind the war.

The historical context of the war also played a significant role, with tensions between nations in the region running high due to territorial disputes and political instability.

However, the war remains an important chapter in the history of the region, and serves as a cautionary tale about the devastating impact of armed conflict on civilian populations.

Anything at all accomplished? One of the lesser-known wars that occurred in the mid-19th century. This war, also known as the Paraguayan War, involved Paraguay fighting against an alliance consisting of Argentina, Brazil, and Uruguay.

First and foremost, it's important to acknowledge that this war was a huge success! At least for two out of the three countries involved in the alliance.

Brazil and Argentina got everything they wanted out of the war, which included Paraguay losing large amounts of territory, significant reparations, and Brazil getting control of the entire Amazon River. Score!

Uruguay, on the other hand, didn't really gain much, but at least they got to hang out with the cool kids.

As for Paraguay, well, they definitely accomplished something. They accomplished becoming the only country in South America to lose over 50% of their population in a single conflict. Congrats!

Additionally, they were completely economically and politically devastated for decades to come. But hey, at least they accomplished something, right?

During the war, there were some other notable accomplishments as well. The Brazilian navy was able to effectively use steam-powered ironclads for the first time, which was really cool.

And the soldiers involved in the war got some serious exercise, which is always important for overall health and wellness.

But let's not forget about the cultural accomplishments of the war. The War of the Triple Alliance inspired some truly beautiful works of art. In particular, there was a painting called "The Battle of Riachuelo" by Pedro Américo that was really quite stunning. It's always great when war can inspire art, don't you think?

And let's not forget about the lasting impact this war had on the region. It set a great example for future generations on how not to conduct a war.

With Paraguay losing so much, the other South American countries realized that they should probably start working together more and not be so quick to go to war with each other. That's a pretty big accomplishment, don't you think?

In the aftermath of the war, Paraguay was left in ruins, but they were able to rebuild over time. They eventually became a republic and were able to start rebuilding their economy.

Brazil and Argentina continued to thrive, and Uruguay... well, they continued to hang out with the cool kids.

Overall, I'd say that the War of the Triple Alliance was a pretty successful war, at least for Brazil and Argentina.

They got what they wanted, Paraguay was left in ruins, and some really beautiful art was created.

And who knows, maybe future generations will look back on this war as a shining example of how to achieve your goals through war.

The Chaco War

The Chaco War, also known as the "Green Hell" due to the harsh and unforgiving terrain, was fought between Bolivia and Paraguay from 1932 to 1935 over the Chaco Boreal region, a sparsely populated area rich in oil and other natural resources.

The war had a significant impact on the political, economic, and social development of both nations, and it still resonates in the collective memories of the people of Bolivia and Paraguay.

The roots of the conflict can be traced back to the late 19th century when both Bolivia and Paraguay claimed ownership of the Chaco Boreal.

The dispute intensified in the early 20th century when the discovery of oil in the region increased its strategic value. In 1928, negotiations between the two nations broke down, and both countries started to militarize the area.

In June 1932, Paraguay launched a surprise attack on Bolivia, starting the Chaco War.

The war was characterized by intense fighting in difficult and inhospitable terrain, with soldiers fighting in temperatures of up to 50 degrees Celsius, dealing with insect swarms and tropical diseases such as malaria and dysentery.

The lack of proper infrastructure made it difficult to transport troops and supplies, and both sides suffered from shortages of food, water, and medical supplies.

The war ended in 1935 with the signing of the Treaty of Buenos Aires, which recognized Paraguay's ownership of most of the Chaco Boreal.

The war had a significant impact on both Bolivia and Paraguay. Bolivia lost a significant amount of territory and suffered an estimated 65,000 casualties, while Paraguay, which had a much smaller population, suffered an estimated 36,000 casualties.

Something accomplished? The Chaco War. A true masterpiece of human folly. What a brilliant idea it was to go to war over a piece of land that's mostly uninhabitable and largely devoid of any resources!
But alas, it happened, and let's dive into what was accomplished.

Both countries wanted it, because, well, why not fight over a hot, dusty, and useless chunk of land?

So, what did the war accomplish? Let's start with the positives.

First and foremost, it was a great way for Bolivia and Paraguay to burn through their respective budgets and resources. It's not like there were any pressing domestic issues to address, so why not just throw money and manpower at a pointless war? Plus, all that weaponry and ammunition wasn't going to use itself, right?

Second, it gave the soldiers on both sides a chance to test out some new military tactics. For example, Bolivia decided to send their troops into battle with no shoes, because why bother with protective footwear when you're marching through a cactus-filled desert?

Paraguay, on the other hand, tried out a bold new strategy of repeatedly charging straight into enemy fire. Spoiler alert: it didn't work out too well for either side.

But the true accomplishment of the Chaco War was the deep and lasting friendship that developed between Bolivia and Paraguay.

After all, nothing brings two nations closer together like fighting a three-year-long war over nothing. And the best part? Neither side even remembers what they were fighting about in the first place.

The aftermath of the war was equally impressive. Bolivia and Paraguay emerged from the conflict as the proud owners of a scorched wasteland, devoid of any significant resources or strategic value.

But hey, at least they didn't have to worry about anyone else trying to steal the Chaco from them, right?

In the end, the Chaco War was a true testament to the power of human stupidity. It was a war fought over nothing, that accomplished nothing, and that no one even remembers anymore.

But hey, at least it was a good way to distract people from the fact that Bolivia and Paraguay had no idea how to address their actual problems. At least it provides a some good questions for some quiz-nights …

The War of the Emboabas

The War of the Emboabas was a conflict that took place in Brazil in the early 18th century, specifically between 1707 and 1709. The conflict was fought between Portuguese settlers and a group of gold miners known as the "Emboabas," who were primarily composed of individuals of mixed-race, indigenous, and African descent.

The war had far-reaching consequences for the colonization of Brazil and the relations between different social and ethnic groups.

The conflict had its origins in the discovery of gold in the region of Minas Gerais, Brazil. The discovery of gold led to a massive influx of Portuguese settlers into the region, who sought to exploit the newly found riches. However, the Portuguese settlers were not the only ones interested in gold.

The region was already home to a group of gold miners known as the "Emboabas," who had been mining gold in the region for several years before the arrival of the Portuguese.

The conflict between the Portuguese settlers and the Emboabas came to a head in 1707 when the Portuguese sought to impose a tax on gold mining in the region.

The Emboabas refused to pay the tax, arguing that they had been mining gold in the region long before the arrival of the Portuguese.

The Portuguese responded by sending a military force to the region, which was met with resistance by the Emboabas.

The war continued for several months, with neither side gaining a decisive advantage. However, the Portuguese were eventually able to gain the upper hand, thanks in part to the support of the local indigenous population.

The Portuguese were able to successfully isolate the Emboabas from their allies, cutting off their supply lines and forcing them to surrender.

Accomplished something, obviously. Let's jump into the hilarity that ensued during and after The War of the Emboabas. The Portuguese colonizers and the Bandeirantes, a group of explorers and adventurers, were fighting for control over gold mines in the region.

The Bandeirantes were mostly composed of people who had migrated to Brazil from other parts of the country, and they called themselves Emboabas. Thus, the war got its name.

The Portuguese eventually won, which means they got control of the gold mines. Hooray for them!

But what did the Emboabas get out of this war? Well, not much. They lost. They were defeated. They were sent back to the regions they came from, with nothing to show for it. At least they got to fight for what they believed in? I mean, what's more, important than that? The answer is gold, but we'll come back to that later.

After the war, tensions between the Portuguese and the Emboabas continued for a while, but eventually, things settled down.
The Portuguese got their gold, and the Emboabas went back to their boring lives, probably wishing they had never left in the first place.

But wait, there's more! Remember that gold I mentioned earlier? Well, it turns out that the Portuguese weren't too good at managing their newfound wealth. The gold mines became overcrowded and overworked, and eventually, they started to run out of gold.

So, what did the Portuguese do? Did they try to find new gold mines? Did they invest in other industries?

Nope. They decided to start taxing the Emboabas who were still living in the region. That's right, the very same people they had defeated in the war were now being forced to pay for the Portuguese's mismanagement of the gold mines.

It's almost as if the Portuguese were saying, "Hey, remember that war we won against you? Well, now we're going to make you pay for it."

And to make matters worse, the taxes were so high that many Emboabas were forced to leave the region altogether. So, not only did they lose the war, but they also lost their homes and their livelihoods.

In the end, the War of the Emboabas accomplished very little, if anything at all. The Portuguese got their gold, but they weren't able to keep it. The Emboabas got nothing, except for a painful reminder of their defeat.

But hey, at least we got a funny name out of it, right? The War of the Emboabas. It just rolls off the tongue. And maybe, just maybe, we can learn a lesson from this war.

Maybe we can learn that fighting over resources is never a good idea. Maybe we can learn that there are better ways to manage wealth than taxing the defeated. Or maybe we can just laugh at how ridiculous it all was.

Either way, the War of the Emboabas will always be remembered as a pointless and absurd conflict, a reminder of how petty and foolish humans can be.

The Anglo-Zanzibar War

The Anglo-Zanzibar War, also known as the shortest war in history, was fought between the British Empire and the Sultanate of Zanzibar on August 27, 1896.

The war lasted for only 38 minutes and resulted in the defeat of the Zanzibar Sultanate.

The war started due to a succession crisis after the death of the pro-British Sultan Hamad bin Thuwaini on August 25, 1896.

The British High Commissioner in Zanzibar, Basil Cave, supported the claim of Hamoud bin Mohammed, who was not recognized by the supporters of the late sultan's cousin, Khalid bin Barghash.

Khalid bin Barghash declared himself the sultan on August 26 and took refuge in the palace. Cave demanded that Khalid abdicate and surrender to the British authorities, but he refused.

Cave gave Khalid an ultimatum that expired at 9:00 am on August 27, after which the British bombardment of the palace began.

The British bombarded the palace for 38 minutes, and by 9:40 am, the Zanzibar flag was taken down, and a white flag was raised, signaling the end of the war.

The Zanzibar Sultanate suffered heavy casualties, with around 500 people killed or wounded, including civilians.

On the other hand, the British forces suffered only one casualty, a sailor injured by a shell fragment. The British also captured Khalid bin Barghash, who was later exiled to St. Helena.

Accomplished anything in that short time? Ah, the Anglo-Zanzibar War, the most epic and glorious conflict in human history! A war that will forever be remembered for its fierce battles, the display of military might, and the heroic deeds of brave soldiers on both sides.

Okay, okay, let's be real. The Anglo-Zanzibar War, also known as the shortest war in history, lasted for a whopping 38 minutes.

Yes, you read that right, 38 MINUTES! But despite its brevity, this conflict left a profound impact on the world, or so we are led to believe.

Firstly, let's talk about what led to this epic battle.
In 1896, the British government had a problem with the sultan of Zanzibar, Khalid bin Barghash, who had taken power in a coup against the British-supported sultan.

The British demanded that Khalid abdicate the throne, but he refused. So, what did the British do? They did what any rational government would do in such a situation: they sent in the big guns, or more specifically, their naval fleet.

On August 27, 1896, the British fleet arrived off the coast of Zanzibar, and they demanded that Khalid step down from power. When he refused, the British began to shell the palace with their cannons.

In just 38 minutes, the British destroyed the palace and killed over 500 people, mostly Zanzibari soldiers and civilians. Khalid managed to escape, but he was later captured and exiled to Seychelles.

So, what did the British accomplish with this short but brutal war? Well, they managed to remove Khalid from power, and they replaced him with a sultan who was more friendly to British interests.

They also demonstrated their military superiority to the world, and they sent a clear message to other African nations that they were not to be messed with.

But perhaps the most significant accomplishment of the Anglo-Zanzibar War was that it cemented the British Empire's position as the world's foremost superpower.

The world watched in awe as the British fleet rained destruction upon the palace in Zanzibar, and they realized that no one could stand up to the might of the British Empire.

The newspapers hailed the British fleet as heroes, and the people of Britain cheered their soldiers as they returned from Zanzibar. The Anglo-Zanzibar War had become a symbol of British power and might, and nothing could take that away.

As for the aftermath of the war, it was mostly uneventful. The new sultan of Zanzibar proved to be a loyal ally of the British, and he helped them in their efforts to establish control over East Africa.

The Zanzibari people, meanwhile, were left to pick up the pieces of their shattered lives, as they tried to rebuild their homes and businesses that had been destroyed by the British shells.

In the end, the Anglo-Zanzibar War was a shining moment in British history, a moment when the empire showed the world what it was capable of.

Sure, some might argue that it was a brutal and unnecessary conflict, but who cares about that when you can brag about winning a war in just 38 minutes?

So, let us raise our glasses to the brave soldiers of the British fleet, who fought so well!

THE BOXER REBELLION

The Boxer Rebellion was a violent anti-foreign and anti-Christian movement that took place in China from 1899 to 1901.

The rebellion was led by a secret society called the Society of Righteous and Harmonious Fists, or the Boxers.

The Boxers were a group of Chinese peasants who were frustrated with the presence of foreigners in China and the perceived spread of Christianity.

The Boxer Rebellion was a significant event in Chinese history and marked a turning point in China's relationship with the Western powers.

The Boxer Rebellion was a complex conflict involving several parties. The Boxers were primarily Chinese peasants who were opposed to foreign influence in China.

The foreign powers involved in the conflict were mainly the Western powers, including the United States, Great Britain, France, Germany, Russia, Italy, Austria-Hungary, and Japan.

The Chinese government, led by Empress Dowager Cixi, was initially sympathetic to the Boxers but eventually declared war on the foreign powers.

The Boxers believed that they were invulnerable to foreign weapons and could perform magical feats that would protect them from harm.

They also believed that the foreign powers were responsible for China's problems, including droughts, floods, and economic difficulties.

The Boxers attacked foreign-owned businesses, Christian churches and schools, and foreign residents. The foreign powers responded by sending troops to protect their citizens and interests in China.

The Chinese government initially supported the Boxers but later declared war on the foreign powers after pressure from the Boxers and other anti-foreign factions.

The Boxer Rebellion resulted in significant casualties on both sides. Estimates of the number of casualties vary, but it is believed that tens of thousands of Chinese civilians and soldiers were killed during the conflict.

The foreign powers also suffered significant losses, with several hundred soldiers and civilians killed in the fighting.

The Boxer Rebellion was one of the deadliest conflicts of the late 19th and early 20th centuries. It ended in 1901 with the defeat of the Boxers and the signing of the Boxer Protocol.

The Boxer Protocol was a treaty signed between the Qing dynasty and the foreign powers that ended the conflict.

The treaty required the Qing government to pay reparations to the foreign powers for the damages caused by the Boxers, disarm the Boxers, and allow foreign troops to be stationed in China to protect foreign interests.

Accomplished stuff? A time when the Chinese people rose up against foreign imperialism and attempted to expel them from their country. But did they succeed? SPOILER ALERT: Do not turn on the news.

First, let's set the scene. The late 19th century was a time of great imperialism, with Western powers carving up Asia and Africa like a Thanksgiving turkey. China was no exception, with the British, French, Germans, and Americans all jostling for control of trade and territory.

But the Chinese people had had enough. They were sick of foreigners coming in and disrupting their way of life, and so they formed a secret society called the "Righteous and Harmonious Fists," or as the Westerners called them, the "Boxers."

The Boxers believed that they were invulnerable to foreign weapons, thanks to their mystical martial arts and spiritual practices.

They went on a rampage, attacking foreign missionaries, traders, and diplomats, and besieging the foreign embassies in Beijing.

This did not sit well with the Western powers, who saw their interests in China threatened. And so they formed a multinational force, led by the British, to crush the rebellion and teach Chinese a lesson.

The war was short but brutal. The foreign troops easily defeated the poorly armed and trained Boxers and then went on a rampage of their own, looting and burning Chinese villages and killing anyone who got in their way.

The Chinese government, which had tacitly supported the Boxers, was forced to sign a humiliating treaty that gave the Western powers even more control over Chinese trade and territory. So, what was accomplished by the Boxer Rebellion?

Well, for one thing, it gave the Western powers an excuse to further exploit China. The Boxers may have had legitimate grievances against foreign imperialism, but their methods were violent and ineffective.

They only served to justify the Western powers' belief that the Chinese were backward and in need of "civilizing."

The Boxer Rebellion also highlighted the weaknesses of the Chinese government and military. Despite having a vast population and a rich cultural heritage, China was unable to defend itself against foreign aggression.

This would have long-lasting consequences, as China would continue to be exploited and humiliated by foreign powers for decades to come.

But surely there must have been some positive outcomes from the Boxer Rebellion. Well, there were a few. For one thing, it led to the creation of the Chinese nationalist movement, which sought to modernize China and free it from foreign domination.

This movement would eventually lead to the fall of the Qing Dynasty and the establishment of the Republic of China.

The Boxer Rebellion also inspired the Chinese people to take a more active role in their own governance. While the Boxers may have been misguided in their methods, they were a clear indication that the Chinese people were no longer willing to sit back and let foreign powers dictate their fate.

And finally, the Boxer Rebellion gave us one of the greatest movie titles of all time: "The Boxer Rebellion."

Seriously, it doesn't get any better than that.
In the end, the Boxer Rebellion accomplished very little. It did not expel foreigners from China, nor did it lead to any meaningful reforms.

It did, however, leave a lasting legacy of violence, humiliation, and distrust between China and the Western powers.

So, let us remember the Boxer Rebellion as a cautionary tale of the dangers of foreign imperialism and the need for all nations to respect the sovereignty and dignity of others. And also as a source of great movie titles!

The First Sino-Japanese War

The First Sino-Japanese War was a conflict that occurred from 1894 to 1895 between the Empire of Japan and the Qing Dynasty of China.

It was the first major war fought between a traditional Asian power and a modernized, Western-style power, and its outcome marked the end of China's centuries-long dominance in East Asia and the emergence of Japan as a major regional power.

The conflict began in July 1894, when a dispute over control of Korea led to fighting between Chinese and Japanese troops.

The Qing government, which regarded Korea as a tributary state, sent troops to Korea to quell an uprising there and to assert its authority over the peninsula. Japan, which saw Korea as within its sphere of influence, responded by sending troops to support the rebels and to protect Japanese citizens and interests in Korea.

The initial fighting was inconclusive, but in January 1895, the Japanese launched a surprise attack on the Chinese fleet at Weihaiwei, a major naval base in northern China.

The Japanese quickly captured the base and destroyed most of the Chinese fleet, effectively ending China's naval dominance in the region.

The Japanese then launched a series of successful land campaigns in Korea and northern China, and by the spring of 1895, the Qing government was forced to sue for peace.

The Treaty of Shimonoseki, signed on April 17, 1895, marked the end of the war. Under its terms, China was forced to recognize the independence of Korea and cede Taiwan, the Pescadores Islands, and the Liaodong Peninsula to Japan.

 China was also required to pay a large indemnity to Japan and to open several treaty ports to Japanese trade and commerce.

Casualty figures for the war vary widely, but it is estimated that tens of thousands of soldiers and civilians were killed or wounded on both sides.

The Japanese suffered around 13,000 casualties, while Chinese losses are believed to have been much higher.

Accomplished something? It's like watching a sumo wrestler fight a ninja—you're not quite sure who's going to win, but it's sure to be entertaining.

Let's take a look at what was accomplished in this classic showdown between two Asian powers, shall we?

First off, the Sino-Japanese War was fought over control of Korea—that's right, Korea. Because when two countries can't agree on something, it's always best to start a war over it, right?

So, what did the Japanese accomplish in this war? Well, they won, for starters. And with that victory came the spoils of war—Taiwan, the Pescadores Islands, and the Liaodong Peninsula. Not bad for a war over Korea…

But wait, there's more! Japan also received a hefty sum of money from China as part of the peace treaty, because apparently, money can buy you love, or at least peace.

But what did China accomplish in this war, you may ask? Well, they got their butts kicked, for one. So, in other words, not much was accomplished on the Chinese side.

But fear not, dear reader, because the aftermath of the Sino-Japanese War is where things really get interesting. Japan emerged as a major world power, establishing itself as a dominant force in Asia and making a name for itself on the world stage.

Meanwhile, China's defeat in the war was a wake-up call for the country, leading to a period of self-reflection and reform.

Of course, that didn't stop them from getting caught up in a few more wars and revolutions over the next few decades, but hey, at least they tried, right?

In the end, the First Sino-Japanese War was a classic case of one country wanting something that another country already had.

And as is often the case with wars, the winners got to write the history books and reap the rewards, while the losers were left to pick up the pieces.

But let's not dwell on the negatives, shall we? The Sino-Japanese War gave us plenty of exciting battles, heroic feats, and political intrigue to keep us entertained for years to come. So, in a way, we're all winners here.

THE SECOND SINO-JAPANESE WAR

The Second Sino-Japanese War, also known as the War of Resistance against Japan, was a military conflict between the Republic of China (ROC) and the Empire of Japan.

The war began on July 7, 1937, and ended on September 9, 1945, with the surrender of Japan to the Allied Powers.

The roots of the conflict can be traced back to the first Sino-Japanese War of 1894–1895, which ended with China's defeat and the ceding of Taiwan and other territories to Japan.

In 1937, an incident known as the Marco Polo Bridge Incident sparked a full-scale invasion of China.

The war was fought on multiple fronts, with major battles taking place in Shanghai, Wuhan, Changsha, and Guangzhou.

The Chinese forces also waged a guerrilla war against the Japanese, with support from local militias and Communist guerrilla forces under the command of Mao Zedong.

In 1941, Japan's attack on Pearl Harbor drew the United States into the war, and the Allies began providing increased military aid to China.

The Chinese forces, now better equipped and trained, launched a major counteroffensive in 1944, recapturing much of southern China and cutting off Japanese supply lines.

With the atomic bombings of Hiroshima and Nagasaki in August 1945, Japan's ability to continue the war was severely crippled.

On September 2, 1945, Japan signed the instrument of surrender, formally ending the war.

The war resulted in significant human and material losses for both sides. Exact casualty figures are difficult to determine, but it is estimated that China suffered between 15 and 20 million civilian and military deaths, while Japan suffered around 2 million deaths.

Ever-lasting peace accomplished? The Second Sino-Japanese War, also known as the Chinese Resistance War or the Asian World War (depending on which side you were on).

The war spanned across China for eight years, causing immense destruction, displacement of millions of people, and loss of countless lives. But, let's not focus on that, shall we?

First off, let's give credit where credit is due. Japan accomplished quite a bit during this war. They managed to expand their empire, invade China, and establish puppet governments.

They also managed to unite the Chinese people in a common cause against them, so, kudos to them for that.

China, on the other hand, accomplished quite a bit as well. They managed to put up a decent fight against a technologically advanced enemy, and in doing so, they gained the respect and admiration of the rest of the world.

They also managed to establish a better relationship with the Soviet Union, which came in handy later on.

But, what about the aftermath of the war? What was accomplished there?

Well, let's start with Japan. They accomplished the destruction of countless Chinese cities, leaving behind a trail of death and destruction that would take years to repair.

They also managed to establish puppet governments in various parts of China, which were about as popular as a root canal.

China, on the other hand, accomplished the establishment of the People's Republic of China in 1949, which was a pretty big deal.

It was a turning point in Chinese history, and it marked the end of years of conflict and turmoil. They also managed to unite the country under the Communist Party, which, depending on who you ask, was either a good thing or a bad thing.

The war led to the rise of Mao Zedong and the eventual establishment of the Communist Party in China. It also paved the way for the Korean War and the eventual involvement of the United States in the affairs of East Asia.

The war caused immense suffering and loss of life for both sides. Perhaps the most significant accomplishment of the war was the lesson it taught us.

The lesson is that war is never the answer, and that we must always strive for peace and understanding between nations. Unfortunately, it's a lesson that we still haven't fully learned.

In conclusion, while the Second Sino-Japanese War may have accomplished some things, it ultimately resulted in a lot of destruction, suffering, and unintended consequences. Hopefully, we can learn from this and work towards a future where wars are a thing of the past.

But, let's be real, we're probably not that enlightened yet.

The First Indochina War

The First Indochina War, also known as the French-Indochina War, was a military conflict that took place from 1946 to 1954 in Southeast Asia.

It was fought between French forces and Vietnamese nationalists seeking independence from French colonial rule. The war was a result of the growing nationalist sentiment in Vietnam and the French attempts to maintain their colonial control over the region.

The war involved several parties, including the French colonial authorities in Vietnam, Laos, and Cambodia, and the Vietnamese forces led by the Communist Party of Vietnam (Viet Minh).

The war also saw the involvement of China, which assisted the Viet Minh, and the United States, which provided aid to the French.

The war began in 1946 with a series of clashes between French forces and Vietnamese nationalists, including the Viet Minh, who had been fighting against Japanese occupation during World War II.

The French were seeking to re-establish their colonial control over the region, while the Vietnamese nationalists were seeking independence.

The war was marked by several major battles and campaigns, including the Battle of Dien Bien Phu in 1954, which resulted in a decisive victory for the Viet Minh forces. The battle lasted for 56 days and ended with the French forces surrendering to the Viet Minh.

The defeat at Dien Bien Phu was a turning point in the war and led to the signing of the Geneva Accords in 1954, which ended the conflict and established the independent states of Vietnam, Laos, and Cambodia.

The First Indochina War resulted in a significant number of casualties on both sides. The exact number of casualties is difficult to estimate, but it is believed that between 300,000 and 400,000 Vietnamese soldiers and civilians were killed, along with around 90,000 French soldiers and colonial troops.

Epic accomplishments? The First Indochina War! This a classic example of the great accomplishments of warfare. So, what was accomplished?

First of all, the French were able to establish their authority in Indochina, something they had been dreaming of for a long time.

They had this strange notion that ruling over other people was a good thing, and what better place to do it than a far-off, exotic land with people who didn't speak their language or share their culture?

Of course, this wasn't an easy task. The Vietnamese people, led by the Viet Minh, were determined to fight for their independence. But the French had a secret weapon: their superior military technology. Yes, they had guns and bombs and all kinds of fancy things that the Vietnamese didn't have.

And so, for eight long years, the French fought the Vietnamese. It was a brutal and bloody conflict, with countless lives lost on both sides. But in the end, the French emerged victorious.

What did this mean for the Vietnamese people? Well, they were now under the rule of a foreign power that didn't care about their needs or desires.

The French were more interested in exploiting the resources of the land and turning a profit than in improving the lives of the people living there. So, while the French saw their victory as a triumph, for the Vietnamese, it was a tragedy.

But let's not focus on the negative! After all, the French accomplished a lot during the First Indochina War. They were able to test out new military strategies and technologies, and they even had the opportunity to try out new chemical weapons like Agent Orange.

It was a great opportunity for the French military to flex their muscles and show off their might to the world.

And what about the aftermath? Well, the French were able to hold onto Indochina for a few more years before they were eventually forced to withdraw.

But even after they left, the damage had been done. The Vietnamese people had suffered through years of war and destruction, and the country was left in ruins.

But hey, at least the French got to show off their military prowess. In conclusion, the First Indochina War was a shining example of the accomplishments of warfare.

The French were able to assert their dominance over a foreign land and try out some cool new weapons in the process.

Sure, the Vietnamese people suffered greatly, but that's just collateral damage, depending on what side you were on during the war.

The Algerian War

The Algerian War, also known as the Algerian War of Independence, was a conflict fought between France and the National Liberation Front (FLN) of Algeria from 1954 to 1962.

The war was fought for Algeria's independence from France and was a significant event in both Algerian and French history.

The origins of the war can be traced back to the late 19th century when France first occupied Algeria in 1830. The French colonizers established a settler society in Algeria, which marginalized and oppressed the indigenous Algerian population.

In the 20th century, a growing sense of Algerian nationalism began to emerge, fueled by anti-colonial sentiment and a desire for independence.

The FLN was formed in 1954 with the goal of achieving Algerian independence through armed struggle.
The war began on November 1, 1954, when the FLN launched a series of coordinated attacks against French targets across Algeria.

The French government responded with a brutal counterinsurgency campaign, deploying the French Army and paramilitary units to Algeria.

French forces used torture, summary executions, and collective punishment against Algerian civilians suspected of supporting the FLN. The war quickly escalated, with both sides committing atrocities against each other.

The war drew international attention and condemnation, with many countries criticizing France for its brutal tactics in Algeria. The United Nations called for an end to the conflict and for Algeria's independence, but France refused to comply.

The war continued for eight years, with the FLN gaining support from the Algerian population and international solidarity movements. In 1958, Charles de Gaulle became the President of France and initiated negotiations with the FLN for a peaceful settlement of the conflict.

The negotiations resulted in the signing of the Evian Accords in 1962, which granted Algeria its independence and recognized the FLN as the legitimate government of Algeria.

The number of casualties in the Algerian War is disputed, with estimates ranging from 350,000 to over 1 million people killed.

Most of the casualties were Algerian civilians, who suffered the greatest toll from the violence and repression of the conflict.

Colonialism accomplished shit here, right? The Algerian War, a classic case of a colonizer trying to maintain their hold on a land they have no business being in.

It's almost comical how many times we've seen this play out throughout history, but let's dive in and see what was "accomplished" with this particular conflict.

First off, we have to commend the French for their incredible patience and dedication to holding onto Algeria.

They arrived in the early 1800s and didn't leave until the 1960s—that's a whole lot of time to spend in a country that doesn't want you there. During the war, the French were really able to showcase their innovative tactics, such as the infamous use of torture and the forced relocation of Algerians into concentration camps. Truly groundbreaking stuff.

Of course, it wasn't all smooth sailing for the French. The Algerians had a pesky habit of fighting back, and there were countless instances of guerrilla warfare and acts of terrorism. But hey, the French were persistent, and they eventually came out on top. Kind of.

So, what was accomplished with this war? Well, the French managed to maintain their hold on Algeria for a few more decades, so there's that.

They also showed the world how effective torture and concentration camps could be when dealing with rebellious populations—a real feather in their cap.

But what about the aftermath? That's where things get a bit messier. You see, the Algerians weren't too thrilled with being subjugated for over a century, and they weren't going to just forgive and forget once the French left.

The country was left in a state of turmoil, with violence and instability plaguing the region for years to come. But hey, at least the French got to pat themselves on the back for a job well done, right?

And they even got to keep their fancy buildings and infrastructure that they built with Algerian labor—that's a pretty sweet deal.

All in all, The Algerian War was a shining example of colonialism at its finest. Who knows, maybe they even inspired some future colonizers to take up the torch and continue the proud tradition of subjugating foreign lands for their own gain.

The Ethiopian Civil War

The Ethiopian Civil War was a prolonged and bloody conflict that lasted from 1974 to 1991. The war involved multiple factions and foreign powers, resulting in significant casualties and suffering for the people of Ethiopia.

The Ethiopian Civil War began with the overthrow of Emperor Haile Selassie in a military coup on September 12, 1974.

The coup was led by a group of military officers known as the Derg, who had grown dissatisfied with the emperor's rule and his handling of Ethiopia's many social and economic problems.

The Derg quickly consolidated power and began implementing a series of socialist reforms, including land redistribution and nationalization of key industries. However, the government's heavy-handed tactics and human rights abuses soon sparked opposition from various groups, including ethnic minorities and religious organizations.

The war initially pitted the Derg against several different rebel groups, each with their own agendas and constituencies. The Ethiopian People's Revolutionary Party (EPRP) was the first major opposition group to emerge, and it quickly gained support.

The EPRP launched a series of assassinations and attacks on government targets, but its tactics alienated potential allies and eventually led to a government crackdown that severely weakened the group.

Another major opposition force was the Tigray People's Liberation Front (TPLF), a Marxist-Leninist group that sought greater autonomy for the Tigray region in northern Ethiopia.

The TPLF gained strength throughout the 1980s and eventually allied itself with other rebel groups to form the Ethiopian People's Revolutionary Democratic Front (EPRDF).

The Ethiopian Civil War resulted in a staggering number of casualties, with estimates ranging from 500,000 to 1.5 million people killed.

The conflict also displaced millions of people and caused widespread famine and poverty.

The war finally came to an end in 1991, when rebel forces led by the EPRDF captured Addis Ababa, the capital of Ethiopia.

Depressing stuff—at least something was accomplished? A classic, almost like a Monthy Python sketch all them liberation peoples front groups! Tale of power struggles, violence, and the joys of victory. The Ethiopian Civil War—what an adventure it was! With its complex web of alliances, military campaigns, and brutal tactics, it was truly a wonder to behold.

The war raged on for years, with both sides committing unspeakable atrocities against each other and the civilian population caught in the crossfire.

The Derg, with their Soviet backing, had the upper hand for much of the conflict, but the rebels, with their guerrilla tactics and strong support from Eritrea and other neighboring countries, were a force to be reckoned with.

But what, you may ask, was actually accomplished in this bloody conflict? First and foremost, the Ethiopian Civil War achieved the goal of getting rid of the old government and replacing it with a new one.

This new government, however, was not exactly what one might call an improvement.

The Derg regime, despite its Marxist rhetoric, was nothing more than a group of power-hungry thugs who had no qualms about killing anyone who got in their way.

But hey, at least it wasn't the old government, right?

In addition to this glorious regime change, the Ethiopian Civil War also saw the birth of several new rebel groups, each with its own ambitions and agendas.

So, in a way, the Ethiopian Civil War accomplished the goal of spreading conflict and instability beyond Ethiopia's borders. Congratulations to all involved!

Of course, we can't forget about the humanitarian accomplishments of the war. The Ethiopian Civil War saw countless atrocities committed against civilians, including massacres, rapes, and forced relocations.

But hey, at least it gave us a new famine to talk about! The famine of the 1980s, which was exacerbated by the war and the Derg's disastrous economic policies, is estimated to have killed over a million people.

But think of all the charity concerts and celebrity activism it inspired! Truly, the war accomplished something great here.

In the end, the Ethiopian Civil War was a masterpiece of destruction, chaos, and general mayhem.

It brought down one government and replaced it with another, spawned new rebel groups and spread conflict across the region, and inspired a famine that still haunts us to this day.

And what did it all amount to? Not much, really. But hey, at least we can look back on it and say the international community did something, right?

The Eritrean War

The Eritrean War of Independence was a 30-year-long conflict that began on September 1, 1961, and ended on May 24, 1991. It was fought between the Eritrean Liberation Front (ELF) and later the Eritrean People's Liberation Front (EPLF) and the Ethiopian government.

Eritrea, a small country located on the Red Sea coast of Africa, was colonized by Italy in the late 1800s. After World War II, Eritrea was under British administration until it was federated with Ethiopia in 1952.

In 1961, the ELF was formed to fight for Eritrean independence from Ethiopia. The war began with a series of attacks by the ELF on Ethiopian targets in Eritrea.

In response, the Ethiopian government launched a counter-offensive, which led to a long and bloody conflict that would last for three decades.

The conflict was characterized by guerrilla warfare, as the Eritrean fighters relied on hit-and-run tactics to strike at Ethiopian forces and then disappear into the countryside.

In 1970, a split occurred within the ELF, leading to the formation of the Eritrean People's Liberation Front (EPLF). The EPLF was led by Isaias Afwerki, who would go on to become the first president of Eritrea after independence.

The EPLF was more organized and disciplined than the ELF and quickly became the dominant force in the Eritrean independence movement.

The war saw numerous atrocities committed by both sides. Ethiopian forces were accused of using chemical weapons against Eritrean fighters and civilians, while the EPLF was accused of committing human rights abuses against Ethiopian soldiers and civilians.

The conflict resulted in a significant number of casualties. Exact numbers are difficult to determine, but it is estimated that tens of thousands of people were killed during the war. Many more were injured or displaced from their homes.

In 1991, the Ethiopian government was overthrown by rebels led by the Ethiopian People's Revolutionary Democratic Front.

The new government recognized Eritrea's right to self-determination, and a referendum on independence was held in 1993.

The referendum saw an overwhelming majority of Eritreans vote in favor of independence, and Eritrea officially became an independent country on May 24, 1993.

The sweet taste of accomplishment? As with many wars, the ultimate goal was to achieve independence and sovereignty, and the Eritrean rebels were successful in their efforts. But what else?

Well, for starters, it accomplished 30 years of death, destruction, and misery for the people of Eritrea. But hey, at least they got their independence, right?

That's definitely worth 30 years of war and suffering. It's not like they could have just negotiated with Ethiopia and peacefully resolved their differences like civilized adults.

And let's not forget the countless atrocities committed on both sides during the war. War crimes, human rights abuses, and other forms of brutality were just par for the course. But again, it was all worth it in the end because Eritrea is now a sovereign nation, and isn't that what really matters?

Of course, the aftermath of the war was not exactly sunshine and rainbows either. The newly independent nation of Eritrea was left with a shattered economy, a devastated infrastructure, and a population traumatized by decades of violence.

But hey, at least they were finally free from Ethiopia's tyrannical rule, right?

And let's not forget about the ongoing political repression and human rights abuses that have characterized Eritrea's government since independence. The country has been ruled by the same authoritarian leader, Isaias Afwerki, since 1993, and he has been accused of numerous human rights violations, including torture, forced labor, and arbitrary detention.

But hey, at least they have their independence, right?
And let's not forget about the ongoing border dispute with Ethiopia, which has resulted in further violence and instability in the region.

In 1998, just seven years after Eritrea gained its independence, a border war broke out between the two countries, resulting in tens of thousands of deaths and the displacement of hundreds of thousands of people. And despite a peace agreement in 2000, tensions between the two countries remain high.

In conclusion, the Eritrean War of Independence was a long and brutal conflict that accomplished little beyond the establishment of a new nation.

The cost of achieving independence was high, and the aftermath has been characterized by ongoing political repression, human rights abuses, and instability.

But hey, at least they have their independence…

The Ethiopian-Eritrean War

The Ethiopian-Eritrean War was a conflict between Ethiopia and Eritrea that lasted from 1998 to 2000. The war erupted over a territorial dispute and long-standing tensions between the two countries.

The roots of the conflict can be traced back to the colonial era when both Eritrea and Ethiopia were ruled by Italy.

In 1952, Eritrea was annexed by Ethiopia, sparking a long and bloody struggle for independence by the Eritrean people. After years of fighting, Eritrea gained independence in 1993, but tensions between Ethiopia and Eritrea remained high, particularly over border disputes.

The Ethiopian-Eritrean War began in May 1998, when Eritrea accused Ethiopia of occupying disputed territory along the border between the two countries.

Both sides suffered heavy casualties, with estimates of over 70,000 people killed on both sides. The war came to an end in June 2000, with the signing of the Algiers Agreement, which established a peacekeeping mission to monitor the ceasefire and a boundary commission to settle the border dispute.

The border commission issued its final ruling in 2002, awarding the disputed town of Badme to Eritrea, which Ethiopia rejected, and that led to a standoff.

The Ethiopian-Eritrean War was a devastating conflict that resulted in significant loss of life and displaced thousands of civilians.

The war highlighted the deep-seated tensions and unresolved border disputes between the two countries.

Despite the signing of a peace agreement, the border dispute remains unresolved and continues to strain relations between Ethiopia and Eritrea.

So what did we accomplish with this war, you ask? The Ethiopian-Eritrean War—a classic case of "my territory is bigger than your territory."

The war lasted for two years, during which both sides engaged in some very impressive feats of stupidity.

Ethiopia, for example, decided to bomb the Eritrean capital of Asmara with cluster bombs. And Eritrea responded by launching a counter-offensive that ended up killing a bunch of Ethiopian civilians.

First of all, we accomplished a whole lot of death and destruction. The exact numbers are a bit fuzzy, but it's estimated that tens of thousands of people died during the conflict.

And for what? To determine whether a strip of land belonged to Ethiopia or Eritrea? I mean, come on, guys, it's not like either country was going to get rich off that land.

Secondly, we accomplished a whole lot of bad blood between Ethiopia and Eritrea. You know how sometimes you have a fight with a friend or family member, and you're both so angry that you just can't seem to let it go?

Well, that's basically what happened here, except on a national scale. Ethiopia and Eritrea are still not on great terms, and there are ongoing disputes over border territories.

And finally, we accomplished a whole lot of nothing. Seriously, what was the point of this war? Did anyone really win? Did anyone really come out ahead? Nope. The Ethiopian-Eritrean War was a complete and utter waste of time, resources, and human life.

We accomplished nothing, and all we're left with is a legacy of violence and bitterness.

Maybe we should all take a lesson from this conflict and remember that sometimes it's better to just let things go. Or maybe we forget that lesson too.

The Rwandian Civil War

The Rwandan Civil War was a conflict that took place from 1990 to 1994, in which the government of Rwanda, led by the Hutu ethnic group, fought against the Tutsi-dominated Rwandan Patriotic Front (RPF).

The conflict culminated in the Rwandan Genocide, in which an estimated 800,000 to 1 million people, primarily Tutsis and moderate Hutus, were killed.

The roots of the conflict go back to the colonial era when Rwanda was divided into two ethnic groups: the majority Hutus and the minority Tutsis.

Under colonial rule, the Tutsis were favored, as they were seen as more "European" in appearance and were believed to be more capable of ruling. This led to tensions between the two groups, which were exacerbated after Rwanda gained independence from Belgium in 1962.

In 1990, the RPF, a group of Tutsi exiles who had been living in Uganda, invaded Rwanda, in an attempt to overthrow the Hutu-dominated government. The RPF's invasion sparked a civil war that would last for the next four years.

In 1993, the Arusha Accords were signed, which called for a power-sharing government between the Hutus and the Tutsis.

However, the Hutu government was unwilling to share power with the RPF, and the peace agreement was never fully implemented.

In April 1994, President Habyarimana's plane was shot down, killing him and the president of Burundi.

This event sparked the Rwandan Genocide, in which Hutu militias, aided by the government and military, began a campaign of mass killing against Tutsis and moderate Hutus.

The genocide lasted for approximately 100 days, during which time an estimated 800,000 to 1 million people were killed.

The international community, including the United Nations, was slow to respond to the crisis, and by the time peacekeeping forces were deployed, much of the killing had already occurred.

What did it accomplish then? What a mess. It's hard to know where to start with this one. So much bloodshed, so much suffering, and for what? Let's see what was accomplished, shall we?

First off, we have to acknowledge that the Rwandan Civil War wasn't just one big conflict. It was a series of wars and insurgencies that spanned several decades, with different factions vying for power and control over the region.

But for the sake of simplicity, we'll focus on the main conflict that most people think of when they hear "Rwandan Civil War": the one that began in 1990 and culminated in the infamous genocide of 1994.

So, what did this conflict accomplish? Well, for starters, it accomplished the deaths of an estimated 500,000 to 1 million people.

Yes, you read that right. Half a million to a million people. That's a staggering number, even by war standards. And for what? To settle political scores and gain power. Lovely. But wait, there's more!

The Rwandan Civil War also accomplished the displacement of millions of people, the destruction of entire communities, and the destabilization of the entire region.

It created a refugee crisis that affected not just Rwanda, but neighboring countries as well. And let's not forget the psychological toll it took on the survivors and their families.

The trauma and PTSD resulting from the genocide will be felt for generations to come.
But what about the aftermath? Surely there were some positive outcomes, right?

Well, let's see. The Rwandan Patriotic Front (RPF) emerged victorious and took control of the country.

President Paul Kagames government has been accused of human rights abuses, including torture, imprisonment of political dissidents, and suppression of free speech.

Opposition leaders have been silenced, journalists have been jailed, and civil society organizations have been shut down.

The government has also been accused of meddling in the affairs of neighboring countries, including the Democratic Republic of Congo.

Some even argue that the RPF's victory in the civil war simply replaced one authoritarian regime with another.

So, what did the aftermath of the Rwandan Civil War accomplish? The consolidation of power in the hands of one man and his ruling party and a facade of progress and development that masks some troubling issues. It's not exactly the happy ending we were hoping for.

In conclusion, the Rwandan Civil War was a tragedy of epic proportions, and the aftermath is a mixed bag at best.

We can only hope that the lessons learned from this conflict will be heeded and that future generations will be spared the horrors that the people of Rwanda endured.

But given the state of the world today, that seems like a pipe dream. Sigh.

THE CONGO WARS

The Congo Wars, also known as the Great War of Africa, were a series of conflicts that occurred between 1996 and 2003 in the Democratic Republic of Congo (DRC).

The wars were fought by many different armed groups, including rebel militias, government forces, and foreign militaries.

The wars were some of the deadliest in African history, with an estimated 5.4 million people losing their lives as a result of the conflicts.

The First Congo War began in 1996, when the forces of Laurent-Désiré Kabila, a rebel leader, marched across the country with the support of neighboring Rwanda and Uganda.

They overthrew the government of President Mobutu Sese Seko, who had been in power since 1965 and installed Kabila as president. However, Kabila soon fell out with his former allies, and the Second Congo War broke out in 1998 when Rwanda and Uganda invaded the country to overthrow him.

Angola, Zimbabwe, and Namibia sent troops to support Kabila, and the war quickly became a regional conflict.

The war officially ended in 2003 with the signing of the Sun City Agreement, which called for the withdrawal of foreign troops and the establishment of a transitional government.

Joseph Kabila, Laurent-Désiré Kabila's son, became president of the DRC.

However, fighting continued in some parts of the country for several more years.

In terms of the human toll, estimates of the number of people killed in the conflict vary widely, but some sources suggest that as many as 5 million people lost their lives due to the fighting and associated causes such as disease and malnutrition.

Must have accomplished a lot then? A time when the Democratic Republic of Congo was plunged into a brutal conflict that lasted for years and resulted in the deaths of millions of people. What could be more fun to write about?

Let's start with the first Congo War, which lasted from 1996 to 1997. The war began when a coalition of African nations invaded the DRC, hoping to overthrow the dictator Mobutu Sese Seko.

The coalition was led by Rwanda and Uganda, who were both unhappy with Mobutu's support for their enemies in the region.

So, what did the coalition accomplish? Well, they managed to capture the capital city of Kinshasa and force Mobutu into exile. But then the coalition fell apart and the various rebel groups turned on each other, plunging the country into even more chaos.

The war officially ended with the signing of the Lusaka Accords in 1999, but that didn't stop the fighting. So, in summary, the first Congo War accomplished...not much.

But wait, there's more! The second Congo War began in 1998 and lasted until 2003. This time, Rwanda and Uganda invaded the DRC again, but this time they were joined by several other African nations.

The war was fought over control of the country's vast mineral resources, which include diamonds, gold, and coltan (a mineral used in electronic devices).

So, did the Second Congo War accomplish anything? Well, it did result in the overthrow of the DRC's new president, Laurent-Désiré Kabila, who had been installed by Rwanda after the first war.

But the fighting continued, with various rebel groups vying for control of the country's resources. The war officially ended with the signing of the Sun City Agreement in 2002, but the violence didn't stop until 2003.

So, in summary, the Second Congo War accomplished…also not much. And what about the aftermath? Well, the DRC is still one of the poorest and most unstable countries in the world.

The conflict led to the deaths of millions of people, and the country is still plagued by violence, corruption, and poverty.

But hey, at least some people got rich off of the conflict, right? The illegal mining of minerals continues to this day, with armed groups controlling the mines and selling the minerals on the black market.

So, if you're in the market for some conflict minerals, look no further than the DRC!

In conclusion, the Congo Wars was a tragic and senseless conflict that accomplished very little, except for enriching a few warlords and leaving a legacy of violence and instability in the region.

But hey, at least we got some sparkling, bloody diamonds out of it!

The Angolan Civil War

The Angolan Civil War was a long and brutal conflict that lasted from 1975 to 2002. The conflict involved several political factions and was fueled by regional and international interests.

The conflict began after Angola gained independence from Portugal in 1975. Three main factions emerged, each with different political ideologies and aspirations for the country.

The Popular Movement for the Liberation of Angola (MPLA), led by Agostinho Neto, wanted a socialist government. The National Union for the Total Independence of Angola (UNITA), led by Jonas Savimbi, was a nationalist movement that sought to establish a capitalist democracy. The National Liberation Front of Angola (FNLA), led by Holden Roberto, was another nationalist movement that sought to establish a democratic government.

The Cold War also played a role in the conflict, as the United States and the Soviet Union backed different factions. The MPLA was backed by the Soviet Union and other socialist countries, while UNITA was backed by the United States and South Africa.

The conflict finally ended in 2002 when UNITA's leader, Jonas Savimbi, was killed in battle. His death marked the end of UNITA as a military force, and the MPLA was able to consolidate its power.

The Angolan Civil War left the country severely damaged. The death toll is estimated to be between 500,000 and 1.5 million people, with many more suffering injuries and displacement.

The war also left Angola with a legacy of landmines, which continue to cause casualties to this day.

Bloody hell, please tell me something good was accomplished… Welcome to the satirical world of The Angolan Civil War, where nothing is too absurd or too impossible. Let's dig into the aftermath of this bloody conflict and see what was accomplished.

First and foremost, the war accomplished the establishment of a one-party state in Angola, with the MPLA emerging as the sole ruling party.

It also accomplished the enrichment of a few elites who managed to amass huge fortunes by exploiting the country's vast natural resources, while the majority of Angolans continued to live in poverty.

The MPLA's victory in the war was largely due to its military superiority, which was made possible by the support of its Soviet and Cuban allies.

But don't worry, UNITA wasn't left out entirely—they received ample support from the United States and South Africa, two countries known for their love of peace and stability.

One major accomplishment of the war was the destruction of Angola's infrastructure. The country's roads, bridges, and buildings were all heavily damaged or destroyed, leaving much of the population without access to basic necessities such as clean water, healthcare, and education.

But hey, at least the warlords got to drive around in their fancy cars and private jets, right?

The Angolan Civil War also accomplished the displacement of millions of people, who were forced to flee their homes and communities in search of safety.

Many of them ended up in squalid refugee camps or makeshift settlements, where they had to endure hunger, disease, and violence. But, at least they got to experience the joy of living in a warzone, right?

Another accomplishment of the Angolan Civil War was the widespread corruption that plagued the country's political and economic systems.

The ruling elite used their positions of power to enrich themselves and their families, while the majority of Angolans remained poor and marginalized.

But hey, at least the corrupt politicians got to live in their luxurious mansions and send their kids to expensive schools, right?

So there you have it, folks—the accomplishments of the Angolan Civil War. A one-party state, the enrichment of a few elites, the destruction of infrastructure, the displacement of millions, the proliferation of landmines, and rampant corruption.

It's almost enough to make you want to start a war yourself! But let's not get carried away—after all, we wouldn't want to accomplish anything meaningful or constructive.

The Mozambican Civil War

The Mozambican Civil War was a prolonged conflict that lasted from 1977 to 1992, pitting the Mozambique Liberation Front (FRELIMO) government against the Mozambique National Resistance (RENAMO) rebels.

The conflict caused a great deal of suffering for the people of Mozambique and resulted in the deaths of hundreds of thousands of people.

The war was fought on various fronts, including guerrilla warfare, political negotiations, and international diplomacy.

The Mozambican Civil War was a result of several factors, including political, economic, and social issues. Mozambique gained its independence from Portugal in 1975, and the country's first president, Samora Machel, was a leader of the FRELIMO party.

Machel's government adopted a socialist ideology, which included the nationalization of land, industries, and the education system.

This policy led to tensions with the West and neighboring countries, particularly South Africa, which saw the FRELIMO government as a threat to its security. The Mozambican Civil War began in 1977 and lasted for 15 years, with both sides committing atrocities against civilians.

The war resulted in the deaths of hundreds of thousands of people, with estimates ranging from 1 million to 1.5 million. The conflict also caused massive displacement, with over 4 million Mozambicans fleeing their homes.

That was a real doozy, wasn't it? At least we can look back and see what was accomplished, right? First and foremost, the war accomplished a lot of death and destruction.

I mean, we're talking about over a million people who died here. That's a pretty impressive body count.

And all that fighting really put Mozambique on the map. Sure, it wasn't the kind of map you want to be on, but hey, any publicity is good publicity, right?

The war also did wonders for the Mozambican economy. I mean, who doesn't love a good war economy, am I right?

All that destruction meant that people needed to rebuild, and that meant jobs for builders, architects, and other construction workers.

Plus, all those weapons and munitions had to come from somewhere, and that meant more jobs in the arms industry. So really, the war was a job-creating machine!

But the war wasn't just about death, destruction, and job creation. It also accomplished a lot in terms of geopolitical strategy. You see, during the Cold War, Mozambique was a bit of a pawn between the Soviet Union and the United States.

FRELIMO was seen as a socialist party, so the Soviets supported them, while RENAMO was seen as a pro-Western party, so the US supported them.

This led to a lot of meddling in Mozambique's internal affairs, which was great for the people of Mozambique because who doesn't love foreign interference in their country's politics?

But the real accomplishment of the Mozambican Civil War was the peace deal that ended it. I mean, sure, it took 15 years of fighting to get there, but hey, better late than never, right? And the peace deal was a real masterpiece. It brought FRELIMO and RENAMO together to form a power-sharing government, which meant that both sides got to share in the spoils of victory.

And best of all, it meant that Mozambique could finally move on from the war and start focusing on other things.

Like rebuilding their country and healing the wounds of the past. Of course, the aftermath of the war wasn't all sunshine and rainbows.

The peace deal was a bit of a shaky one, and there were still occasional flare-ups of violence between FRELIMO and RENAMO.

And let's not forget the landmines. Mozambique is still one of the most heavily mined countries in the world, and those landmines continue to kill and maim innocent people to this day.

So, it did accomplish giving the world a lot of beautiful pictures of Princess Diana in the country—and leaving kids without legs, families without their mums, and so on…

Sure, the Mozambican Civil War was a brutal, destructive conflict that left a trail of death and destruction in its wake. But it also accomplished a lot of things, like job creation, geopolitical maneuvering, and a peace deal that brought an end to the fighting. So really, when you think about it, the war was a bit of a mixed bag.

But hey, those pictures of Princess Diana. She looked so beautiful in that white hat and must have brought in a millions to the magazines who printed the images of her.

The Guatemalan Civil War

The Guatemalan Civil War was a conflict that lasted from 1960 to 1996 and involved the government of Guatemala and various guerrilla groups.

The war resulted in the deaths of an estimated 200,000 people, with many more suffering human rights abuses and displacement.

The conflict began on November 13, 1960, when a group of left-wing militants attacked the Guatemalan army in the town of San Juan Sacatepéquez.

The militants, who were members of the Guatemalan Labor Party (PGT), were attempting to spark a revolution to overthrow the government of President Miguel Ydígoras Fuentes.

The government responded with a heavy-handed crackdown, arresting and torturing suspected leftist militants and supporters.

In 1962, a group of military officers led by Colonel Carlos Castillo Armas overthrew President Ydígoras in a coup.

The new government, which was strongly anti-communist, received support from the United States, which saw leftist movements as a threat to its strategic interests in the region.

The conflict escalated in the 1970s, as the government expanded its counterinsurgency campaign.

The government established paramilitary groups known as the Civil Defense Patrols (PAC) to combat the guerrilla threat, which often resulted in human rights abuses and the displacement of civilians.

The guerrillas, for their part, resorted to terrorist tactics, such as bombings and assassinations. In 1982, General Efraín Ríos Montt seized power in a coup and implemented a brutal counterinsurgency campaign that included massacres of indigenous peoples suspected of supporting the guerrillas.

This period, known as the "scorched earth" campaign, resulted in the deaths of thousands of people and the displacement of many more. The government's campaign was aided by U.S. military and intelligence support. In terms of casualties, the exact number of people who died during the conflict is difficult to estimate, but it is believed to be around 200,000.

The majority of the victims were indigenous peoples, who were targeted by both the government and guerrilla groups. The war also resulted in the displacement of around 1 million people, many of whom fled to neighboring countries.

While the conflict officially ended with a peace agreement in 1992, the legacy of the war continues to be felt in Guatemala today, as the country struggles to address issues of inequality.

Civil wars, are famous for accomplishments, aren't they? Ladies and gentlemen, step right up and get ready for a wild ride through the history of The Guatemalan Civil War!

A conflict that was so messy, so convoluted, and so downright ridiculous that it could only have been the product of a bunch of bickering politicians and trigger-happy military generals.

Let's start with the good news—after 36 years of violence, death, and destruction, the Guatemalan Civil War finally came to an end in the 90s. The bad news? Not much else was accomplished.

The United States, never one to pass up an opportunity to meddle in Latin America, got involved as well. They trained Guatemalan military officers in counterinsurgency tactics, provided weapons and funding, and generally made a mess of things.

But despite all this, the EGP managed to hold its own for decades, and the war became a stalemate. That is, until the mid-1990s when a peace agreement was finally signed.

But wait, there's more! Even after the war ended, the aftermath was just as messy as the war itself. The peace agreement included provisions for land reform, indigenous rights, and the demobilization of rebel fighters.

But surprise, surprise, the government didn't follow through on most of these promises. Land reform was half-hearted at best, and many indigenous people are still fighting for their rights today.

The demobilization of rebel fighters was also a mess, with many former rebels being left without jobs or support.

The country has one of the highest homicide rates in the world, and politicians regularly engage in shady deals and backroom politics.

So, in the end, what was accomplished with The Guatemalan Civil War and its aftermath? Not much, folks. Just a lot of death, destruction, and political maneuvering.

But, at least they can say they are famous for more things than Oscar Isaac? Never heard of him, actually. Never heard of The Guatemalan Civil War before now either, to be honest.

The Salvadoran Civil War

The Salvadoran Civil War was a conflict that took place in El Salvador from 1980 to 1992. The war was fought between the government of El Salvador, which was supported by the United States, and leftist guerrilla groups.

The war resulted in the deaths of tens of thousands of people and left the country in ruins.

The origins of the conflict can be traced back to the early 20th century when a small group of wealthy families controlled most of the land and wealth in El Salvador. These families were opposed to any form of land reform that would give the country's poor and working-class greater access to land and resources.

In the 1970s, a coalition of left-wing political parties and guerrilla groups began to organize and call for land reform, workers' rights, and an end to the country's military dictatorship. The government responded with violence, including the use of death squads, to suppress the movement.

In 1980, a group of left-wing guerrilla groups formed the Farabundo Marti National Liberation Front (FMLN) and launched an armed uprising against the government.

The war quickly escalated, with the government receiving significant support from the United States in the form of military aid and training.

The US government feared that the Salvadoran conflict was part of a larger Communist conspiracy to spread revolution throughout Central America. The war had a devastating impact on the country, with an estimated 75,000 people killed and hundreds of thousands more displaced from their homes.

Well, this was a conflict that truly accomplished... well, something. Once upon a time, in a small Central American country called El Salvador, a civil war broke out between the government and left-wing guerrilla groups.

The war lasted for over a decade but at least something was accomplished, right?

1. Lots of people died Yes, this may seem like a negative thing, but hear me out. By the end of the conflict, over 75,000 people had been killed, which means there were a lot fewer mouths to feed. Plus, it gave the local funeral industry a much-needed boost.

2. The economy was stimulated. With all the fighting and destruction going on, there was plenty of work to be done in terms of rebuilding infrastructure. The construction industry thrived, as did the arms trade.

3. The military got some exercise. The Salvadoran Armed Forces had been itching to test out their new weaponry, and the civil war gave them the perfect opportunity. Plus, it was a great way for the soldiers to stay in shape.

4. People learned new skills. In order to survive during the war, people had to become experts in a variety of fields. Some became skilled at hiding from bombs and bullets, while others became proficient in treating injuries and illnesses without proper medical equipment. It was like one big survivalist training camp!

After over a decade of violence and destruction, the Salvadoran government and the guerrilla groups finally signed a peace agreement in 1992.

But what did they accomplish?

1. They stopped fighting. Well, that's certainly something.

2. They formed a commission. To address some of the human rights violations that had occurred during the war, the government created a Truth Commission. It was meant to investigate the crimes committed by both sides and bring those responsible to justice. Unfortunately, not much came of it.

3. The country remained poor. Despite all the rebuilding efforts, the economy of El Salvador remained pretty much the same. The war had destroyed much of the country's infrastructure, and the government was too busy buying new guns and bombs to worry about fixing things. Plus, with so many people dead, there were fewer consumers to stimulate the economy.

4. The people remained divided. The war had left a deep divide between the government and the people. The guerrilla groups had fought for social justice and equality, while the government had fought to maintain the status quo. The peace agreement did little to bridge this divide, and many people continued to feel shit in general.

The Nicaraguan Revolution

The Nicaraguan Revolution was a political upheaval that occurred between 1961 and 1990, leading to the ousting of the Somoza dynasty, a family that had ruled Nicaragua for over 40 years.

The revolution involved a range of social, economic, and political factors, including the oppression of the working class, rampant corruption, and the struggle for democratic reforms.

The revolution began in the early 1960s with the formation of the Sandinista National Liberation Front (FSLN), a Marxist-Leninist group that aimed to overthrow the Somoza regime. The FSLN was named after Augusto Cesar Sandino, a Nicaraguan revolutionary who led a rebellion against U.S. occupation of Nicaragua in the 1920s and 1930s.

In the late 1970s, the FSLN gained significant support from the Nicaraguan population, who were fed up with the Somoza regime's corruption and repression. In 1978, the FSLN launched a successful military offensive against the government, which led to the ousting of the Somoza regime in July 1979.

The Nicaraguan Revolution was marked by significant violence and casualties. The war led to the death of an estimated 50,000 people, including combatants and civilians. Many others were injured or displaced from their homes.

So many deaths, so much accomplished? The Nicaraguan Revolution was a tumultuous period in the country's history, spanning from 1978 to 1990. It was marked by political upheaval, violence, and international meddling, and in the end, it's unclear what was actually accomplished.

It all started with the Sandinistas, a group of left-wing revolutionaries who had been fighting against the Somoza dictatorship for years. In 1978, they launched a massive offensive against the regime, with support from the broader population.

They were successful, and by July 1979, they had taken control of the capital city, Managua. But the victory was short-lived. The Sandinistas quickly found themselves facing opposition from various quarters, both domestically and abroad.

The US government, in particular, was not pleased with the leftist turn in Nicaragua, and they launched a campaign of economic and military sabotage against the new government.

The Contras were a group of counter-revolutionaries, funded and trained by the US government, who fought against the Sandinistas. The conflict was marked by atrocities on both sides, with civilians caught in the crossfire. In the end, it's hard to say what was accomplished.

The Sandinistas were eventually voted out of power in 1990, after an election that was widely regarded as fair. But the Contra War had left the country devastated, thousands dead and billions of dollars in damage. And to this day, Nicaragua remains one of the poorest countries in the Western Hemisphere.

But let's take a closer look at what was "accomplished" during this period. First and foremost, the US government accomplished the goal of stopping a leftist revolution in its backyard. They poured millions of dollars into the Contras, who in turn committed countless atrocities against the Nicaraguan people. And for what?

To prevent a socialist government from taking hold in a small Central American country? Was it really worth it?

The people of Nicaragua suffered greatly during this period, caught between warring factions and subjected to violence and repression. And in the end, the country was left in shambles, with a shattered economy and a fractured society.

Also in the end, the Sandinistas were defeated, and the Contras succeeded in their mission to prevent socialism from taking root in Nicaragua. So what was the aftermath of this glorious victory?

Well, Nicaragua was left in ruins. The country was devastated by the conflict, with infrastructure destroyed and the economy in shambles. But at least the US got what they wanted, right?

Oh, and let's not forget about the Iran-Contra scandal. This was a delightful little subplot in the conflict worty of its own chapter in this book, where the US government secretly sold weapons to Iran (yes, the same Iran that they were also publicly condemning) in order to fund the Contras.

What could go wrong? Turns out, a lot. When this little scheme was discovered, it led to a massive scandal that rocked the Reagan administration.

But hey, at least they got to stick it to those commies in Nicaragua, right? So, what was accomplished in the Sandinista-Contra Conflict? A lot of death, destruction, and political maneuvering. And the aftermath?

A devastated country and a massive scandal that tarnished the reputation of the US government. But hey, at least they won, right?

The First Sudaanese Civil War

The First Sudanese Civil War was a conflict that lasted from 1955 to 1972 between the government of Sudan and Southern Sudanese rebels.

The conflict was primarily a result of tensions between the north and south over political, economic, and cultural differences.

It resulted in the deaths of hundreds of thousands of people and the displacement of millions.

At the time of independence from British colonial rule in 1956, Sudan was a country deeply divided along ethnic, religious, and regional lines. The north was predominantly Arab and Muslim, while the south was made up of various African tribes and was predominantly Christian or animist.

These differences were further exacerbated by the lack of development in the south, which was largely ignored by the northern-based government. The spark that ignited the civil war was a dispute over land and grazing rights between the Dinka and Nuer tribes in the southern province of Equatoria.

In August 1955, southern soldiers of the Equatorial Corps mutinied in the town of Torit after they were ordered to disarm by the northern-dominated Sudanese army. The mutiny quickly spread to other southern towns, and soon a full-scale insurgency was underway.

In 1972, after 17 years of fighting, the Addis Ababa Agreement was signed, granting the south autonomy and the right to self-determination. The agreement was brokered by the Ethiopian government and was supported by the international community.

It is estimated that between 500,000 and 1.5 million people died as a result of the First Sudanese Civil War, while millions more were displaced or became refugees.

The war also caused significant damage to the country's infrastructure, further exacerbating poverty and underdevelopment in the south. The legacy of the First Sudanese Civil War continues to be felt in Sudan today, with ongoing conflicts in Darfur, South Kordofan, and Blue Nile states.

Accomplished something, but what? It began in 1955 and lasted for over two decades (which is war terminology for «it still continues». Just like all good civil wars, it featured ethnic, religious, and economic tensions that boiled over into a brutal armed conflict and accomplished...

First off, it was a fantastic opportunity for both sides to engage in some good old-fashioned bloodshed. Who doesn't love a bit of fighting, am I right?

The government forces, supported by the North, were able to show off their military might and put down any rebellions with force. The rebels, supported by the South, were able to show their tenacity and willingness to fight for their cause.

So really, everyone was a winner. But what about the actual outcome of the war? Well, it did result in the Addis Ababa Agreement in 1972, which granted autonomy to the South.

However, this was short-lived, as the agreement was ultimately broken and the war resumed in 1983.

Again, it gave both sides a chance to showcase their military prowess. The government forces were able to continue their brutal crackdown on any rebellious elements, while the rebels were able to continue fighting for their cause.

But in the end, it was the government forces that emerged victorious, with the signing of the Comprehensive Peace Agreement in 2005.

And what did this agreement accomplish? Well, it officially ended the war, which is a pretty big deal. It also granted the South semi-autonomous status and allowed for the creation of a government of national unity.

But let's not forget the real winner of the war: the arms dealers. After all, what's a civil war without a healthy supply of guns and ammunition?

In terms of the aftermath, well, it's a mixed bag. On the one hand, the South was granted autonomy and eventually gained independence in 2011.

On the other hand, the country has been plagued by ongoing conflict and political instability to this day. And let's not forget about the atrocities committed during the war, including the use of child soldiers and widespread human rights abuses.

But hey, at least we can say that the First Sudanese Civil War accomplished something, right? It gave us all an opportunity to witness some good old-fashioned violence, and isn't that what life is all about?

The Second Sudanese Civil War

The Second Sudanese Civil War, which lasted from 1983 to 2005, was one of the longest and deadliest conflicts in Africa's history. It resulted in the death of an estimated 2 million people, and the displacement of millions more.

The conflict pitted the Sudanese government, dominated by Arab Muslims in the north, against rebels in the predominantly Christian and animist south.

The Second Sudanese Civil War officially began in 1983, when the Sudanese government, under the leadership of President Jaafar Nimeiri, imposed Sharia law throughout the country, including in the south. This move was seen as a direct attack on the predominantly Christian and animist south and led to widespread protests.

In response to the imposition of Sharia law, a rebel group called the Sudan People's Liberation Movement/Army (SPLM/A) was formed. Led by John Garang, the SPLM/A sought to overthrow the government and establish a separate state in the south.

The war quickly escalated, with the government launching a brutal campaign against the rebels and civilians in the South.

The government forces used scorched earth tactics, burning villages and crops, and displacing millions of people.

The SPLM/A, for its part, also committed numerous human rights cases of abuse, including the recruitment of child soldiers, and attacks on civilians in the north.

The war came to an end in 2005, with the signing of the Comprehensive Peace Agreement (CPA) between the Sudanese government and the SPLM/A. The agreement granted the South a degree of autonomy and provided for a referendum on independence in 2011.

In 2011, the people of South Sudan voted overwhelmingly for independence, and the new state was officially established on July 9, 2011.

What was accomplished? One of the most thrilling and captivating wars in modern history. It's no surprise that so many people are still talking about it today.

I mean, who could forget the non-stop action, the thrilling battles, and the inspiring leaders?

First of all, let's talk about what caused the war in the first place. The Second Sudanese Civil War was fought between the Sudanese government and rebel groups, primarily in the south of the country.

The government, led by the charismatic Omar al-Bashir, wanted to maintain control over the whole country, while the rebels, led by John Garang, wanted more autonomy for the south.

The war began in 1983 and lasted for 22 years, making it one of the longest-running conflicts in Africa. So it did achieve some claim to the African Hall of Fame for long-running conflicts.

So, what was accomplished during those 22 years of bloodshed and violence? Well, let's start with the positives.

The Sudanese government did manage to maintain control over the country, at least for the most part. They also managed to secure valuable resources, such as oil, which helped to fuel the country's economy.

As for the rebels, they were able to gain some degree of autonomy for the South, with the signing of the Comprehensive Peace Agreement in 2005.

However, this autonomy was short-lived, as South Sudan eventually gained independence in 2011, creating a separate nation altogether. But let's not focus too much on the positives, because there were plenty of negatives to go around.

For starters, as we mentioned earlier, over 2 million people lost their lives during the conflict. That's 2 million people who will never get to experience the joys of life, such as eating ice cream or watching a sunset.

The war also left countless others injured or displaced, with many families being torn apart as a result. It's hard to imagine the pain and suffering that these people went through, and it's even harder to imagine what they must have felt when they realized that all of this was for nothing.

And what about the economic impact of the war? Well, it's safe to say that it wasn't exactly positive. The country's infrastructure was severely damaged, and many businesses were forced to shut down as a result. This had a devastating effect on the economy, which is still struggling to recover today.

But hey, at least the government and rebel leaders were able to live in relative luxury throughout the conflict, right? I mean, sure, the average Sudanese citizen was struggling to survive, but at least the people in power were doing just fine. It's always nice to know that your leaders are looking out for your best interests, isn't it?

So, what was accomplished with the Second Sudanese Civil War? Well, not much, really. The government managed to maintain control over the country, but at a huge cost in terms of human lives and suffering. The rebels were able to secure some degree of autonomy, but this was short-lived, and the eventual independence of South Sudan created a whole new set of problems.

And what about the aftermath of the war? Well, it's not exactly a happy story. The country is still struggling to recover from the devastation caused by the conflict, and many people are still living in poverty and struggling to survive.

It's a sad reminder that war never really accomplishes anything, except for destruction and suffering.

So, there you have it, folks. The Second Sudanese Civil War: a 22-year-long conflict that accomplished very little, except for the loss of 2 million lives and counting…

The Somali Civil War

The Somali Civil War, also known as the Somali conflict, is an ongoing conflict in the Horn of Africa country of Somalia. The war has been raging since the overthrow of former dictator Siad Barre in 1991, and it is still ongoing today, with various factions fighting for power and control.

The origins of the conflict can be traced back to the colonial era, when Somalia was divided into five territories: British Somaliland, Italian Somaliland, French Somaliland, Ethiopian Somaliland, and Kenyan Somaliland.

After independence, the newly formed Somali government attempted to unite all of these territories, but this proved difficult due to various clan rivalries and other factors.

This ultimately led to Siad Barre seizing power in a military coup in 1969 and ruling the country as a dictator until his ouster in 1991.

After the fall of Siad Barre's regime, Somalia descended into chaos as various factions fought for control of the country. The main actors in the conflict include warlords, clan militias, Islamic militants, and the internationally recognized government.

The conflict has been marked by widespread violence, displacement, famine, and humanitarian crises.

One of the most prominent factions in the conflict is Al-Shabaab, an Islamist militant group that emerged in the early 2000s and is aligned with Al-Qaeda.

The group has carried out numerous attacks against the Somali government, African Union peacekeeping forces, and civilians.

In addition to Al-Shabaab, there are several other militant groups that operate in Somalia, including ISIS, which has been active in the country since 2015.

The number of casualties in the Somali conflict is difficult to estimate due to the ongoing nature of the conflict and the lack of reliable data.

However, it is believed that tens of thousands of people have been killed since the conflict began in 1991.

Additionally, millions of Somalis have been displaced, and the country has experienced multiple famines and humanitarian crises. Efforts to end the conflict have been ongoing since the early 1990s, but progress has been slow and often unsuccessful.

In recent years, there have been some positive developments in Somalia, including the establishment of regional administrations and the holding of national elections. However, the conflict is still ongoing, and there is no clear end in sight.

The war that never accomplished? The war that began in 1991 and ended...well, technically it's still ongoing. But don't worry, I'm sure there's been plenty of progress and accomplishments made in the last few decades.

First off, let's start with the positive news. After years of violence and chaos, Somalia is now one of the most peaceful and stable countries in the world... said no one ever.

In fact, Somalia is still considered one of the most dangerous places on the planet, with warlords, terrorist groups, and pirates all vying for control. So, it did not accomplish a boost in tourism.

But hey, let's not focus on the negative. Surely there have been some accomplishments in the last thirty years.

Well, for starters, the Somali people have become incredibly resilient. I mean, how many people can say they've survived decades of civil war, famine, and terrorism? Talk about a tough crowd.

And let's not forget about the progress made in the realm of piracy. Somali pirates used to be all the rage, hijacking ships and holding crews for ransom. But now, thanks to increased international naval patrols and security measures, piracy in the region has decreased significantly.

Of course, that doesn't mean piracy has been completely eradicated, but hey, progress is progress, right?

As for the rest of the country, the situation is a bit murkier. The central government has struggled to maintain control over the various regions of Somalia, with some areas falling under the control of warlords or Islamist militants.

But hey, at least the government has a presence in the capital city of Mogadishu. Sure, it's a heavily fortified compound surrounded by miles of razor wire, but it's a start.

But let's not forget the humanitarian aid that's been poured into Somalia over the years. Of course, that aid hasn't always reached the people who need it most, and there have been accusations of aid organizations funding militant groups. But hey, at least someone's trying, right?

All in all, it's been a wild ride for Somalia over the last few decades. But, at least there's been progress...right? Okay, maybe not. But, there's always hope for the future. Maybe someday Somalia will be a stable, peaceful country.

Or maybe it'll just keep limping along, surviving against all odds. Who knows?

THE SOMALI-ETHIOPAN WAR

The Somali-Ethiopian War was a short-lived conflict that took place between Somalia and Ethiopia in 1977–1978. The war was sparked by Somalia's claim to the Ethiopian Somali Region (Ogaden), which was home to a predominantly ethnic Somali population.

The war ended in a decisive victory for Ethiopia, and Somalia was forced to withdraw its forces from Ethiopian territory.

The origins of the conflict can be traced back to the colonial period when the Ogaden region was divided between Ethiopia and Italian Somaliland.

After World War II, the United Nations granted Italy trusteeship over Italian Somaliland, with the aim of preparing the territory for independence.

In 1960, the former Italian Somaliland gained independence and merged with British Somaliland to form the Somali Republic. Meanwhile, Ethiopia retained control of the Ogaden region.

Somalia had long sought to reunite the ethnic Somali population in Ogaden with its own territory.

The issue came to a head in the mid-1970s when Somalia, under the leadership of President Siad Barre, launched a campaign to annex the Ogaden region.

The campaign began with a series of cross-border raids by Somali forces, who encountered little resistance from Ethiopian troops. In July 1977, Somalia officially declared war on Ethiopia.

With the help of Soviet military advisors and Cuban troops, the Ethiopian military was able to turn the tide of the war.

The Soviet Union saw Ethiopia as an important ally in the Horn of Africa, and provided extensive military aid to the Ethiopian government during the conflict.

The Somali military was accused of massacring Ethiopian civilians and prisoners of war, while the Ethiopian military was accused of using chemical weapons against Somali soldiers and civilians.

So much fighting, what was achieved?
The Somali-Ethiopian War, A tale of two neighbors who just can't seem to get along.

They say good fences make good neighbors, but it seems like these two countries never got the memo. I mean, who needs boundaries when you can have a war?

Also known as the Ogaden War, it all started when Somalia, under the rule of the famous Siad Barre, decided they wanted to take back the Somali-inhabited Ogaden region from Ethiopia.

You know, just a friendly neighborhood takeover.

So, what did the war accomplish? Well, let's see. Somalia got to flex its military muscles and invade its neighbor, Ethiopia. That's a pretty big accomplishment, right? I mean, who needs peace when you can have a good old-fashioned invasion?

But wait, there's more! Ethiopia managed to fight back and repel the Somali invasion. So, they got to show off their military prowess as well.

And let's not forget the Soviet Union, who supplied both sides with weapons and ammunition. I mean, it's always good to have a proxy war going on…

In the end, surprisingly, the war didn't really accomplish much.

The two countries continued to have a rocky relationship, with occasional border skirmishes and tension, but, at least they got to have a war.

But let's not forget the real winners of the Somali-Ethiopian War: the arms dealers. Yes, the war provided a great opportunity for weapons manufacturers and dealers to make some serious money. And who doesn't love a good profit, right?

In conclusion, the Somali-Ethiopian War was a great opportunity for both countries to show off their military strength, receive aid from the Soviet Union, and make some arms dealers very happy.

But in the end, it didn't really accomplish much except leaving Somalia weakened and unstable. Maybe next time, they should try a game of Monopoly or Risk instead.

The Russo-Georgian War

The Russo-Georgian War was a short-lived conflict that occurred between Russia and Georgia in August 2008. The conflict arose as a result of tensions between Georgia and its breakaway regions of Abkhazia and South Ossetia.

The origins of the Russo-Georgian War date back to the early 1990s, when the Soviet Union collapsed, and the newly independent Republic of Georgia sought to assert its control over the regions of Abkhazia and South Ossetia.

Both regions had substantial populations of ethnic minorities, and tensions between them and the central government in Tbilisi were high.

In the years that followed, separatist movements emerged in both regions and 1992, Abkhazia declared its independence.

In the early 2000s, the Georgian government under President Mikheil Saakashvili sought to reassert its control over Abkhazia and South Ossetia.

Tensions between Georgia and Russia increased, and in 2008, the conflict erupted into full-scale war.

The war resulted in significant casualties on both sides, with estimates suggesting that up to 1,600 people were killed.

International efforts to mediate the conflict were unsuccessful, and a ceasefire agreement was not reached until August 12, 2008.

Under the terms of the ceasefire agreement, Russian forces were to withdraw from Georgian territory, and Georgia agreed to not use force against Abkhazia and South Ossetia.

Despite the ceasefire agreement, tensions between Russia and Georgia remained high in the years following the war.

Everyone is friends and ever-lasting peace was accomplished? The war lasted only five days but was enough to make the world question why Georgia and Russia were fighting in the first place.

The war began when Georgia decided to get back control of South Ossetia, a breakaway region that had declared independence. But as soon as Georgia set its sights on South Ossetia, Russia got involved, and the two countries found themselves in a full-blown conflict.

Georgia tried to play it cool and act tough, but it didn't take long for Russia to show them who's boss, and guess what! So much was accomplished!

1. The world got to see some impressive military hardware. Russia showed off its tanks, jets, and troops, while Georgia showed off…well, not much. Maybe some nice uniforms?

2. The war was a great distraction from other problems. The global economy was tanking, and the world was in the midst of a financial crisis. But hey, at least we had the Russo-Georgian War to focus on, right?

3. The conflict made for some great news coverage. Journalists from all over the world were there, cameras in hand, ready to capture the action. It was like watching an action movie – but with real-life consequences.

4. Georgia got to feel tough for a little while. Sure, they got their butts handed to them by the Russians, but at least they stood up to a big, bad country, right?

5. The war helped strengthen the bond between Russia and its allies. Russia's buddies in the region – Belarus, Kazakhstan, and Armenia – got to show their support for their big brother by sending in some troops.

But what about the aftermath of the war?

1. Georgia learned the hard way that they can't mess with Russia. After the war, Georgia was forced to recognize South Ossetia and Abkhazia as independent states. It was a tough pill to swallow, but hey, at least they learned their lesson, right?

2. The conflict helped Russia flex its muscles in the region. After the war, Russia was seen as a big, powerful country that won't take any crap from anyone. The other countries in the region took notice and thought twice before crossing Putin.

3. The war brought attention to the plight of the people of South Ossetia and Abkhazia. Before the war, most people had never heard of these regions. Now, thanks to the conflict, the world knows that these people exist – even if they're not recognized by most countries.

4. The war provided plenty of fodder for political pundits and armchair analysts to argue about. Was Georgia justified in its actions? Did Russia overreact? Who was right and who was wrong? It was a great opportunity for people to pretend like they knew what they were talking about.

In the end, the Russo-Georgian War accomplished…not much.

The conflict was a brief blip in history that left behind a lot of destruction and heartache. And well, the war was successful in not ending the conflict.

THE CHECHEN WARS

The Chechen Wars were a series of armed conflicts between the Russian Federation and the Chechen Republic of Ichkeria, a separatist region in the North Caucasus, which sought independence from Russia.

The First Chechen War took place from 1994 to 1996, while the Second Chechen War occurred from 1999 to 2009.

The First Chechen War began in December 1994, when Russian forces invaded Chechnya in an attempt to re-establish control over the region, which had declared independence in 1991.

The conflict quickly escalated into a full-scale war, with the Chechen forces using guerrilla tactics to fight the Russian military. The war was marked by brutal fighting, including indiscriminate shelling of civilian areas by Russian forces and hostage-taking by Chechen fighters.

The war ended in 1996 with a ceasefire agreement, which granted de facto independence to Chechnya, although it remained part of the Russian Federation.

The Second Chechen War began in August 1999, when a group of Chechen militants led by Shamil Basayev and Ibn al-Khattab crossed the border into the neighboring Russian republic of Dagestan, intending to establish an independent Islamic state.

This triggered a massive Russian military response, with troops being deployed to the region to quell the insurgency.

The conflict quickly spread to Chechnya, with Russian forces launching a massive air and ground offensive against the region.

The conflict continued until 2009 when Russian forces declared victory over the separatist forces. The Chechen Wars resulted in significant casualties on both sides.

The exact number of casualties is disputed, but it is estimated that tens of thousands of people were killed or wounded. Russian forces suffered heavy losses, with estimates ranging from 5,000 to 14,000 soldiers killed.

Chechen losses were even higher, with estimates ranging from 30,000 to 100,000 people killed.

The Chechen Wars officially ended in 2009, with the Russian government declaring victory over the separatist forces. However, the conflict has left deep scars on the region, with the legacy of the wars continuing to be felt today.

So, it accomplished something? This war is a classic example of what happens when you mix a bunch of nationalism, religious extremism, and political instability.

First off, let's start with the First Chechen War. The Russians were fighting against Chechen separatists who wanted to break away from Russia and form their own country.

The Russians sent in their troops, and what followed was a brutal conflict that resulted in the deaths of tens of thousands of people.

So, what did the Russians accomplish with all that bloodshed? Well, they did manage to officially regain control of Chechnya, but at what cost?

The conflict left the region in ruins, with entire cities reduced to rubble and civilians displaced from their homes.

It also created a whole new generation of angry, embittered Chechens who had been traumatized by the violence and felt even more strongly about their desire for independence.

This time, the Russians were fighting against Islamic extremists who had taken over the region and were using it as a base for launching terrorist attacks across Russia.

The Russians claimed that they were fighting against terrorism and protecting their citizens, but the reality was that the conflict was just as brutal as the first one.

Thousands of civilians were killed, and the Russians were accused of using excessive force and committing war crimes.

In the end, what did the Russians accomplish? Well, they did manage to regain control of Chechnya once again, but the region was left in a state of chaos and violence.

The conflict also fueled anti-Russian sentiment not just in Chechnya but across the entire North Caucasus region.

And let's not forget about the impact that the Chechen Wars had on the rest of the world.

The wars helped to radicalize many Muslims around the world, who saw the conflict as a classic example of a powerful, oppressive state crushing the aspirations of weaker, marginalized people.

It also gave rise to a whole new wave of terrorism, as Chechen militants began launching attacks not just in Russia but in other parts of the world as well.

So, all in all, what did we accomplish with the Chechen Wars? Well, we managed to cause untold suffering, death, and destruction, radicalize a generation of Chechens, fuel anti-Russian sentiment across the North Caucasus, and give rise to a whole new wave of terrorism.

Bravo, everyone—job well done!

The Libyan Civil War

The Libyan Civil War was a major conflict that took place in Libya from 2011 to 2020. The conflict began as a popular uprising against the regime of longtime dictator Muammar Gaddafi and quickly escalated into a civil war involving a variety of factions, both domestic and foreign.

The conflict finally came to an end with the defeat of Gaddafi's regime in 2011, but political instability and violence continued to plague the country for years to come.

Muammar Gaddafi came to power in Libya in 1969 through a military coup. He ruled the country for over 40 years with an authoritarian regime, which was characterized by political oppression, human rights abuses, and corruption.

The Libyan economy was heavily dependent on oil exports, which contributed to Gaddafi's power and influence in the region.

However, the Libyan people became increasingly dissatisfied with Gaddafi's rule, and protests broke out across the country in early 2011.

In February 2011, the opposition established a transitional government in the eastern city of Benghazi, and the conflict quickly escalated into a full-scale civil war.

Gaddafi's regime, supported by loyalist militias, launched a brutal crackdown on the opposition, leading to widespread violence and human rights abuses.

The exact number of casualties in the Libyan Civil War is difficult to determine. However, estimates suggest that between 10,000 and 30,000 people were killed, and thousands more were injured or displaced.

The conflict officially came to an end in October 2011, with the death of Gaddafi. However, the country remained unstable, with various factions and militias vying for power.

The transitional government established in Benghazi struggled to assert control over the country, and rival governments emerged in the east and west of the country.

In 2014, a civil war broke out between the Libyan National Army (LNA), led by General Khalifa Haftar, and the Government of National Accord (GNA), led by Prime Minister Fayez al-Sarraj.

The conflict drew in a number of regional and international actors, with Haftar receiving support from Egypt, the United Arab Emirates, and Russia, while the GNA was backed by Turkey and Qatar.

In 2020, after years of conflict and political instability, the GNA and LNA agreed to a ceasefire, which was brokered by the United Nations. However, the situation remains fragile.

It did accomplish something? Ah, the Libyan Civil War, or as some people call it, "Gaddafi's Last Stand." What a wild ride that was.

Muammar Gaddafi, the eccentric and flamboyant dictator of Libya, was feeling the heat, so to speak, as his people began to demand political reform and greater freedom.

At first, Gaddafi tried to quell the protests with force, but that only made things worse. The rebels, armed with little more than homemade weapons and a lot of determination, rose up against him and soon had control of large swaths of the country.

NATO, seeing an opportunity to intervene in yet another foreign conflict, launched airstrikes against Gaddafi's forces and helped the rebels to eventually topple the regime.

And what did we accomplish, you might ask?

Well, for starters, we got rid of Gaddafi. That's something, right? The guy was a real pain in the ass, always dressed in those ridiculous outfits and ranting about how he was the "King of Kings" and how the Libyan people loved him.

He was a megalomaniac, plain and simple, and we were all better off without him. But what came next was a whole other mess.

The country was in chaos, with various factions vying for power and militias running rampant. It was like a game of thrones, but with less dragons and more AK-47s.

So, what did we accomplish with the Libyan Civil War? We got rid of one dictator, but we created another mess in the process.

The country is still in turmoil, with no end in sight. We've learned that military intervention isn't always the best solution, and that toppling a regime is just the beginning of a long, difficult process of rebuilding.

At least we can say we tried, right?

The Western Sahara War

The Western Sahara War was a conflict fought between Morocco and the Polisario Front from 1975 to 1991 over the sovereignty of Western Sahara. The war resulted in a ceasefire in 1991 but the conflict remains unresolved.

Western Sahara, formerly known as Spanish Sahara, was a colony of Spain from the late 19th century until 1975. In the early 1970s, the Polisario Front, a national liberation movement formed by Sahrawi activists, began an armed struggle against Spanish colonial rule.

Meanwhile, Morocco and Mauritania also laid claim to the territory. In 1975, as Spain prepared to withdraw from the territory, Morocco and Mauritania signed a secret agreement with Spain known as the Madrid Accords, in which Spain agreed to transfer control of Western Sahara to Morocco and Mauritania.

This move was opposed by the Polisario Front, who declared the Sahrawi Arab Democratic Republic (SADR) as an independent state on February 27, 1976.

The Moroccan military began to occupy Western Sahara in 1975, leading to the outbreak of a guerrilla war between the Polisario Front and the Moroccan armed forces.

Mauritania withdrew from the conflict in 1979 after suffering a series of defeats at the hands of the Polisario Front, which led to the complete control of Western Sahara by Morocco.

In 1991, the United Nations brokered a ceasefire between the Polisario Front and Morocco, which ended the armed conflict. The ceasefire called for a referendum on self-determination for the people of Western Sahara, which has yet to take place.

A UN peacekeeping mission, known as the United Nations Mission for the Referendum in Western Sahara (MINURSO), was established to monitor the ceasefire and prepare for the referendum.

As of today, the status of Western Sahara remains unresolved, with Morocco still maintaining control over the majority of the territory. The Polisario Front continues to call for self-determination for the Sahrawi people.

Did they ever accomplish anything of value? A story of territorial disputes, political tensions, and, of course, sand. I can already feel the excitement building.

Let's start at the beginning, shall we? Back in 1975, the Western Sahara was a colony of Spain. However, both Morocco and Mauritania claimed the land as their own, because apparently having enough land already just isn't cool enough.

And so, the Western Sahara War began. At first, it was just Morocco and Mauritania against a group called the Polisario Front, who were fighting for an independent Western Sahara.

But then, Mauritania got cold feet (or sand in their boots, who knows) and decided to withdraw from the conflict.

Morocco, however, was not deterred and continued to fight the Polisario Front until 1991, when a ceasefire was finally agreed upon.

So, what was accomplished in all of this? Well, let's see. Morocco ended up controlling about 80% of the sand Western Sahara, while the Polisario Front controlled the other 20% or so.

The conflict also led to the displacement of thousands of Sahrawi people, who were forced to flee the fighting and seek refuge in neighboring countries.

But fear not, dear reader, for this is not the end of the story. In 2020, tensions between Morocco and the Polisario Front once again reached a boiling point, with the latter declaring the 1991 ceasefire null and void.

Morocco responded by sending troops into the Western Sahara and engaging in a series of skirmishes with the Polisario Front.

And so, the Western Sahara War lives on, because apparently nothing says "progress" quite like fighting over a piece of land that's mostly made up of sand. Who needs resources, stability, or peace when you can have sand...

But let's not forget the true winners in all of this—the sand merchants. Yes, those brave souls who risked life and limb to smuggle sand out of the Western Sahara and sell it to unsuspecting buyers around the world.

Who needs diamonds or gold when you can have sand from a disputed territory, am I right? In conclusion, the Western Sahara War has accomplished...well, not much, really.

Sure, some people have a bigger sandbox to play in now, but at what cost? The displacement of thousands of people, the ongoing conflict, and the general sense of instability in the region are hardly worth it.

The Israel-Lebanon Conflict

The Israel-Lebanon conflict of 1982–2000 was a prolonged and complex conflict that took place between the state of Israel and various Lebanese groups, most notably Hezbollah.

The conflict began in 1982 when Israel launched a military invasion of Lebanon, which aimed to push back Palestinian militants who had been using southern Lebanon as a base for attacks against Israel.

The conflict was marked by significant levels of violence, with both sides engaging in heavy fighting and sustained periods of bombardment.

In addition, there were multiple rounds of negotiations and ceasefire agreements, which ultimately failed to bring a lasting end to the conflict.

The roots of the conflict can be traced back to the decades-long Israeli-Palestinian conflict,
which began in the late 1940s with the establishment of the state of Israel and the displacement of hundreds of thousands of Palestinian refugees.

Over the years, Palestinian militant groups had established a presence in southern Lebanon, where they launched attacks against Israeli targets across the border.

In 1982, Israel launched a large-scale invasion of Lebanon, which aimed to drive out the Palestinian militants and establish a pro-Israeli government in Beirut.

The conflict quickly escalated, drawing in multiple actors and leading to a protracted and bloody conflict that lasted for nearly two decades.

During this time, Israeli forces occupied large parts of southern Lebanon, while Hezbollah and other Lebanese militias launched a sustained campaign of guerrilla warfare against Israeli troops and the pro-Israeli government in Beirut.

In 2000, Israel finally withdrew its forces from southern Lebanon, ending its long-term military occupation of the country. Hezbollah claimed victory, arguing that its sustained campaign of guerrilla warfare had forced Israel to withdraw.

So, it accomplished nothing? The Israel-Lebanon conflict, where two neighboring countries spent nearly two decades taking turns attacking each other and achieving...well, let's see what they accomplished, shall we?

In 1982, Israel decided that they weren't content with just occupying Palestine, they wanted to expand their territory and take over Lebanon as well. So they invaded, because why not? It's not like there are any real-world consequences for constantly violating international law.

The Israelis quickly established a "security zone" in southern Lebanon, which they promptly filled with Israeli soldiers and their allies, the South Lebanese Army (SLA). The SLA was a group of Lebanese soldiers who were basically puppets of the Israeli government, so they happily did whatever the Israelis told them to do. Like a good little lapdog.

Of course, the Lebanese people were none too pleased about being occupied by a foreign army, so they formed their own resistance group, Hezbollah.

So for nearly two decades, Israel and Hezbollah went back and forth, attacking each other and accomplishing absolutely nothing. Israel would bomb Beirut, Hezbollah would launch rockets into Israel, and both sides would claim victory.

It's like a never-ending game of "who can cause the most destruction." But wait, there's more!

In 2000, Israel finally decided that they had had enough and withdrew their troops from southern Lebanon. So what did they accomplish in nearly two decades of occupation and conflict?

Well, they managed to kill a lot of Lebanese people and destroy a lot of infrastructure. And what did Hezbollah accomplish? They managed to kill a lot of Israeli soldiers and launch a lot of rockets into Israel.

And, since Israel left, they claimed victory and bragging rights! It is a bit like calling shotgun before a car ride.

So all in all, it was a big ol' waste of time and human life. But at least they can all pat themselves on the back for a job well done, right?

Oh, and let's not forget about the thousands of Lebanese and Palestinian refugees who were forced to flee their homes and become displaced. They probably accomplished a whole lot of suffering and trauma, if nothing else.

So what's the aftermath of all this? Well, Lebanon is still recovering from the devastation that was wrought upon it, and Hezbollah is still a political force in the country.

Israel is still occupying Palestine, and the conflict between the two sides shows no signs of ending anytime soon. It's almost like all that violence and bloodshed accomplished absolutely nothing. But they probably did try.

THE ISRAEL-PALESTINIAN CONFLICT

The Israeli-Palestinian conflict is a protracted and ongoing conflict that has lasted for decades and involves the state of Israel and various Palestinian groups.

The conflict began in 1948 with the establishment of the state of Israel, and has since been marked by multiple rounds of violence, negotiations, and failed peace agreements.

The conflict can be traced back to the early 20th century when Zionist Jewish immigrants began to settle in Palestine, then part of the Ottoman Empire.

As Jewish immigration increased, tensions between Jews and Arabs grew, and the two sides engaged in a series of violent clashes.

In 1947, the United Nations voted to partition Palestine into two separate states, one for Jews and one for Arabs.

The Jews accepted the plan, but the Arabs rejected it, leading to the outbreak of violence and the first Arab-Israeli War.

During the war, Israel gained control of a significant portion of Palestine, including the areas that would become the West Bank and Gaza Strip.

Hundreds of thousands of Palestinians were displaced from their homes, becoming refugees in neighboring countries.

In the years that followed, the conflict continued to simmer, with Palestinians seeking independence and Israel seeking to maintain its security and control over the occupied territories.

The conflict was marked by multiple rounds of violence, including the Six-Day War in 1967, which saw Israel gain control of the West Bank, Gaza Strip, and other territories.

The conflict has also been marked by ongoing negotiations and attempts at peace agreements. The most notable of these was the Oslo Accords of 1993, which aimed to establish a framework for Israeli-Palestinian negotiations and the eventual creation of a Palestinian state.

However, the peace process has been repeatedly derailed by violence and political disagreements, and the conflict remains unresolved.

The conflict has taken a significant toll on both Israelis and Palestinians, with estimates suggesting that tens of thousands of people have been killed or injured over the decades.

The majority of casualties have been Palestinians, who have borne the brunt of Israeli military operations and the ongoing Israeli occupation of the West Bank and Gaza Strip.

In recent years, the conflict has become increasingly polarized and entrenched, with both sides appearing to be more committed to their positions than ever before.

The rise of right-wing Israeli politics, and the continued expansion of Israeli settlements in the West Bank, have fueled Palestinian anger and frustration, while Palestinian political disunity and weak leadership have undermined efforts to negotiate a lasting peace agreement.

As of now, the Israeli-Palestinian conflict remains ongoing, with both sides continuing to engage in sporadic violence and tension.

However, there have been some recent positive developments, such as the normalization of relations between Israel and several Arab countries, which may offer some hope for a possible resolution to the conflict in the future.

So, they have accomplished nothing? Shit, welcome to the chapter of the book that will get me sued if every other chapter failed...

The Israeli-Palestinian conflict. A source of endless debate, conflict, and irony. For decades, the world has watched as these two groups of people engage in a seemingly endless cycle of violence, peace talks, and broken promises.

So, what has been accomplished with this conflict? Let's take a sarcastic journey through the history of this never-ending saga.

It all started back in the early 20th century when Zionists began to immigrate to Palestine with the goal of creating a Jewish homeland.

As you can imagine, the native Palestinian Arabs weren't too thrilled about this idea. But despite the inevitable conflict that arose, the Zionists managed to establish the state of Israel in 1948. Hooray! The problem was, the Palestinians didn't exactly agree with this plan, and so began a series of wars, intifadas, and negotiations that continue to this day.

Over the years, both sides have achieved a great deal.
For one, they've become incredibly skilled at propaganda. Each side has managed to paint itself as the righteous underdog fighting against an oppressive enemy.

Never mind that they've both committed their fair share of atrocities, including suicide bombings, targeted assassinations, and military strikes on civilian areas. No, no, it's all about who's the real victim here (the Palestinians).

And speaking of victims, both sides have managed to produce quite a few of them. Palestinian refugees have been displaced from their homes and forced to live in refugee camps for generations, while Israelis have been killed and injured in terrorist attacks and rocket fires.

But hey, at least they've gotten really good at building walls!

Israel has erected a massive wall separating itself from the West Bank, effectively annexing Palestinian territory and making peace even more unlikely.

And the Palestinians? They've built tunnels to smuggle in weapons and goods, because why bother negotiating when you can just dig underground? And let's not forget about the peace talks. Oh, the peace talks. Every few years, the international community gets together and tries to broker a peace agreement between Israel and Palestine. And every time, it ends in failure.

But that's okay because it's not really about finding a solution, it's about making it look like everyone is trying really hard. And besides, the negotiators get to stay in fancy hotels and eat gourmet food, so it's not a total loss.

But surely something positive has come out of this conflict, right? Well, Israel has become a thriving democracy with a strong economy and a powerful military.

And the Palestinians? They've become experts in resilience and resourcefulness. They've learned to make do with very little, and to keep fighting even when the odds are stacked against them. It's a valuable lesson, really. After all, who needs peace when you have determination?

In the end, it's hard to say what has been accomplished with the Israeli-Palestinian conflict. Both sides have achieved their fair share of victories and suffered their fair share of losses.

But one thing is for sure: they've both become really good at perpetuating the conflict.

So here's to another century of fighting, negotiating, and wall-building. Who needs peace when you can have irony?

The Six-Day War

The Six-Day War was a short but intense conflict that took place in June 1967 between Israel and a coalition of Arab states led by Egypt.

The war resulted in a decisive Israeli victory and had far-reaching consequences for the Middle East, shaping the political and military landscape of the region for decades to come.

The origins of the conflict can be traced back to the early 1960s, when tensions between Israel and its Arab neighbors began to rise.

In particular, the Egyptian leader Gamal Abdel Nasser emerged as a leading opponent of Israel, seeking to unite the Arab world against what he saw as Zionist aggression. In 1967, Nasser announced a blockade of the Strait of Tiran, a crucial waterway through which Israel received most of its oil supplies.

Israel saw this as a major provocation and a threat to its national security, and launched a preemptive strike against Egypt on June 5, 1967. The Israeli Air Force launched a surprise attack on Egyptian airfields, destroying most of the Egyptian air force on the ground.

The war ended on June 10, 1967, with a decisive Israeli victory. Israel had captured the Sinai Peninsula from Egypt, the Gaza Strip and West Bank from Jordan, and the Golan Heights from Syria.

The war had also resulted in significant casualties, with estimates suggesting that around 15,000 people were killed or wounded.

What can you accomplish in just six days of war? The Six-Day War, this masterpiece of military strategy and geopolitical maneuvering! What could be better than taking your neighbors by surrise and grabbing their land before they even know what hit them?

In case you've been living under a rock for the past 50+ years, let me fill you in: Israel decided to launch a preemptive attack against Egypt, Syria, and Jordan, and in just six days, they managed to capture the West Bank, the Gaza Strip, the Sinai Peninsula, and the Golan Heights.

And what did they accomplish with all this land? First off, Israel got to show off their military might to the world, proving that they were a force to be reckoned with.

Sure, they had already won the 1948 Arab-Israeli War, but this victory was on a whole new level. They had defeated three Arab armies in just six days, and they did it with style.

But what about the actual land they captured? Well, the West Bank and Gaza Strip gave Israel control over a large Palestinian population, and they've been struggling to figure out what to do with them ever since.

They've built settlements, which are illegal under international law, and they've created a system of checkpoints and restrictions that make life difficult for Palestinians. But hey, at least they got some nice real estate out of the deal, right?

As for the Sinai Peninsula, Israel gave that back to Egypt in 1982 as part of the Camp David Accords. So they managed to hold onto it for 15 years, but at least they got some sweet beachfront property for a while.

The Golan Heights are still under Israeli control, and they've built settlements there too. They've also started to exploit the area for its natural resources, such as water, which has caused tension with Syria.

But hey, who needs diplomatic relations when you've got the high ground?

In the aftermath of the Six-Day War, Israel became a major player in the Middle East, and they were able to use their newfound power to their advantage. They've managed to negotiate peace treaties with Egypt and Jordan.

And they've done it all while maintaining their status as the only democracy in the Middle East (if you ignore that whole "apartheid" thing in the West Bank and Gaza Strip).

But despite all of their accomplishments, Israel still faces plenty of challenges. The Palestinian-Israeli conflict continues to simmer, with no end in sight.

And the international community is growing increasingly critical of Israel's treatment of the Palestinians. Plus, there's always the looming threat of war with their neighbors, because let's face it, the Middle East is a powder keg just waiting to explode.

So what did Israel really accomplish with the Six-Day War? Well, they got some land, they flexed their military muscles, and they became a major player in the region. But they also created a whole host of new problems for themselves, and they've yet to find a solution to many of them.

At least they can look back on those six days in 1967 and feel like they really kicked some Arab butt.

THE YOM KIPPUR WAR

The Yom Kippur War, also known as the October War, was a major conflict that took place in 1973 between Israel and a coalition of Arab states led by Egypt and Syria.

The war was fought over a number of strategic territories, including the Sinai Peninsula, the Golan Heights, and the Suez Canal, and had significant implications for the political and military landscape of the Middle East.

The origins of the Yom Kippur War can be traced back to the ongoing conflict between Israel and its Arab neighbors.

Following Israel's victory in the Six-Day War in 1967, tensions remained high in the region, with Arab states seeking to regain lost territory and assert their dominance over Israel.

In 1973, Egypt and Syria launched a coordinated surprise attack on Israel on the Jewish holy day of Yom Kippur.

The attack came as a shock to the Israeli military and resulted in significant initial gains for the Arab forces, particularly in the Sinai Peninsula and the Golan Heights.

The conflict quickly escalated into a full-scale war, with both sides committing significant resources to the fight. Israel launched a major counterattack and eventually succeeded in repelling the Arab forces and regaining control of key territories.

The war was marked by significant casualties on both sides. Estimates suggest that between 8,000 and 18,000 people were killed, with much more injured or displaced.

The Yom Kippur War ended in a ceasefire agreement, with Israel regaining control of the territories it had lost and both sides agreeing to a return to the pre-war status quo.

So, nothing accomplished? The Yom Kippur War was a time of great accomplishment, if you ask the people who like to pat themselves on the back for causing death and destruction.

Let's start with the war itself. Israel, with its superior military, might, managed to fend off the combined forces of Egypt and Syria. Sure, it was a bit touch and go there for a while, what with Israel being caught off guard and all, but they managed to come out on top in the end.

Hooray for Israel, the plucky underdog who somehow manages to always come out on top, despite having the backing of the most powerful country in the world.

And what did Israel accomplish with this victory? Well, they managed to hold onto the land they had already stolen from the Palestinians and even took a bit more for good measure. Nothing like a good old land grab to really get the blood pumping.

But let's not forget about the aftermath of the war. Israel was hailed as a hero by its allies (read: the United States), while Egypt and Syria were left to lick their wounds.

But don't worry, it wasn't all bad for them. They got to experience the joy of having their cities and infrastructure destroyed by bombs and missiles. Who needs functioning hospitals and schools when you can have rubble and death?

And of course, the aftermath of the war also saw the continuation of the Israeli occupation of Palestine. The Palestinians, who had nothing to do with the Yom Kippur War, were once again left to suffer the consequences.

More land was stolen, more homes were destroyed, and more people were killed. But hey, at least Israel got to feel good about itself …

But let's not forget about the other great accomplishment of the Yom Kippur War: it paved the way for even more violence and bloodshed in the Middle East!

The war created even more tensions between Israel and its neighbors, leading to more wars, more death, and more destruction.

It's like a never-ending cycle of violence and suffering, at least some people are making money off of it…

And let's not forget about the United States, who was more than happy to supply Israel with all the weapons and support they needed to win the war.

Because nothing says "democracy" like arming a country that routinely violates the human rights of the people it occupies.

So yes, the Yom Kippur War was truly a great accomplishment. It allowed Israel to continue its occupation of Palestine, destroyed the lives of countless people in the Middle East, and paved the way for even more violence and bloodshed in the future.

Hooray for humanity!

The Gulf of Sidra Incident

The Gulf of Sidra Incident of 1981 was a military conflict between the United States and Libya, centered around the Gulf of Sidra, a body of water off the Libyan coast.

The incident arose from a longstanding dispute over the extent of Libyan territorial waters, with the United States challenging Libya's claims of sovereignty over the Gulf.

The conflict began on August 19, 1981, when two U.S. Navy F-14 Tomcat fighter jets were intercepted by Libyan fighter jets while conducting a routine patrol of the Gulf of Sidra.

The U.S. planes were ordered to leave the area by the Libyan pilots but instead engaged in a dogfight, resulting in the shooting down of two Libyan planes.

The incident marked a significant escalation in tensions between the United States and Libya, with both sides accusing each other of violating international law and territorial sovereignty.

The conflict also had significant implications for regional geopolitics, with Libya emerging as a major antagonist of the United States and the West.

The Gulf of Sidra Incident resulted in several casualties on both sides, with at least two Libyan pilots killed and two U.S. Navy personnel injured.

The incident also had significant economic consequences, with the United States imposing sanctions on Libya and limiting its access to U.S. markets and technology.

The conflict did not lead to a full-scale war or military engagement, but it did contribute to a broader pattern of tensions between the United States and Libya.

In the years following the Gulf of Sidra Incident, Libya continued to be a major source of conflict and instability in the region, with the United States and other Western powers taking steps to isolate and undermine the Gaddafi regime.

It was a time of great accomplishment, if you ask the people who like to play with their toys in the ocean and pretend they're big, tough sailors.

And in 1981, the United States decided it would be a great idea to send a bunch of ships and planes into that area, just to show Libya who's boss.

Because nothing says "diplomacy" like flexing your military muscles and trying to intimidate a sovereign nation.

And what did the United States accomplish with this little stunt? Well, they managed to provoke Libya into firing a missile at one of their planes, which then resulted in the United States retaliating by blowing up some Libyan boats. Hooray for escalation!

But let's not forget about the aftermath of the Gulf of Sidra Incident. The United States was hailed as a hero by its allies (read: other countries that like to play with their toys in the ocean), while Libya was left to lick its wounds.

But don't worry, it wasn't all bad for them. They got to experience the joy of having their boats blown up by a much larger and more powerful military. Who needs functioning infrastructure and a stable government when you can have death and destruction?

And of course, the aftermath of the incident also saw the continuation of the United States meddling in the affairs of other countries. Because why bother with things like diplomacy and cooperation when you can just blow stuff up and pretend you're a big, tough country?

But let's not forget about the other great accomplishment of the Gulf of Sidra Incident: it paved the way for even more tension and conflict in the Middle East.

The incident created even more animosity between the United States and Libya, leading to more skirmishes and conflicts in the future. It's like a never-ending cycle of provocation and retaliation, but hey, at least some people are making money off of it, right?

And let's not forget about the United States military, who were more than happy to play with their toys in the ocean and pretend they were big, tough sailors.

Because nothing says "bravery" like bombing a smaller and weaker country from the safety of your ships and planes.

So yes, the Gulf of Sidra Incident of 1981 was truly a great accomplishment. It allowed the United States to continue its pattern of aggression and meddling in the affairs of other countries, destroyed the lives of countless people in Libya, and paved the way for even more tension and conflict in the Middle East.

One more time, say it with me: Hooray for humanity!

The Iran-Contra Affair

The Iran-Contra Affair was a political scandal that occurred in the mid-1980s during the Reagan administration. The scandal involved secret arms sales to Iran, which was then under an arms embargo, and the use of the profits from those sales to fund Contra rebels in Nicaragua, who were seeking to overthrow the Sandinista government.

The affair began in 1985, when members of the Reagan administration secretly initiated contact with Iranian officials, hoping to secure the release of American hostages being held in Lebanon by Iranian-backed groups.

These officials, including National Security Advisor Robert McFarlane and Lieutenant Colonel Oliver North, believed that the Iranian government might be willing to negotiate the release of the hostages in exchange for arms.

The negotiations with Iran eventually led to a series of secret arms sales, in which the United States sold weapons to Iran through Israel, which was acting as an intermediary.

The profits from these sales were then funneled to the Contra rebels in Nicaragua, who were fighting against the socialist Sandinista government.

The affair came to light in late 1986 when a Lebanese newspaper published an article revealing arms sales to Iran.

The revelations sparked a major political scandal, with members of Congress and the media accusing the Reagan administration of violating U.S. law and undermining American foreign policy objectives.

The Iran-Contra Affair had significant political and legal consequences for those involved. Several high-ranking officials, including Lieutenant Colonel Oliver North, were indicted on charges of perjury, obstruction of justice, and other crimes. North was eventually convicted on three counts, although his convictions were later overturned on appeal.

In terms of casualties, the Iran-Contra Affair did not result in significant military casualties, as the arms sales were conducted covertly and did not involve direct military engagement.

However, the scandal did have significant human and political costs, as it eroded public trust in the government and damaged the reputation of the United States on the international stage. The Iran-Contra Affair ultimately ended with a series of legal proceedings and political fallout.

It was a time of great accomplishment if you ask the people who like to play fast and loose with the law and the Constitution.

And what did the United States accomplish with this little scheme? Well, they managed to sell weapons to a country that had been designated as a state sponsor of terrorism, and they managed to funnel money and weapons to a group of rebels who had been implicated in several human rights violations.

Hooray for ethical and legal violations!

But let's not forget about the aftermath of the Iran-Contra Affair. The United States was embarrassed on the world stage, with its dirty laundry being aired for all to see. But don't worry, it wasn't all bad for them.

They got to experience the joy of having their top officials implicated in illegal activities, and they got to pretend that they were still a shining beacon of democracy and freedom in the world.

And of course, the aftermath of the affair also saw the continuation of the United States meddling in the affairs of other countries.

Because why bother with things like international law and sovereignty when you can just sell weapons to anyone who promises to help you with your shady activities?

But let's not forget about the other great accomplishment of the Iran-Contra Affair: it paved the way for even more corruption and lawlessness in the United States government.

The affair demonstrated that high-ranking officials could engage in illegal activities and get away with them, as long as they had enough power and influence.

It's like a never-ending cycle of abuse of power and impunity, but hey, at least some people are making money off of it, right? Because nothing says "patriotism" like betraying your own country's laws and values for a quick buck or a political advantage.

So yes, the Iran-Contra Affair was truly a great accomplishment. It allowed the United States to continue its pattern of corruption and lawlessness, sold weapons to a designated state sponsor of terrorism, and paved the way for even more abuse of power and impunity in the future.

The American Way, baby!

The Cenepa War

The Cenepa War, also known as the Alto Cenepa War, was a brief military conflict fought between Peru and Ecuador in early 1995. The conflict arose over a disputed border area known as the Cenepa Valley, which both countries claimed as their own.

Peru and Ecuador have a long history of territorial disputes, dating back to the colonial period. The dispute over the Cenepa Valley began in the early 20th century when both countries claimed the region as part of their own territory.

The dispute escalated in the 1980s when both Peru and Ecuador began to increase their military presence in the area.

The conflict began in January 1995, when Ecuadorian troops launched a surprise attack on a Peruvian army outpost in the Cenepa Valley. The attack led to a major military engagement, with both sides deploying troops and artillery to the region.

The fighting was intense and lasted for several weeks, with both sides suffering significant casualties. Estimates of the total number of casualties vary, but most sources agree that several hundred soldiers were killed or wounded during the conflict.

The Cenepa War was notable for its use of advanced military technology, including precision-guided missiles and unmanned aerial vehicles.
The use of this technology contributed to the high level of casualties on both sides.

The conflict drew international attention, with several countries, including Brazil, Argentina, and the United States, offering to mediate a resolution to the dispute.

Ultimately, a ceasefire was negotiated, and both sides agreed to withdraw their troops from the region.

The Cenepa War had significant political and diplomatic consequences for both Peru and Ecuador.

In Peru, the conflict led to the downfall of the government of President Alberto Fujimori, who was criticized for his handling of the crisis.

To accomplish, or not to accomplish, that is…? Well, Ecuador and Peru managed to achieve a whole lot of nothing, really. They spent millions of dollars and put thousands of soldiers at risk to fight over a patch of land that no one wanted.

But hey, at least they got to pretend that they were doing something important, right?

During the war, both sides engaged in a game of "who can build the most ridiculous military installations". Peru built an airbase that looked like it belonged in a sci-fi movie, complete with giant radar dishes and underground tunnels.

Ecuador, not to be outdone, built a bunker that looked like something out of a bad video game, with a giant tower that served no discernible purpose. Truly, these were the shining achievements of the Cenepa War.

But let's not forget about the aftermath of the conflict. Ecuador and Peru managed to sign a peace treaty that essentially amounted to "let's just forget this ever happened". They agreed to some minor border adjustments, but nothing that solved the underlying issues.

In the end, the Cenepa War was just a big waste of time and resources, a distraction from the real problems facing both countries.

And let's not forget about the role of the international community in the Cenepa War. They watched from the sidelines, wringing their hands and issuing sternly worded statements that no one paid attention to.

Because nothing says "we care about global peace and stability" like sitting back and letting two countries fight over a meaningless patch of land.

But hey, at least the Cenepa War gave us some great stories to tell. Like the time when Ecuadorian soldiers dressed up in fake foliage to try and blend in with the jungle (spoiler alert: it didn't work).

Or the time when Peruvian soldiers accidentally bombed their troops (whoops!). Truly, these were the shining moments of the conflict.

In the end, the Cenepa War accomplished nothing but wasted resources and a few good war stories. It was a reminder that sometimes, even the most meaningless conflicts can drag on for far too long.

But hey, at least both sides got to pretend that they were important for a little while. And isn't that what matters? Nothing matters!

THE ECUADORIAN-PERUVIAN WAR

The Ecuadorian-Peruvian War of 1941 was a brief conflict fought between Ecuador and Peru over disputed territory along their mutual border.

The conflict began in July of 1941 and lasted for just over a month, with both sides suffering significant casualties.

The conflict arose over a long-standing border dispute between the two countries. The border between Ecuador and Peru had been in dispute since the late 19th century, with both countries claiming a region known as the Zarumilla Triangle as their own.

The dispute was exacerbated in the early 20th century when oil was discovered in the region, leading both countries to intensify their claims.

Tensions between the two countries came to a head in July of 1941 when an Ecuadorian military unit crossed the Zarumilla River and occupied a Peruvian border post.

The Peruvian government responded by mobilizing its armed forces and launching a counterattack against Ecuadorian troops. The fighting was intense and lasted for several weeks, with both sides deploying troops, artillery, and air power.

The war was characterized by intense jungle warfare and a high level of brutality, with both sides committing atrocities against civilians and prisoners of war.

The exact number of casualties from the conflict is difficult to determine, but estimates suggest that between 2,000 and 4,000 soldiers were killed, along with an unknown number of civilians.

The conflict also resulted in significant economic damage, particularly to the oil industry in the region.

The war ended in August of 1941, with both sides agreeing to a ceasefire and negotiations to resolve the border dispute.

The peace talks were mediated by the United States and Argentina and resulted in a peace treaty signed in 1942.

The treaty recognized Peru's claim to the disputed territory but also established a demilitarized zone along the border to prevent future conflicts.

Mission accomplished? The Ecuadorian-Peruvian War of 1941. A classic in the annals of meaningless conflicts.
First and foremost, the war accomplished the impressive feat of lasting all six weeks.

Six whole weeks! It's a wonder they didn't need a nap halfway through. In that time, both sides managed to achieve...not much of anything.

They fought over a few chunks of land that no one cared about, and then they stopped. Talk about anticlimactic.
But let's not forget about the real accomplishment of the war: setting a new standard for petty disputes.

The whole conflict was sparked by a border dispute that had been simmering for years. Rather than sit down and talk it out like adults, Ecuador and Peru decided to escalate things to the point of armed conflict.

Because nothing says "mature diplomacy" like throwing a temper tantrum and starting a war.

And let's not forget about the role of the international community in the Ecuadorian-Peruvian War. They watched from the sidelines, issuing sternly worded statements that no one paid attention to. Because when it comes to meaningless conflicts, why bother getting involved? It's not like anyone was invested in the outcome.

In the end, the war accomplished nothing but wasted resources and a few good war stories.

It was a reminder that sometimes, even the most insignificant border disputes can turn into full-blown conflicts if no one bothers to communicate.

But hey, at least both sides got to play with their shiny new tanks and guns for a little while. And isn't that what matters?

And let's not forget about the aftermath of the war. Ecuador and Peru managed to sign a peace treaty that essentially amounted to "let's just forget this ever happened". They agreed to some minor border adjustments, but nothing that solved the underlying issues.

In the end, the Ecuadorian-Peruvian War of 1941 was just a blip on the radar of history, a footnote in the grand scheme of things.

Like the time when Ecuadorian soldiers tried to sneak across the border by disguising themselves as Peruvian troops (spoiler alert: it didn't work).

Or the time when Peruvian troops accidentally invaded Ecuadorian territory because they got lost (whoops!). Truly, these were the shining moments of the conflict.

In the end, the Ecuadorian-Peruvian War of 1941 accomplished nothing but a few laughs and a lot of head-scratching.

It was a reminder that sometimes, even the most pointless conflicts can drag on for far too long. And it has possibly helped some with the knowledge that these countries lie in South America.

The Venezuelan Crisis

The Venezuelan Crisis, which began in 2013, is an ongoing political and economic crisis that has plunged the country into a state of chaos and instability.

The crisis has been marked by hyperinflation, shortages of basic goods, political polarization, human rights abuses, and a mass exodus of Venezuelans from the country. It had far-reaching consequences not only for Venezuela but also for the wider region and international community.

The crisis began in 2013 when Nicolas Maduro, the successor to long-time leader Hugo Chavez, was elected as President of Venezuela in a controversial election.

Maduro's presidency has been marked by allegations of electoral fraud, repression of political opposition, and the gradual erosion of democratic institutions.

The economic crisis in Venezuela began in 2014 when falling oil prices, the country's main source of revenue, led to a sharp decline in government revenues. This led to widespread shortages of basic goods such as food, medicine, and gasoline, as well as hyperinflation that rendered the national currency virtually worthless.

The economic crisis has also led to a humanitarian crisis, with many Venezuelans struggling to access necessities such as food, water, and healthcare.

The United States and other countries have recognized Guaido as Venezuela's legitimate interim president, but Maduro has refused to step down, leading to a protracted power struggle.

The number of casualties resulting from the Venezuelan Crisis is difficult to determine, but reports suggest that there have been numerous deaths resulting from protests and clashes with security forces.

The crisis has also contributed to a rise in crime and violence in the country, and led to a mass exodus of Venezuelans from the country, with an estimated 5 million people leaving since 2015.

Was anything at all accomplished? The Venezuelan Crisis is a classic tale of political drama, economic disaster, destroyed life, and...well, not much else!

First and foremost, the Venezuelan Crisis accomplished the impressive feat of turning a once-prosperous country into a dumpster fire. Under the leadership of Nicolas Maduro, the economy has tanked, necessities are in short supply, and inflation is through the roof. But hey, at least the government can blame it all on the imperialist United States, right?

Speaking of the US, the Venezuelan Crisis accomplished the task of reigniting the age-old debate of " Should we get involved in other countries' affairs?"

On one hand, you have people who argue that we need to support democracy and human rights around the world. On the other hand, you have people who argue that we have our problems to deal with, and getting involved in other countries' business is just asking for trouble.

And then there's the whole issue of oil. Venezuela has some of the largest oil reserves in the world, which makes it a valuable commodity in the eyes of many countries. So of course, everyone wants a piece of the pie.

The US wants to "liberate" Venezuela and get access to its oil. Russia wants to prop up Maduro and continue to have a foothold in the region.

China wants to invest in Venezuela's oil industry and use it to expand its global influence. It's like a geopolitical game of musical chairs, but with oil instead of chairs.

But let's not forget about the real accomplishment of the Venezuelan Crisis: inspiring countless hot takes and think pieces from armchair political analysts.

Everyone has an opinion on Venezuela, whether they know anything about the country or not.

You've got people arguing that Maduro is a socialist hero fighting against imperialist aggression. You've got people arguing that he's a brutal dictator oppressing his people. And you've got people arguing that it's all just a big conspiracy orchestrated by lizard people. (Okay, maybe not that last one. But you get the idea.)

The international community issued plenty of statements condemning Maduro and calling for democratic reforms, but so far, nothing has changed. It's like a giant game of "who can virtue signal the loudest", but with no actual results to show for it.

The Venezuelan Crisis accomplished nothing but a whole lot of hand-wringing and finger-pointing. And let's not forget about the aftermath of the crisis.

So far, Maduro is still in power, the economy is still a mess, and the people of Venezuela are still suffering.

In the end, the Venezuelan Crisis accomplished nothing but a lot of posturing and rhetoric. It was a reminder that sometimes, even the most well-meaning attempts to help can end up being a complete disaster.

But at least we got some good memes out of it, like "Socialism works until you run out of other people's money".

The Colombian Conflict

The Colombian Conflict is a protracted armed conflict that has been ongoing in Colombia since 1964. It involves several armed groups, including the Colombian government, left-wing guerrillas, right-wing paramilitaries, and drug cartels.

The conflict has resulted in the deaths of thousands of people and the displacement of millions of others. In this article, we will discuss the origins, participants, casualties, and current status of the Colombian Conflict.

The conflict began in the mid-1960s when the Revolutionary Armed Forces of Colombia (FARC) was formed.

The Colombian government viewed them as a threat to national security and launched several military operations against them.

This led to the creation of other leftist guerrilla groups, including the National Liberation Army (ELN) and the Popular Liberation Army (EPL). They might have inspied some dialogue in the movie Life of Brian.

During the 1980s and 1990s, the Colombian conflict became more complex with the emergence of right-wing paramilitary groups. These groups were formed by wealthy landowners, drug traffickers, and members of the Colombian military to counter the leftist guerrilla groups.

The paramilitary groups were notorious for their brutality and were responsible for numerous human rights cases of abuse, including massacres and forced disappearances.

The drug trade also played a significant role in the Colombian Conflict. Colombia is the world's largest producer of cocaine, and drug cartels have used the conflict to protect their interests.

The most infamous of these cartels was the Medellin Cartel, led by Pablo Escobar. The cartel waged a violent war against the Colombian government and other drug traffickers, leading to the deaths of thousands of people.

The Colombian Conflict involves several groups, including the Colombian government, left-wing guerrilla groups, right-wing paramilitary groups, and drug cartels.

The Colombian military is supported by the United States, which has provided billions of dollars in aid to the government to fight drug trafficking and leftist guerrilla groups. The FARC was the largest and most well-known of the leftist guerrilla groups, but other groups such as the ELN and EPL also played a significant role.

The paramilitary groups, such as the United Self-Defense Forces of Colombia (AUC), were formed to counter the leftist guerrilla groups but eventually became involved in the drug trade.

The Colombian Conflict has resulted in the deaths of over 220,000 people, with millions more displaced from their homes. Civilians have been disproportionately affected, with many caught in the crossfire between the various armed groups.

Human rights abuses, such as massacres and forced disappearances, have been committed by all sides. The Colombian government has been accused of collaborating with paramilitary groups and turning a blind eye to human rights abuses committed by the military.

Leftist guerrilla groups have also been responsible for kidnappings and bombings targeting civilians.

The Colombian government has made significant progress in recent years, particularly with the signing of the peace agreement with FARC in 2016. This agreement has led to a reduction in violence and the demobilization of thousands of guerrilla fighters.

However, other armed groups continue to operate in the country, and the implementation of the peace agreement has faced challenges.

Anyything accomplished or accomplishments in sight? The ultimate example of a never-ending war. First and foremost, the Colombian Conflict accomplished the task of turning a beautiful country into a war zone.

For decades, armed groups have been fighting for control of Colombia's territory, resources, and people. But hey, at least they're keeping the country interesting, right?

Speaking of armed groups, the Colombian Conflict accomplished the impressive feat of having more factions than you can shake a stick at.

You've got the government, the guerrillas, the paramilitaries, the drug cartels, and probably a few others I'm forgetting. It's like a game of whack-a-mole, except the moles are heavily armed and have political agendas.

And let's not forget about the role of the United States in the Colombian Conflict. They've been pouring billions of dollars into anti-drug efforts, but so far, the results have been...mixed, to say the least. On one hand, coca production has decreased in some areas. On the other hand, drug trafficking has just moved to other countries, and armed groups are still running rampant. But hey, at least the US can say they tried, right?

Meanwhile, the Colombian government has been negotiating with the guerrillas to try and bring an end to the conflict. But those negotiations have mostly resulted in a lot of photo ops and handshakes.

The guerrillas still have their guns, the government still has its corruption, and the people of Colombia are still caught in the crossfire. And let's not forget about the role of the international community in the Colombian Conflict.

They've issued plenty of statements condemning the violence and calling for peace, but so far, nothing has changed. It's like a giant game of "who can virtue signal the loudest", but with no actual results to show for it. Sounds familiar, right?

But let's not forget about the real accomplishment of the Colombian Conflict: inspiring countless Netflix series and documentaries. From Narcos to Wild District to El Chapo, there's no shortage of entertainment about the drug cartels and armed groups of Colombia.

Who needs peace and stability when you can have gritty dramas and true crime thrillers, am I right?

And let's not forget about the aftermath of the Colombian Conflict. So far, there's been some progress in demobilizing the armed groups, but it's still a long way from peace. The drug trade is still a major problem, and the government is still struggling with corruption and inequality. But hey, at least there's plenty of beautiful scenery for tourists to enjoy, right?

In the end, the Colombian Conflict accomplished nothing but a whole lot of suffering and destruction.

It was a reminder that sometimes, even the most well-intentioned efforts to promote peace and stability can end up being a total mess. But at least we got some good TV shows out of it …

The War in Darfur

The War in Darfur is an ongoing conflict that began in 2003 and is still ongoing. It is a complex conflict involving multiple parties and has caused significant loss of life and displacement in the region.

The conflict in Darfur is rooted in a history of tensions between various ethnic groups in the region. Darfur is located in western Sudan and is home to a diverse population that includes Arab nomads and non-Arab farming communities.

The region has long been marked by political and economic marginalization, as well as conflict over access to land and resources.

In the early 2000s, tensions between Arab and non-Arab groups in Darfur escalated. The government of Sudan, led by President Omar al-Bashir, responded to this unrest by arming Arab militias, known as Janjaweed, to suppress the non-Arab rebels.

These militias have been accused of carrying out a campaign of violence and terror against non-Arab communities in the region, including killings, rape, and destruction of property.

The conflict in Darfur involves multiple parties, including the government of Sudan, rebel groups, and international organizations.

The United Nations, have also been involved in the conflict. The UN has deployed a peacekeeping mission, known as the United Nations-African Union Mission in Darfur (UNAMID), to protect civilians and promote peace in the region.

Estimates of the number of casualties in the War in Darfur vary widely, but it is widely recognized as one of the deadliest conflicts of the 21st century.

According to the UN, over 300,000 people have been killed in the conflict, while over 2.7 million have been displaced from their homes.

The War in Darfur is still ongoing. Like an absolute masterpiece of a conflict it accomplish little of value. This one has yet to end and is a shining example of everything that can be accomplished when people really put their minds to it.

First and foremost, the War in Darfur accomplished the impressive feat of causing untold amounts of suffering and displacement.

It's estimated that around 300,000 people have died as a result of the conflict, and over two million have been forced to flee their homes. But hey, at least they got to see some beautiful scenery along the way, right?

And let's not forget about the role of the international community in the War in Darfur. They've issued plenty of statements condemning the violence and calling for peace, but so far, nothing has really changed. It's like watching a bunch of people shout into the void, except the void is filled with bloodshed and human rights abuses.

Meanwhile, the government of Sudan has been trying to negotiate a peace deal with the rebels. But so far, those negotiations have mostly resulted in a lot of posturing and finger-pointing. The rebels still have their guns, the government still has its corruption, and the people of Darfur are still caught in the crossfire.

But let's not forget about the real accomplishment of the War in Darfur: inspiring countless think pieces and op-eds. From The New York Times to The Guardian to Al Jazeera, there's no shortage of hot takes about the conflict.

Who needs peace and stability when you can have a good old-fashioned debate?

And let's not forget about the aftermath of the War in Darfur. So far, there's been some progress in bringing attention to the conflict, but it's still a long way from peace. The government has made some attempts to bring the rebels to the negotiating table, but those attempts have mostly been met with skepticism.

Meanwhile, the people of Darfur continue to suffer, and the world continues to turn a blind eye. In the end, the War in Darfur accomplished nothing but a whole lot of suffering and destruction. It was a reminder that sometimes, even the most well-intentioned efforts to promote peace and stability can end up being a total mess.

But hey, at least we got some good think pieces out of it, right?

The Boko Haram Insurgency

The Boko Haram insurgency is an ongoing conflict in northeastern Nigeria and surrounding areas, which began in 2009.

It is named after the jihadist militant group Boko Haram, which seeks to establish an Islamic state in the region and has been responsible for numerous terrorist attacks, kidnappings, and other atrocities.

Boko Haram was founded in 2002 by a radical Islamist preacher, Mohammed Yusuf, who established a mosque and Islamic school in Maiduguri, the capital of Borno state in northeastern Nigeria.

The group's initial aim was to oppose Western-style education and promote Islamic fundamentalism, but it soon turned to violent means to achieve its goals.

In 2009, Boko Haram launched an armed rebellion against the Nigerian government, attacking police stations, prisons, and other government buildings. The Nigerian government responded with a military crackdown, but this only intensified the conflict, leading to further violence and bloodshed.

Boko Haram expanded its activities to other states in northeastern Nigeria, including Yobe, Adamawa, and Gombe, as well as neighboring countries such as Cameroon, Chad, and Niger.

The group has also carried out attacks on churches, schools, and other civilian targets, as well as kidnappings of foreign workers and schoolgirls.

According to the United Nations, more than 36,000 people have been killed and over 2 million people have been displaced since the conflict began.

The Nigerian government has struggled to contain the insurgency, despite the support of international partners such as the United States and France.

In 2015, Muhammadu Buhari was elected as Nigeria's president, and he promised to make defeating Boko Haram a top priority. Under his leadership, the Nigerian military has made some gains against the group, retaking territory and freeing hostages.

However, the group continues to launch attacks, and the conflict remains ongoing.

So, anything accomplished? First and foremost, the Boko Haram insurgency accomplished the impressive feat of terrorizing innocent civilians.

With bombings, kidnappings, and mass killings, Boko Haram showed what it means to be a ruthless terrorist organization. I mean, who needs peace and stability when you can have fear and chaos, right?

And let's not forget about the role of the Nigerian government in the Boko Haram insurgency. They've been trying to fight the group for years, but so far, nothing has changed.

It's like watching a bunch of people chase their tails, except the tail is made of bombs and extremist ideology. Meanwhile, the international community has been doing its best to assist Nigeria.

They've offered military aid, intelligence support, and even drone surveillance. But so far, those efforts have mostly resulted in a lot of posturing and finger-pointing.

Boko Haram still has its guns, the government still has its corruption, and the people of Nigeria are still caught in the crossfire. But let's not forget about the real accomplishment of the Boko Haram insurgency: inspiring countless hashtags and social media campaigns.

From #BringBackOurGirls to #StopBokoHaram, there's no shortage of catchy slogans to show solidarity with the victims of the conflict. Who needs concrete action when you can have a good old-fashioned tweetstorm?

And let's not forget about the aftermath of the Boko Haram insurgency. So far, there's been some progress in pushing the group back, but it's still a long way from peace.

The government has made some attempts to negotiate with the militants, but those attempts have mostly been met with skepticism. Meanwhile, the people of Nigeria continue to suffer, and the world continues to scroll past their pain on their social media feeds.

In the end, the Boko Haram insurgency accomplished nothing but a whole lot of suffering and destruction. It was a reminder that sometimes, even the most well-intentioned efforts to fight terrorism can end up being a total mess.

But hey, at least we got some catchy hashtags out of it, right? #Winning.

The Nigerian Civil War

The Nigerian Civil War, also known as the Biafran War, took place between 1967 and 1970.

It was fought between the government of Nigeria, led by General Yakubu Gowon, and the secessionist state of Biafra, led by Colonel Odumegwu Ojukwu.

The conflict was characterized by violence and famine, resulting in the deaths of hundreds of thousands of people.

The origins of the conflict can be traced back to the political and economic marginalization of the Igbo people, who are the majority in the southeastern part of Nigeria. The Igbo felt that they were not given a fair share of political power and economic resources by the Nigerian government, which was dominated by the Hausa-Fulani and Yoruba ethnic groups.

The situation was exacerbated by the discovery of oil in the Niger Delta, which further widened the economic gap between the regions. In 1966, a group of army officers, mostly Igbo, overthrew the government of Nigeria in a coup d'état.

However, this was followed by a counter-coup in July of the same year, which led to the deaths of many Igbo officers and civilians.

In response to the violence, Colonel Ojukwu declared the independence of Biafra on May 30, 1967, citing the need to protect the Igbo people from persecution.

The Nigerian government, led by General Gowon, responded by declaring war on Biafra. The conflict quickly escalated, with both sides committing atrocities and the international community largely ignoring the situation.

The Nigerian military, supported by British and Soviet arms, launched a blockade of Biafra, causing widespread famine and malnutrition.

It is estimated that between 500,000 and 2 million people died from starvation and disease during the conflict.

The war ended on January 15, 1970, when General Ojukwu fled to Ivory Coast and Biafra surrendered to the Nigerian government.

Problem solved and everything accomplished? The Nigerian Civil War is the perfect example of how to solve political and ethnic differences through violence and destruction.

First and foremost, the Nigerian Civil War accomplished the impressive feat of killing over a million people.

Yes, you read that right, a million people. Who needs diplomacy and negotiation when you can just start shooting?

The war also accomplished the creation of a new country, the Republic of Biafra. I mean, sure, it only lasted for a few years before being crushed by the Nigerian government, but hey, at least they tried.

But let's not forget about the real accomplishment of the Nigerian Civil War: the destruction of infrastructure and the displacement of millions of people. Who needs hospitals and schools anyway...

And let's not forget about the aftermath of the Nigerian Civil War. Sure, there was some effort to reconcile the warring factions, but that mostly amounted to a few speeches and some half-hearted apologies.

The wounds of the conflict still run deep, and the people of Nigeria are still grappling with the scars of their violent past.

But at least we learned some valuable lessons from the Nigerian Civil War. We learned that sometimes it's better to just shoot first and ask questions later. We learned that it's okay to ignore the root causes of a conflict and focus solely on military solutions.

And most importantly, we learned that sometimes it's easier to just walk away from the mess we created and pretend as if nothing happened.

In the end, the Nigerian Civil War accomplished nothing but death and destruction.

It was a reminder that sometimes, violence is not the answer and this knowledge will be put right in the lessons never learned box.

The Lebanese Civil War

The Lebanese Civil War was a complex and protracted conflict that took place in Lebanon between 1975 and 1990.

The conflict involved a range of political and social groups, including political parties, religious factions, and militia groups.

The war began on April 13, 1975, when an altercation between Christian and Muslim factions in Beirut led to a series of violent clashes throughout the city.

The conflict quickly spread throughout the country, with different factions vying for control over different areas of Lebanon.

The conflict was marked by significant sectarian violence, with Christian and Muslim factions engaging in brutal acts of violence against each other. The war was also marked by significant external intervention, with Israel, Syria, and other countries becoming involved in the conflict.

The conflict resulted in a significant loss of life, with estimates of the number of casualties varying widely. According to the Lebanon-based Centre for Research on the Lebanese Economy and Society, at least 150,000 people were killed in the conflict, including both civilians and combatants. Other estimates put the number of casualties much higher, with some suggesting that up to 300,000 people were killed.

The conflict officially ended on October 13, 1990, with the signing of the Taif Agreement, which was negotiated in the Saudi Arabian city of Taif.

The agreement established a new power-sharing arrangement between the different factions, with an emphasis on national unity and reconciliation.

ACCOMPLISHED! What a shining example of conflict resolution that war was! I mean, who needs peaceful negotiation and diplomacy when you can just start shooting at each other?

Well, first and foremost, it accomplished the destruction of the beautiful city of Beirut. Who needs iconic landmarks and historic buildings when you can have rubble and bricks for free?

The war also accomplished the displacement of hundreds of thousands of people and the creation of a generation of refugees. But hey, at least they got a front-row seat to the stunning display of human brutality and senseless violence.

And let's not forget about the factionalism that arose during the war. It's always nice when a conflict can pit different religious and ethnic groups against each other. Because who needs unity and cooperation when you can have division and hatred?

But let's not stop there. The aftermath of the Lebanese Civil War was just as impressive as the war itself. It accomplished the establishment of Hezbollah, a militant group that continues to spread peace and love throughout the region.

And who can forget about the Syrian occupation of Lebanon, which brought a whole new level of peace and stability to the country?

And let's not forget about the amazing reconstruction efforts that followed the war. I mean, sure, some buildings were rebuilt and some semblance of order was restored, but at what cost?

The country is still dealing with the economic and political fallout from the conflict, but at least they have some shiny new buildings to show for it.

In the end, the Lebanese Civil War accomplished nothing but death, destruction, and division.
At least we can look back on it and appreciate the stunning display of human cruelty and senseless violence.

And who knows, maybe someday we'll have another conflict that's just as successful at achieving absolutely nothing.

The Yemeni Civil War

The Yemeni Civil War began in 2015 and is ongoing, with no clear end in sight.

The conflict has involved a range of different groups and has had significant humanitarian consequences, with millions of people displaced and in need of assistance.

The conflict began when Houthi rebels, who are aligned with Iran, seized control of the capital city of Sana'a in September 2014.

This led to the ouster of President Abd Rabbuh Mansur Hadi, who fled to Saudi Arabia. In response to the Houthi takeover, a coalition of Arab states led by Saudi Arabia launched a military intervention in Yemen in March 2015.

The coalition's stated goal was to restore Hadi to power and prevent Iranian influence from spreading in the region.

The conflict has been marked by significant fighting and human suffering, with both sides engaging in acts of violence against civilians. The United Nations has described the conflict as one of the worst humanitarian crises in the world, with millions of people in need of humanitarian assistance.

Estimates of the number of casualties vary widely, with some suggesting that tens of thousands of people have been killed in the conflict. The conflict has also led to significant displacement, with millions of people forced to flee their homes as a result of the fighting.

Efforts to negotiate an end to the conflict have been ongoing, with several different peace talks held in recent years. However, these efforts have thus far been unsuccessful, and the conflict continues to rage on.

So, does this conflict continue to deliver accomplishments? The Yemeni Civil War is the perfect example of how to solve political differences through violence and mayhem.

Well, first and foremost, it accomplished the destruction of the Yemeni infrastructure. Who needs roads, hospitals, and schools anyway?

The war also accomplished the displacement of millions of people, the loss of thousands of lives, and the proliferation of armed groups throughout the country. But at least they got a front-row seat to the stunning display of human brutality and senseless violence.

And let's not forget about the proxy war between Saudi Arabia and Iran that fueled the conflict. It's always nice when other countries can get involved in a conflict and make things even more complicated.

But let's not stop there. The aftermath of the Yemeni Civil War was just as impressive as the war itself. It accomplished the establishment of the Houthi rebels as a major player in Yemeni politics, a group that continues to spread peace and stability throughout the region.

And who can forget about the humanitarian crisis that followed the conflict, which brought a whole new level of suffering and despair to the country?

And let's not forget about the amazing reconstruction efforts that followed the war. The country is still dealing with the economic and political fallout from the conflict, but hey, at least they have some humanitarian aid to show for it.

In the end, the Yemeni Civil War accomplished nothing but death, destruction, and despair. At least we can look back on it and appreciate the stunning display of human cruelty and senseless violence.

And who knows, maybe someday we'll have another conflict that's just as successful at achieving absolutely nothing.

THE SAUDI-LED INTERVENTION IN YEMEN

The Saudi Arabian-led intervention in Yemen began in March 2015 and is ongoing, with no clear end in sight.

The conflict has involved a range of different groups and has had significant humanitarian consequences, with millions of people displaced and in need of assistance.

The conflict began when Houthi rebels, who are aligned with Iran, seized control of the capital city of Sana'a in September 2014. This led to the ouster of President Abd Rabbuh Mansur Hadi, who fled to Saudi Arabia. In response, a coalition of Arab states led by Saudi Arabia launched a military intervention in Yemen in March 2015.

The coalition's stated goal was to restore Hadi to power and prevent Iranian influence from spreading in the region. The coalition included several other Arab states, including Egypt, the United Arab Emirates, Bahrain, Kuwait, Jordan, Morocco, and Sudan.

The intervention began with a series of airstrikes on Houthi targets, followed by a ground offensive by coalition forces.

The coalition has been accused of committing a range of human rights abuses, including the bombing of civilian targets such as hospitals and schools.

The conflict has been marked by significant fighting and human suffering, with both sides engaging in acts of violence against civilians.

The United Nations has described the conflict as one of the worst humanitarian crises in the world, with millions of people in need of humanitarian assistance.

What was accomplished, you ask? The Saudi Arabian-led intervention in Yemen is truly a shining example of how to intervene in another country's civil war and make everything better.

Well, for starters, the intervention accomplished the destruction of the Yemeni infrastructure. The intervention also accomplished the displacement of millions of people, the loss of thousands of lives, and the proliferation of armed groups throughout the country.

And let's not forget about the amazing diplomacy efforts that followed the intervention. I mean, sure, some attempts were made to broker peace, but at what cost? The conflict only escalated, and the situation in Yemen continued to deteriorate.

But let's not stop there. The aftermath of the intervention was just as impressive as the intervention itself.

It accomplished the establishment of the Houthi rebels as a major player in Yemeni politics, a group that continues to spread peace and stability throughout the region.

And who can forget about the humanitarian crisis that followed the intervention, which brought a whole new level of suffering and despair to the country?

And let's not forget about the amazing reconstruction efforts that followed the intervention. I mean, sure, some aid was sent to help the people, but at what cost?

The country is still dealing with the economic and political fallout from the intervention, but hey, at least they have some humanitarian aid to show for it.

In the end, the Saudi Arabian-led intervention accomplished nothing but death, destruction, and despair.

But, at least we can look back on it and appreciate the stunning display of human cruelty and senseless violence.

And who knows, maybe someday we'll have another intervention that's just as successful at achieving absolutely nothing.

The Islamic State Insurgency

The Islamic State insurgency in Iraq and Syria is an ongoing conflict that began in 2014 and has had significant consequences for the region and the world.

The conflict has involved a range of different groups and has had a major impact on the civilian population, with millions of people displaced and thousands killed.

The origins of the conflict can be traced back to the US-led invasion of Iraq in 2003, which led to the ouster of Saddam Hussein's regime and the establishment of a new government.

The new government was unable to provide adequate security and services to the population, leading to widespread dissatisfaction and unrest.

In 2011, a civil war broke out in neighboring Syria, which provided an opportunity for extremist groups to gain a foothold in the region. ISIS emerged from the remnants of Al-Qaeda in Iraq and other extremist groups and quickly established control over large areas of both Iraq and Syria.

The group's initial success was due in part to its sophisticated use of social media and propaganda, which helped to attract thousands of foreign fighters to its cause.

The group's brutal tactics included mass executions and the enslavement of women and children

The conflict also involved significant external intervention, with the US and its allies launching airstrikes against ISIS targets and providing military and logistical support to local forces.

The conflict has had a significant human toll, with estimates of the number of casualties ranging from tens of thousands to over a hundred thousand.

Despite the significant military campaign against ISIS, the group has not been fully defeated and continues to carry out attacks in both Iraq and Syria. The group has also expanded its operations to other regions, including Afghanistan and Libya.

Efforts to negotiate an end to the conflict have been ongoing, but have thus far been unsuccessful.

The conflict has been complicated by the involvement of multiple groups and external actors, and by the complex sectarian and ethnic tensions in the region.

The Islamic State accomplished so much during its brief reign of terror, it's hard to know where to start. They were useless, cowardly scumbags. Of course, their accomplishments didn't stop there.

The group was also responsible for some of the most heinous crimes against humanity in recent memory, including mass executions, beheadings, and the enslavement of women and girls.

And who could forget about their social media prowess? The Islamic State insurgency was an expert at using Twitter and other platforms to spread its message of hate and terror. The group's reign of terror was finally brought to an end thanks to a coalition of international forces, including the United States and its allies.

And while the group may no longer hold territory, they continue to inspire acts of terror around the world.

As for the aftermath of the Islamic State insurgency, well, it's a mixed bag. On the one hand, the group's defeat was a major victory for the forces of democracy and freedom.

On the other hand, the region is still dealing with the fallout from the conflict, including the displacement of millions of people and ongoing violence and instability.

And let's not forget about the long-term impact of the insurgency. The group's ideology continues to inspire people around the world, and there are concerns that a new generation of terrorists could rise to take their place.

So while the Islamic State insurgency may be over, the fight against terrorism is far from over.

In the end, the Islamic State insurgency accomplished a lot during its brief time in power. They showed the world what true evil looks like, and they inspired fear and terror in the hearts of millions. But they were ultimately defeated, and their legacy will be one of violence and destruction.

THE SINAI INSURGENCY

The Sinai insurgency is an ongoing conflict that began in 2011 in the Sinai Peninsula, a region that lies in northeastern Egypt and borders Israel and the Gaza Strip.

The conflict has involved a range of different groups, including militants affiliated with the Islamic State and other extremist organizations, as well as government forces.

The origins of the conflict can be traced back to the 2011 Egyptian revolution, which led to the overthrow of longtime President Hosni Mubarak.

The resulting political instability in Egypt allowed extremist groups to gain a foothold in the Sinai, and they began carrying out attacks against government and military targets in the region.

In 2013, the Egyptian military carried out a coup against the government of President Mohamed Morsi, who was a member of the Muslim Brotherhood.

The military crackdown on the Muslim Brotherhood and other Islamist groups led to increased support for extremist groups in the Sinai, as many disillusioned members of these organizations turned to more radical groups like the Islamic State.

The conflict has been marked by a series of violent attacks against government and military targets, as well as against civilians perceived to be collaborating with the government.

The Egyptian government has responded to the insurgency with a series of military operations, including the deployment of tens of thousands of troops to the region.

The military has also carried out airstrikes and ground operations against militant targets and has reportedly engaged in extrajudicial killings and other human rights abuses in its efforts to suppress the insurgency.

The conflict has had a significant human toll, with estimates of the number of casualties ranging from several hundred to several thousand. The conflict has also led to significant displacement, with tens of thousands of people forced to flee their homes as a result of the fighting.

Efforts to negotiate an end to the conflict have been ongoing, but have thus far been unsuccessful.

This little-known conflict accomplished so much in such a short amount of time, it's hard to know where to start. For one thing, the insurgency managed to make the Sinai Peninsula one of the most dangerous places in the world.

They were responsible for countless terrorist attacks, including bombings, shootings, and kidnappings. They even managed to shoot down an Egyptian military helicopter—talk about a feat!

But it wasn't just about violence and chaos. The Sinai insurgency also accomplished some truly impressive feats of organization.

They managed to coordinate attacks across a wide geographic area, often using sophisticated tactics like improvised explosive devices and suicide bombers.
They even had their propaganda wing, which produced slick videos and social media content to promote their cause.

And let's not forget about the insurgency's impact on the Egyptian economy.

The conflict made the Sinai Peninsula a no-go zone for tourists, which had a devastating impact on the local economy. Hotels and resorts went bankrupt, and thousands of people lost their jobs. But hey, at least the insurgency accomplished something, right?

As for the aftermath of the Sinai insurgency, well, it's a bit of a mixed bag. On the one hand, the Egyptian government was eventually able to restore order to the region, and violence has decreased significantly in recent years.

On the other hand, the insurgency may have accomplished its main goal: to sow chaos and undermine the authority of the Egyptian state.

And let's not forget about the impact of the insurgency on the people of the Sinai Peninsula.

The conflict has left many people traumatized and displaced, and the government's heavy-handed response to the insurgency has led to accusations of human rights abuses.

The Sinai insurgency brought nothing but misery and suffering to the people of the region. And while the violence may have died down for now, there are concerns that the insurgency could flare up again at any moment.

So let's raise a glass to the Sinai insurgency, a conflict that accomplished so much, yet left so much devastation in its wake. Here's hoping that the people of the Sinai Peninsula can finally find some peace and stability after years of turmoil.

THE SOMALI-KENYAN BORDER CONFLICT

The Somali-Kenyan Border Conflict is an ongoing conflict that started in 2012 between the Somali-based extremist group Al-Shabaab and the Kenyan government.

The conflict has primarily taken place in the border regions between Somalia and Kenya and has resulted in significant violence and instability in the region.

The origins of the conflict can be traced back to the involvement of the Kenyan military in Somalia in 2011.

The Kenyan government launched an operation, known as Operation Linda Nchi, in response to a series of kidnappings and attacks on Kenyan soil that were attributed to Al-Shabaab.

The operation was aimed at rooting out Al-Shabaab militants from Somalia and securing the border region between the two countries. The conflict escalated significantly in 2012 when Al-Shabaab began carrying out a series of attacks in Kenya in retaliation for the Kenyan military's involvement in Somalia.

The attacks included bombings and shootings targeting civilian and government targets and resulted in significant casualties among both Kenyan and Somali civilians and military personnel.

The Kenyan government responded to the attacks with a series of military operations aimed at weakening Al-Shabaab's presence in the region.

The Kenyan military, along with other forces including the African Union Mission in Somalia (AMISOM), has carried out airstrikes and ground operations against Al-Shabaab targets and has reportedly killed several high-ranking members of the group.

The conflict has had a significant human toll, with estimates of the number of casualties ranging from several hundred to several thousand.

The conflict has also led to significant displacement, with tens of thousands of people forced to flee their homes as a result of the fighting. Efforts to negotiate an end to the conflict have been ongoing, but have thus far been unsuccessful.

The conflict has been complicated by the involvement of multiple groups and external actors, including the United States, which has provided military support and training to the Kenyan military.

The Somali-Kenyan border conflict was truly a sight to behold. It had everything you could want in a conflict: rival factions, international meddling, and of course, a healthy dose of senseless violence.

So much must have been accomplished? First and foremost, the conflict accomplished the destruction of countless homes, businesses, and lives.

Both sides engaged in brutal fighting, with no regard for the innocent civilians caught in the crossfire. This included everything from targeted killings and bombings to forced displacement and famine.

And let's not forget about the impact on the environment. The conflict led to the general destruction of wildlife and natural resources, with both sides using the land for their purposes.

This included everything from poaching to illegal logging and mining. But surely the conflict accomplished something, right? Well, it did manage to highlight the deep-rooted issues plaguing both Somalia and Kenya.

This included everything from corruption and poverty to political instability and tribalism. However, any progress made in these areas was quickly overshadowed by the sheer scale of the violence and destruction wrought by the conflict.

As for the aftermath of the conflict, well, it's a bit of a mixed bag. On the one hand, both Somalia and Kenya were able to restore some semblance of order to their respective regions.

Violence has decreased significantly in recent years, and there have been some attempts at reconciliation between the two sides.

On the other hand, the damage has already been done. The conflict left deep scars on both sides, with many people traumatized and displaced.

The environmental damage will take years—if not decades—to repair. And there are concerns that the underlying issues that led to the conflict in the first place have not been adequately addressed.

So in the end, what was accomplished with the Somali-Kenyan border conflict? Not much, it seems. It was a brutal and senseless conflict that accomplished nothing.

The South Sudanese Civil War

The South Sudanese Civil War was a conflict that lasted from 2013 to 2018 and resulted in significant loss of life and displacement of civilians.

The conflict was primarily fought between the government of South Sudan, led by President Salva Kiir, and opposition forces led by former Vice President Riek Machar.

The origins of the conflict can be traced back to a long-standing power struggle between Kiir and Machar. The two men had been allies during South Sudan's struggle for independence from Sudan, but tensions began to rise following the formation of the new country in 2011.

Machar was dismissed from his position as Vice President in July 2013, and soon thereafter he began to mobilize opposition forces against the government. The conflict quickly escalated into a full-scale civil war, with both sides carrying out violent attacks against one another.

The war was characterized by significant human rights abuses, including massacres, sexual violence, and forced displacement. It was also marked by significant ethnic tension, with Kiir's Dinka ethnic group pitted against Machar's Nuer ethnic group.

The conflict resulted in significant loss of life, with estimates of the number of casualties ranging from 50,000 to 383,000. It also led to significant displacement, with millions of South Sudanese forced to flee their homes as a result of the fighting.

The war had significant economic consequences, with oil production –
South Sudan's primary source of revenue – severely disrupted.

Efforts to negotiate an end to the conflict were ongoing throughout the war
but were frequently derailed by continued violence and mistrust between the
two sides.

The conflict was also complicated by the involvement of external actors,
including the United Nations and neighboring countries such as Uganda
and Ethiopia.

In September 2018, a peace agreement was signed between Kiir and Machar,
bringing an end to the conflict. The agreement called for the establishment
of a unity government, with Machar returning as Vice President.

While the agreement was hailed as a significant step forward, it has faced
significant challenges in implementation, and fighting has continued in
some parts of the country.

There were factions galore, government corruption, and of course, plenty
of senseless violence. But what did the conflict accomplish?

First and foremost, the civil war accomplished the displacement and
suffering of millions of people.
The fighting between the government and opposition forces led to countless
deaths, with both sides using brutal tactics like ethnic cleansing and forced
displacement.

This resulted in one of the largest refugee crises in the world, with millions
of South Sudanese fleeing their homes in search of safety.

But surely the civil war accomplished something? Well, it did manage
to highlight the deep-seated issues plaguing South Sudan. This included
everything from political corruption and economic instability to tribalism
and human rights abuses.

However, any progress made in these areas was quickly overshadowed by
the sheer scale of the violence and destruction wrought by the conflict. It's
hard to imagine anyone looking back on the South Sudanese Civil War with
anything but horror and disgust.

As for the aftermath of the conflict, well, it's a bit of a mixed bag. On the
one hand, a peace deal was signed in 2018 between the government and
opposition forces, bringing an end to the fighting.

But the deal has been fragile at best, with continued violence and human rights abuses being reported.

On the other hand, the damage has already been done. The civil war left deep scars on South Sudan, with many people traumatized and displaced. The country's infrastructure was also severely damaged, with hospitals, schools, and other essential services either destroyed or in disrepair.

So in the end, what was accomplished with the South Sudanese Civil War? Not much, it seems. It was a brutal and senseless conflict that accomplished nothing but death, destruction, and misery.

Let's hope that the peace deal holds and that South Sudan can start the long, hard road to recovery. But given the country's history, it's hard to be optimistic.

The Mexican Drug War

The Mexican Drug War, also known as the Mexican War on Drugs, is an ongoing conflict that began in 2006 between the Mexican government and various drug cartels operating in the country.

The war has resulted in tens of thousands of casualties and has had a significant impact on the political and social landscape of Mexico.

The Mexican Drug War started as a result of the Mexican government's efforts to combat drug trafficking and organized crime in the country.

In December 2006, newly elected President Felipe Calderon announced that he was deploying the military to several Mexican states to combat drug trafficking organizations.

The move was a response to rising violence and the increasing power of the drug cartels, which had become major players in the drug trade in Mexico and had started to challenge the government's authority.

The conflict quickly escalated, with the drug cartels responding to the government's crackdown with a wave of violence that has continued to this day.

The cartels have engaged in a range of criminal activities, including drug trafficking, kidnapping, extortion, and murder. They have also been responsible for several high-profile attacks on government officials, police officers, and civilians.

The Mexican Drug War has had a devastating impact on the country. According to estimates, the conflict has resulted in more than 250,000 deaths, with many more people being injured or displaced.

The violence has had a significant impact on the economy, with businesses and tourism suffering as a result.

It has also had a significant impact on the political landscape of the country, with many politicians and government officials being targeted by cartels.

Accomplished some highs?
Ah, the Mexican Drug War. A conflict that has been raging for over a decade and has accomplished...well, what exactly?

Let's start with the basics. The Mexican Drug War is a conflict between the Mexican government and various drug cartels operating in the country. It's estimated that the war has resulted in over 200,000 deaths, with many more people displaced or forced to flee their homes.

So, what was accomplished with all of this violence and bloodshed? Well, for starters, the drug cartels managed to maintain their hold on the Mexican drug trade, which is estimated to be worth billions of dollars.

The government has made some progress in cracking down on the cartels, but for the most part, the drug trade continues to thrive.

The Mexican Drug War has arguably made the drug trade even more lucrative. With the government cracking down on the cartels, the price of drugs like cocaine and methamphetamine has skyrocketed, leading to even greater profits for the cartels.

But surely the Mexican Drug War has accomplished something positive, right? Well, there have been some successes. For example, the Mexican government has managed to capture or kill many high-profile cartel leaders, including Joaquín "El Chapo" Guzmán, the former leader of the Sinaloa Cartel.

But these successes have been overshadowed by the sheer scale of the violence and destruction caused by the conflict. The drug cartels have shown themselves to be incredibly resilient, quickly replacing any leaders who are captured or killed.

And of course, the human toll of the conflict has been devastating. The war has led to the deaths of countless innocent people, including journalists, activists, and even children.

Many more people have been displaced, with entire communities uprooted and forced to flee in the face of cartel violence.

As for the aftermath of the conflict, well, it's a bit of a mess. The Mexican government has struggled to maintain control over the country, with corruption and political instability hampering efforts to bring the cartels to justice.

Meanwhile, the violence continues, with many people living in fear of cartel reprisals.

So, in the end, what was accomplished with the Mexican Drug War? Not much, it seems. The conflict has resulted in untold suffering and loss of life, with little progress made in terms of bringing the cartels to justice or ending the drug trade.

It's a sad state of affairs, but until something changes, it seems that the violence and chaos will continue unabated.

The Salvadoran Gang War

The Salvadoran Gang War, also known as the Maras War, is a long-standing conflict that has been ongoing in El Salvador since the early 1990s.

The conflict involves two rival gangs, MS-13 and Barrio 18, who have been fighting for control of territory and drug trafficking routes.

This conflict has led to a high number of casualties and has had a significant impact on the social and economic development of El Salvador.

The MS-13 and Barrio 18 gangs both originated in the United States in the 1980s, formed by Salvadoran immigrants who fled the civil war in their country.

These gangs became notorious for their involvement in drug trafficking and violent crimes, and their influence spread throughout Central America, particularly in El Salvador, Guatemala, and Honduras.

The Salvadoran government began a crackdown on the gangs in the early 2000s, leading to increased violence as the gangs fought back. The government's approach was criticized for its heavy-handedness and its failure to address the underlying social and economic issues that contributed to the gangs' growth.

Gang violence reached its peak in El Salvador in 2015, with a murder rate of 104 per 100,000 people, making it the most violent country in the world outside of a war zone.

The Salvadoran government responded by implementing a series of security measures, including the deployment of the military in gang-controlled areas and the establishment of special courts to prosecute gang members.

The government also negotiated a truce with the gangs in 2012, but it quickly fell apart, leading to increased violence.

Accomplished some lows then? The Salvadoran Gang War, or as it's locally known, "La Mara Salvatrucha." What a shining example of humanity's capacity for conflict and violence.

Let's see, what was accomplished in this glorious chapter of history. Well, for starters, the Salvadoran government managed to create a situation where entire neighborhoods are controlled by ruthless gangs, turning the country into a living hell for the people who live there.

I mean, who needs functioning public services and safe streets when you can have machete-wielding gang members running the show?

Of course, the Salvadoran government couldn't have achieved this level of chaos without the help of the United States, which has a long history of meddling in Central American affairs.

Through its policies of intervention and destabilization, the U.S. helped create the conditions for the gang war to thrive, ensuring a steady flow of refugees fleeing to the U.S. border.

And what about the gangs themselves? Well, they've accomplished quite a lot. They've established a thriving underworld economy built on extortion, drug trafficking, and human trafficking, creating a generation of young people who see no other options for survival.

They've also managed to cultivate a terrifying image, with their tattoos, violence, and disregard for human life. If you're looking for an efficient PR campaign, you could do worse than a gang that tattoos its name on its members' faces.

But surely, there must be some positive outcomes, right? Well, the Salvadoran government has tried various strategies to combat the gangs, including a truce in 2012 that lasted for about a year before falling apart.

They've also poured money into the police and military, with mixed results.

The gangs themselves have occasionally shown a willingness to negotiate, but these efforts have been sporadic and ultimately unsuccessful.

After all, when you're making millions of dollars a year through illegal means, why bother with compromise?

Meanwhile, the Salvadoran people are left to suffer the consequences of their government's failures, trapped in a cycle of poverty, violence, and corruption.

In conclusion, the Salvadoran Gang War is a perfect example of what happens when governments and outside forces prioritize their interests over the well-being of the people they're supposed to serve.

The result is a never-ending cycle of violence and despair, with no easy solutions in sight. But hey, at least we got some cool tattoos out of it.

The Mozambican Islamist Insurgency

The Mozambican Islamist insurgency, also known as the Cabo Delgado insurgency, began in October 2017 in the northern region of Cabo Delgado, Mozambique.

The conflict involves an Islamist militant group known as Ahlu Sunnah Wal Jamaah, also referred to as Ansar al-Sunna or simply as Al-Shabaab (although it has no known connection to the Somali-based group of the same name). The group has been linked to the Islamic State of Iraq and Syria (ISIS) and is seeking to establish an Islamic caliphate in the region.

The insurgency began with a series of attacks on police stations and military installations in the town of Mocimboa da Praia. The group then proceeded to attack civilian targets, such as villages and towns, killing and displacing thousands of people.

The Mozambican government responded with a military campaign to root out the insurgents, but the conflict has continued to escalate with reports of human rights violations and the displacement of thousands of people.

The Mozambican government has received support from the Southern African Development Community (SADC), with neighboring countries such as South Africa, Tanzania, and Zimbabwe offering military assistance to help quell the insurgency.

The government has also hired private military contractors from Russia and South Africa to aid in the fight against the militants.

The number of casualties in the Mozambican Islamist insurgency is difficult to ascertain due to the ongoing conflict, but estimates suggest that thousands of people have been killed or displaced since the conflict began.

Does nothing say accomplished like insurgency? This a perfect example of how a war can be won and accomplished, leaving behind a peaceful and prosperous nation. Or not.

First of all, what is The Mozambican Islamist insurgency? Well, it's pretty much what it sounds like—a group of Islamist militants who want to establish an Islamic state in Mozambique.

They've been operating in the northern part of the country since 2017, carrying out attacks on civilians and government forces. So, what was accomplished with this insurgency? Let's find out.

The insurgency began in October 2017, and since then, it has killed over 3,000 people and displaced over 800,000. That's quite an accomplishment. The militants have also destroyed infrastructure, including schools and hospitals, and made it difficult for people to access basic services.

But wait, there's more. In response to the insurgency, the Mozambican government decided to take action. They enlisted the help of Russian mercenaries, who were more than happy to get involved in yet another conflict.

These mercenaries were supposed to help the government forces defeat the militants and restore order to the affected areas. And what an outstanding job they did.

Sure, they may have committed human rights abuses, including torture and extrajudicial killings. And yes, they may have caused even more displacement and destruction. But at least they were getting paid, right? And they did manage to kill some militants, so that's something.

In 2020, the Mozambican government declared victory over the militants. Hooray!

They had accomplished their goal of defeating the insurgents and bringing peace to the affected areas. But wait, why does it still seem like there's violence and displacement in the region?

Oh, that's right. The government forces and the mercenaries may have killed some militants, but they certainly didn't get them all.

The insurgency is still going on, and it doesn't look like it's going to end anytime soon.

In the aftermath of the conflict, the Mozambican government has been trying to rebuild the affected areas and provide assistance to those who have been displaced.

But with the insurgency still going on, it's a difficult task. And let's not forget the lingering trauma and fear that many people in the region still feel.

So, what can we learn from The Mozambican Islamist insurgency? Well, for one thing, war is never the answer. It only leads to destruction and suffering.

And for another, sometimes the "accomplishments" of a conflict are not what they seem. It's important to look beyond the surface and consider the long-term effects.

In conclusion, The Mozambican Islamist insurgency was an example of what can go wrong when a government decides to use violence to solve a problem.

The conflict accomplished little in the way of peace and stability but accomplished to leave behind a trail of death and destruction.

THE WAR OF THE FIRST DIADOCH

The War of the First Diadoch War was a conflict that occurred between 322 and 320 BC after the death of Alexander the Great.

The term "diadochi" means "successors" in Greek, and the war was fought between Alexander's former generals, known as the diadochi, who were fighting over control of his vast empire.

The conflict began when Alexander died without an heir, and his generals began to fight over who would succeed him.

The main participants in the war were the diadochi Antigonus, Ptolemy, Seleucus, Cassander, and Lysimachus. These generals split the empire into several kingdoms, with each vying for control of the others.

The war ended in 320 BC when the Diadochi agreed to a peace settlement that divided Alexander's empire among them.

The outcome was that Ptolemy received Egypt and Cyprus, Seleucus received Babylon and parts of Syria, Lysimachus received Thrace and parts of Asia Minor, Cassander received Macedonia, and Antigonus received much of Asia Minor.

It is difficult to estimate the number of casualties in the War of the First Diadoch War, but it was likely significant. The conflict marked the beginning of a long period of warfare among Alexander's former generals, which lasted for several decades.

The result of the war was the establishment of several Hellenistic kingdoms, which lasted for several centuries after the death of Alexander.

The conflict also marked the end of the period of Greek city-states, as the Hellenistic kingdoms were larger and more centralized.

So, what was accomplished? The War of the First Diadoch War! What a time to be alive! Or not, depending on whether you were one of the unfortunate souls caught up in this mess and is now arguably the oldest person on the earth at the age of 2500 and then some years.

Let's take a look at what was accomplished in this great, glorious war, and the aftermath that followed. It was a war fought between the generals of Alexander the Great, also known as the Diadochi, after he died in 323 BC.

These guys couldn't agree on who should be the next ruler of the empire, so they decided to fight it out like a bunch of schoolyard bullies. And thus, the War of the First Diadoch War was born.

Well, let's see. Millions of people died, countless cities were destroyed, and the once-great empire of Alexander the Great was torn apart.

Oh, and the Diadochi still couldn't agree on who should be the next ruler, so they just split the empire up into a bunch of smaller kingdoms. Yeah, real productive stuff.

But wait, there's more! The aftermath of the war was just as much of a disaster as the war itself. The kingdoms that were formed after the war were constantly at war with each other, fighting over territory and power.

It was like a never-ending game of Risk, but with real people and real consequences.

And let's not forget about the cultural impact of the War of the First Diadoch War. It was a time of great upheaval and change, as the once-great empire of Alexander the Great was replaced by a bunch of squabbling kingdoms.

It was a time of great uncertainty and fear, as people wondered what would happen next and who would come out on top.

But, at least we got some cool stories out of it, right? I mean, who doesn't love hearing about generals like Seleucus, Ptolemy, and Antigonus going at it like a bunch of medieval knights?

And let's not forget about the elephants! There were elephants in this war, people! You don't get that kind of entertainment in modern warfare.

In conclusion, the War of the First Diadoch War was a total disaster. It accomplished nothing but death and destruction, and the aftermath was just as bad. But hey, at least we got some cool stories out of it, right?

So, the next time you're feeling down about the state of the world, just remember that it could be worse. We could be living in the time of the Diadochi, fighting over who gets to be king of the sandbox.

THE PUNIC WARS

The Punic Wars were a series of three wars fought by Rome and Carthage from 264 BC to 146 BC. The wars were named after the Latin and Punic words for "Phoenician," which was the term used to describe the people of Carthage.

The First Punic War (264–241 BC) started as a dispute over the island of Sicily. Carthage, a powerful city-state in North Africa, had established a presence on the island, and Rome saw this as a threat to their interests.

The war was fought mostly at sea, with Rome ultimately emerging as the victor. As a result of the war, Carthage was forced to pay a large indemnity to Rome, cede Sicily to Rome, and give up its naval supremacy.

The Second Punic War (218–201 BC) was the most famous of the three wars. It began when Carthage, led by the brilliant general Hannibal, invaded Italy by crossing the Alps with a large army of men and elephants.

Hannibal won several impressive victories against the Romans, but ultimately he was defeated by the Roman general Scipio Africanus in the Battle of Zama.

As a result of the war, Carthage was forced to pay a large indemnity to Rome, cede Spain to Rome, and give up their elephants and their naval supremacy.

The Third Punic War (149–146 BC) was fought after Rome accused Carthage of breaking the terms of their treaty. The Romans laid siege to the city of Carthage, which eventually fell.

The city was destroyed and its inhabitants were either killed or sold into slavery. As a result of the war, Carthage ceased to exist as a city-state and the territory of Carthage became a Roman province.

It is difficult to estimate the number of casualties in the Punic Wars, but they were likely significant. The wars were fought over more than 100 years and involved many battles and sieges.

The result of the wars was the expansion of Rome's territory and influence, as well as the decline of Carthage as a major power in the Mediterranean.

War, after the war, after war … a classic example of a long and drawn-out conflict that accomplished...well, what did it accomplish?

First of all, let's start with the reasons for the war. Was it over resources? Land? Power?

No, no, it was all about honor and pride, of course! The Carthaginians had a bit of a grudge against the Romans after they were forced to pay some hefty reparations following the First Punic War, so they decided to pick a fight.

Because what's a little petty vengeance between ancient Mediterranean powers? So, off to war, they went. And boy, did they go. The Punic Wars lasted a whopping 118 years, spanning from 264 BC to 146 BC. That's longer than most modern countries have been around!

And what did all that time and effort accomplish?
Well, for starters, it decimated the populations of both Carthage and Rome, leading to untold suffering and death. But hey, at least they got to feel like big, powerful nations for a while, right?

As for actual tangible accomplishments, the First Punic War did manage to secure Sicily for the Romans, which was nice.

But then the Second Punic War happened, and Hannibal, the Carthaginian general, decided to march his army from Spain to Italy, crossing the Alps with elephants and everything.

It was quite the feat but ultimately didn't accomplish much other than some temporary victories for Carthage. It ended with Rome pretty much stomping all over Carthage and burning their city to the ground. Oops.

The Third Punic War was just Rome finishing the job and salting the earth where Carthage once stood, just to drive home the point that they were the winners.

So, what was accomplished with all this destruction and death? Well, Rome did gain control over a bunch of new territories, including Spain, North Africa, and parts of Greece.

They also became the undisputed superpower of the Mediterranean for a while, which I'm sure made them feel pretty good about themselves.

But in the long run, what did all this really accomplish? Sure, Rome got some new territory and felt tough and powerful for a while, but eventually, their empire fell apart anyway.

And Carthage? Well, they were completely wiped out, so I guess they didn't accomplish much at all. It's almost like all that bloodshed and destruction were for nothing.

The legacy of the Punic Wars is more of a cautionary tale about the dangers of pride, ego, and the lengths to which people will go to prove they're better than someone else.

And let's not forget about the massive toll it took on the people involved, both soldiers and civilians alike.

So if you're ever thinking about starting a 118-year-long war just to prove a point, maybe take a step back and reconsider. It's probably not worth it.

THE JUGURTHINE WAR

The Jugurthine War was a Roman military campaign waged in Numidia (present-day Algeria) from 112–106 BC. It was fought between Rome and Jugurtha, the king of Numidia.

The war began when Jugurtha, who had been adopted by the Roman Republic, was accused of murdering his half-brothers and seizing the throne of Numidia.

Rome sent a commission to investigate the matter, but Jugurtha bribed several of its members and was able to escape punishment. This led to tensions between Numidia and Rome, and Jugurtha began attacking Roman allies in the region.

In 111 BC, Rome sent an army to Numidia under the command of the consul Lucius Calpurnius Bestia. However, Bestia was also bribed by Jugurtha and agreed to a peace treaty that was favorable to the Numidian king.

This angered the Roman Senate, which sent another army under the command of Quintus Caecilius Metellus in 109 BC.

Metellus was able to achieve some early successes against Jugurtha, but the war dragged on for several years.

In 106 BC, the Roman general Gaius Marius took over command of the campaign and was able to defeat Jugurtha in a series of battles. Jugurtha was eventually captured and taken to Rome, where he was executed.

The casualties of the war are not known, but it is believed that several thousand Romans and Numidians were killed.

So anything lasting accomplished? The Jugurthine War was a classic tale of greed, deception, and pointless bloodshed. The war was so senseless and convoluted that even the Romans, who were pretty well-versed in pointless wars, were left scratching their heads.

It all started when Rome decided it wanted to expand its empire into North Africa. Jugurtha, the king of Numidia, wasn't too keen on this idea and started causing trouble.

The Romans sent a general named Metellus to deal with him, but Jugurtha proved to be a wily opponent and kept evading capture.

So the Romans sent in another general, Marius, who managed to capture Jugurtha by bribing one of his allies. But the war wasn't over yet. Jugurtha's allies continued to resist Roman rule, and Marius was forced to spend several more years fighting a guerrilla war against them.

Eventually, Marius was replaced by another general, Sulla, who managed to crush the remaining resistance and bring the war to an end.

So what was accomplished with this war, you may ask? Well, let's see:

1. Rome got a new province: Yes, that's right—after all that bloodshed and turmoil, Rome managed to add Numidia to its growing empire. Because nothing says "victory" like conquering a country and enslaving its people.

2. A lot of people died: This one's a bit of a downer, but it's hard to ignore the fact that the Jugurthine War resulted in the deaths of thousands of people. Roman soldiers, Numidian rebels, innocent civilians caught in the crossfire—they all paid the ultimate price for this pointless conflict.

3. Some people got rich: Ah, the spoils of war. While most people suffered during the Jugurthine War, there were a few lucky individuals who managed to profit from it. Bribes, loot, and plunder—are all the hallmarks of a successful military campaign.

4. Marius and Sulla got famous: Both generals managed to score some major victories during the war, and their names went down in history as great Roman conquerors. Of course, this didn't stop them from eventually turning on each other and plunging Rome into another bloody conflict, but that's a story for another time.

5. It set the stage for future Roman conquests: The Jugurthine War proved that Rome was a force to be reckoned with, and it paved the way for future conquests in North Africa and beyond. So I guess you could say that, in a way, the Jugurthine War was a valuable learning experience for Rome.

Overall, the Jugurthine War was a classic case of a powerful nation flexing its muscles and getting embroiled in a conflict that had no real purpose or endgame.

Sure, Rome got a new province out of it, but at what cost?

Countless lives were lost, and the region was plunged into chaos and instability for years to come. But hey, at least a few people got rich and famous, right?

THE ROMAN CIVIL WAR

The Roman Civil War, also known as Caesar's Civil War, was a conflict that occurred from 49 BC to 45 BC in ancient Rome.

It was fought between the forces of Julius Caesar, a prominent Roman general, and the forces of the Roman Senate, led by Gnaeus Pompey.

The conflict began when Julius Caesar, who had been appointed as governor of Gaul (modern-day France) by the Senate, was ordered to disband his army and return to Rome.

Caesar, however, refused to comply with this order and instead led his army across the Rubicon River into Italy, a move that marked the beginning of the civil war.

The war was fought across several battles and campaigns, with Caesar eventually emerging as the victor.

The Battle of Pharsalus in 48 BC was a particularly significant battle in which Caesar's forces decisively defeated the army of Pompey, who fled to Egypt and was later assassinated.

The war resulted in significant casualties on both sides, with estimates ranging from tens of thousands to hundreds of thousands of deaths.

The Roman Republic was effectively destroyed as a result of the conflict, with Caesar becoming the sole ruler of Rome and ushering in the period of Roman history known as the Roman Empire.

What did the Romans accomplish? One of the greatest achievements of the Roman Republic, and a true testament to the power of political infighting and backstabbing. The Roman Civil War had it all!

First of all, we have to acknowledge the sheer chaos and destruction that the Roman Civil War wrought upon the Republic. What an accomplishment! It was a time of great upheaval, as various factions fought for control and supremacy, and the blood of countless Romans was spilled in the streets.

For starters, it allowed Julius Caesar to march triumphantly into Rome and declare himself dictator for life. So, I guess you could say that the Civil War was a success in that regard.

After all, what could be more glorious than having one man wield absolute power over an entire nation?

Of course, Caesar's reign was cut tragically short when he was assassinated by a group of senators who were jealous of his supreme power.

But don't worry, the chaos didn't end there! The subsequent power struggle between Caesar's heir Octavian (later known as Augustus) and his rivals Mark Antony and Cleopatra was another shining example of Roman political brilliance.

After several years of intrigue, double-crossing, and epic battles, Octavian emerged victorious, and the Roman Republic was officially transformed into the Roman Empire.

So, I guess you could say that the Civil War accomplished the ultimate goal of any great war: creating an entirely new form of government!
But let's not forget the other achievements of the Roman Civil War. For one thing, it gave us some truly unforgettable historical figures, such as Caesar, Antony, and Cicero.

Who wouldn't want to read about these larger-than-life characters and their epic feats of daring and cunning?

And let's not overlook the cultural impact of the Civil War. It inspired countless works of literature, from Shakespeare's "Julius Caesar" to HBO's "Rome."

And let's not forget the impact it had on modern political discourse. After all, what better way to make a point than to compare your opponents to Brutus and his fellow conspirators?

So, in conclusion, what was accomplished with the Roman Civil War? Well, it gave us some great historical figures, inspired countless works of literature and art, and ultimately led to the creation of the Roman Empire. Not bad for a few years of political infighting and bloodshed, right?

Of course, some might argue that the cost of all this was too high. After all, the Roman Republic was one of the greatest political achievements of the ancient world, and its downfall marked the beginning of centuries of imperial rule and decline.

But let's not focus on the negative, shall we?

Instead, let's celebrate the sheer audacity and brilliance of the Roman Civil War, and remember it as one of the greatest achievements of Western civilization! Cheers!

The Armenian War

The Armenian War was a military conflict between the Roman Empire and the Parthian Empire over control of the Kingdom of Armenia. The war started when the Roman general Gnaeus Domitius Corbulo marched into Armenia and installed Tigranes VI as king, replacing the Parthian-backed King Tiridates.

This move was seen as a provocation by the Parthians, who sent an army under the command of general Surena to retake Armenia.

The war lasted for several years, with both sides scoring victories and suffering defeats. However, in 63 AD, the Roman general Lucius Caesennius Paetus suffered a crushing defeat at the Battle of Rhandeia and was forced to sign a humiliating peace treaty with the Parthians.

Under the terms of the treaty, the Romans agreed to withdraw their forces from Armenia and recognize Tiridates as the legitimate king.

However, the treaty also required Tiridates to travel to Rome and receive his crown from the Roman emperor Nero, effectively making Armenia a client state of the Roman Empire.

It is difficult to determine the exact number of casualties, but both sides suffered significant losses during the war.

The result of the Armenian War was the establishment of a client kingdom in Armenia, firmly under Roman influence.

This situation would continue for several centuries, with Armenia becoming a key buffer state between the Roman and Parthian Empires.

So much for achievement then? So, the story goes that the Roman Empire, under the rule of Emperor Nero, decided to conquer Armenia because, well, why not?

Armenia was a strategic location and it would look great on their resume of conquered territories. But the Parthian Empire also had its eyes on Armenia and didn't want to give up its claim to the land. And thus, the Armenian War began.

What did the Romans accomplish in this war, you ask? Well, they did manage to invade Armenia and capture the capital city of Artaxata. But it wasn't without its challenges. The Parthians put up a good fight, and the Roman general in charge of the invasion, Gnaeus Domitius Corbulo, faced setbacks and obstacles throughout the campaign.

But ultimately, the Romans emerged victorious and installed a new king, Tigranes VI, who was loyal to the Roman Empire. So, I guess you could say they accomplished their goal of gaining control over Armenia. But at what cost?

The aftermath of the Armenian War was a mixed bag. On one hand, the Romans had gained a new territory and could add it to their list of conquered lands.

But on the other hand, the war had taken a toll on their resources and soldiers. And let's not forget the fact that they now had to deal with an entirely new region of people who may not have been too thrilled about their new Roman overlords.

And what about the Armenians themselves? Well, they were left in a state of confusion and disarray. Their land had been invaded and they were now under the control of a foreign power.

And while Tigranes VI may have been a puppet king loyal to Rome, that didn't necessarily mean that he had the best interests of the Armenian people in mind. The aftermath of the war led to increased tensions and unrest within Armenia.

The Armenian people didn't take kindly to being conquered by the Romans and were eager to fight back. This led to a series of rebellions and uprisings throughout the region, which only served to make the situation worse.

So, what did the Romans accomplish with the Armenian War? They gained new territory, but at a high cost. And they later lost it.

They had to deal with the aftermath of the war and the turmoil it provoked, and it's not like they were particularly well-liked by the people they had conquered.

And let's not forget the fact that they were now responsible for governing and maintaining control over a new region, which would require even more resources and soldiers.

All in all, the Armenian War may have looked like a good idea on paper, but it ultimately led to more problems than it solved. But hey, at least they got a cool new territory out of it until it was lost.

THE JEWISH-ROMAN WAR

The Jewish-Roman War was a major conflict that took place in the eastern Mediterranean region between the Roman Empire and the Jews of Judea from 66 to 73 AD.

The war began when a group of Jewish rebels, led by the Zealots, launched a revolt against Roman rule in Judea. The Romans, under the command of governor Gessius Florus, responded with harsh repression, and the situation quickly spiraled out of control.

The Jewish rebels took control of Jerusalem, and the Roman emperor Nero dispatched his general Vespasian to quell the rebellion.

Vespasian arrived in Judea in 67 AD and began a campaign of siege warfare against the Jewish rebels. The siege of Jerusalem lasted for several months, during which the city was subjected to intense bombardment and starvation.

In 70 AD, the Romans breached the walls of Jerusalem and sacked the city, destroying the Second Temple and killing or capturing many of the rebels. The war continued for several more years, with the remaining rebels retreating to the fortress of Masada. In 73 AD, the Romans besieged

Masada and eventually breached its walls, only to find that the Jewish defenders had committed mass suicide rather than surrender to the Romans.

It is estimated that the Jewish-Roman War resulted in the deaths of hundreds of thousands of people, with the vast majority of them being Jewish civilians.

The war had a profound impact on Jewish history, leading to the dispersal of Jews throughout the Roman Empire and the eventual rise of Rabbinic Judaism in the centuries that followed.

For the Romans, the war marked a significant military victory and the end of the Jewish state until the modern era.

Accomplished a lot then? The Jewish-Roman War was a classic example of a conflict with a great outcome for everyone involved. Well, maybe not everyone.

It all started when the Jews rebelled against Roman rule and took control of Jerusalem, and from there, things just spiraled out of control.

So, what was accomplished with this war? Well, for starters, the Roman Empire was able to put down the rebellion and reestablish control over Jerusalem.

And isn't that what every empire dreams of? The ability to crush rebellions and assert their dominance over their subjects.

But let's not forget about the Jews. They accomplished a lot too. Like... um... well, they certainly showed the Romans that they weren't going to go down without a fight! That counts for something, right?

And they managed to hold out against the Roman siege of Jerusalem for three whole years before finally succumbing to starvation and disease. That's... impressive, in a way.

And then there's the aftermath. What did the Jewish-Roman War leave behind? Oh, just a little thing called the Diaspora.

You know, the forced dispersal of the Jewish people from their homeland and the beginning of centuries of persecution and oppression? Yeah, that's all thanks to the Jewish-Roman War.

But hey, at least everyone learned a valuable lesson, right? The Romans learned that crushing rebellions are always the way to go, and the Jews learned that rebelling against your oppressors is a great way to get yourself scattered to the winds and hated by everyone.

And let's not forget about the legacy of the Jewish-Roman War. It's inspired countless other conflicts throughout history, proving that if there's one thing people love more than peace and harmony, it's fighting and killing each other over religious and cultural differences.

So, in conclusion, the Jewish-Roman War was a resounding success for everyone involved.

The Romans got to put down a rebellion and establish their dominance, the Jews got to... show some spunk, and the world got to learn a valuable lesson about the futility of war and the lasting impact of conflict.

Truly a triumph of human achievement.

The Arab-Byzantine Wars

The Arab-Byzantine Wars were a series of wars fought between the Arab Muslim Caliphates and the Eastern Roman Empire (Byzantine Empire) from 634 to 750 AD.

The first Arab-Byzantine War began in 634 AD when the Arab Muslims under the leadership of Caliph Abu Bakr launched an invasion of Syria, which was then a province of the Byzantine Empire.

The Arab Muslims quickly conquered Syria, Palestine, and Egypt, and continued their advance into Anatolia (modern-day Turkey), where they were eventually stopped by the Byzantine Emperor Heraclius at the Battle of Nineveh in 627 AD.

After Heraclius' death, his successors were unable to prevent further Arab-Muslim incursions into Byzantine territory. The Arabs captured the important city of Damascus in 635 AD and continued to advance, conquering much of Anatolia by the mid-7th century.

The war saw several significant battles, including the Battle of Yarmouk in 636 AD, in which the Byzantines suffered a major defeat and lost control of Syria.

The Byzantines were also defeated at the Battle of Heliopolis in 640 AD, which allowed the Arabs to capture Egypt. The war continued for over a century, with both sides gaining and losing territory.

The Byzantines were able to regain some of their lost territories in the early 8ᵗʰ century under Emperor Leo III, but by this time the Arab Muslims had established a strong presence in the region.

In 750 AD, the Arab Abbasid Caliphate overthrew the Umayyad Caliphate, which had been responsible for the initial conquests.

The new Abbasid rulers focused on consolidating their power within the Islamic world and did not launch any major attacks on the Byzantine Empire. As a result, the Arab-Byzantine Wars came to an end.

The total number of casualties in the war is difficult to estimate, but it is believed to have been signed on both sides.

The war had a profound impact on the region, leading to the Arabization of much of the Eastern Mediterranean and the decline of the Byzantine Empire.

Achieved a whole lot?
The Byzantine-Sassanid War began when Emperor Phocas of the Byzantine Empire decided to execute his predecessor, Emperor Maurice, along with his entire family.

The Sassanid Empire, under the leadership of King Khosrow II, saw this as an opportunity to invade and reclaim territories that were once under their rule. And so, the war began.

The two empires went back and forth, with battles and skirmishes spanning over twenty years.

The Byzantine Empire was led by a series of incompetent leaders who couldn't seem to get their act together, while the Sassanid Empire was led by King Khosrow II, who was more interested in building extravagant palaces than actually winning the war.

As the years went on, the war became less about territorial gain and more about petty squabbles and personal vendettas.

At one point, the Byzantine general Narses was recalled by Emperor Heraclius because he was jealous of Narses' popularity among the troops. The Sassanids, for their part, were more interested in killing each other than killing Byzantines.

By the time the war ended in 628 AD, both empires were exhausted and bankrupt. The Sassanid Empire was left in ruins, and King Khosrow II was deposed and murdered by his son. The Byzantine Empire, on the other hand, was left with a massive power vacuum, and would eventually fall to the Islamic conquests less than a century later.

So, what was accomplished with the Byzantine-Sassanid War? Absolutely nothing. Both empires were weakened and destabilized, leading to their eventual collapse. The war was a pointless and costly exercise in futility, with no clear winners or losers.

But let's not forget the comedic moments of this war. There was a time when the Byzantines supposedly used war elephants to charge into Sassanid lines, only for the elephants to panic and run back into their ranks.

And who could forget the time when the Sassanids tried, so it is said, to invade Byzantine territory with a herd of war camels, only for the camels to get spooked by a passing rabbit and stampede back towards their lines?

In the end, the Byzantine-Sassanid War was a lesson in the futility of war and the dangers of incompetent leadership.

Let's hope that future generations will learn from our mistakes and avoid similar pointless conflicts. But knowing humanity, we'll probably never learn and will continue to make the same mistakes over and over again.

The First Fitna

The First Fitna was a civil war in the early Islamic Caliphate that lasted from 656 to 661 AD.

It arose from a succession dispute following the assassination of Caliph Uthman ibn Affan in 656 AD, which led to a power struggle among the early Muslim community.

The war began with the emergence of two factions: one supporting Uthman's cousin and son-in-law, Caliph Ali ibn Abi Talib, as the rightful successor, and the other supporting Muawiyah I, the governor of Syria.

The dispute quickly turned into a full-blown civil war, with both factions gathering armies and engaging in battles across the caliphate.

The war came to a head with the Battle of Siffin in 657 AD, in which Ali's forces faced Muawiyah's forces in a brutal conflict that lasted for months. The battle ended in a stalemate, with neither side emerging as the clear victor.

This led to a split within Ali's army, with some of his supporters accusing him of compromising with Muawiyah.

The First Fitna ended with the assassination of Ali in 661 AD, followed by the establishment of the Umayyad Caliphate under Muawiyah's leadership.

The war resulted in significant casualties on both sides, including the deaths of several prominent figures of the early Islamic community.

It accomplished something, it was the first! The First Fitna is the classic tale of a family feud that spiraled out of control and plunged the Islamic world into chaos.

It's like the Hatfields and McCoys, but with swords and a lot more bloodshed. So, what was accomplished with this whole mess apart from being the first Fitna war?

The First Fitna war erupted in the Islamic Caliphate following the assassination of the third caliph, Uthman.

A power struggle ensued between two factions: one supporting Uthman's successor, Ali, and the other advocating for the rule of Muawiyah, the governor of Syria.

The conflict lasted for several years and resulted in a lot of death and destruction. Now, let's get to the meat of the matter. What was accomplished with all this infighting and bloodshed? Well, let's see...

First of all, the Islamic world was thrown into turmoil, with various factions vying for power and control. That's always a good thing, right? Chaos is the spice of life, after all.

Secondly, thousands of people lost their lives in the fighting. But hey, that's just collateral damage, right?

Thirdly, the conflict set the stage for further divisions and sectarianism within the Islamic world. Who doesn't love a good religious schism?

Fourthly, the First Fitna paved the way for the rise of the Umayyad Caliphate, which would go on to become one of the most powerful empires of its time. So, I guess you could say that the war was good for business, in a way.

Fifthly, the First Fitna gave rise to a lot of fascinating historical anecdotes and trivia.

For example, did you know that during the Battle of Siffin, Muawiyah's troops hung copies of the Quran from their spears to trick Ali's army into thinking they were surrendering? That's some next-level trolling right there.

And finally, the aftermath of the First Fitna set the stage for future conflicts and tensions within the Islamic world. So, you know, it's like the gift that keeps on giving.

In conclusion, what was accomplished with the First Fitna?

A lot of death, destruction, chaos, sectarianism, and historical trivia.

Was it worth it? Who knows? But hey, at least it made for a good story, I mean they were first, right?

THE SECOND FITNA

The Second Fitna was a civil war that occurred within the Islamic Caliphate from 680 to 692 AD.

It was a succession crisis that arose after the death of the Umayyad Caliph, Mu'awiya I, and led to a power struggle between two rival claimants to the caliphate: Abd Allah ibn al-Zubayr and the Umayyad Caliph, Yazid I.

The conflict began when Ibn al-Zubayr declared himself the Caliph in Mecca after the death of Mu'awiya I.

This move was opposed by Yazid I, who had also declared himself the Caliph in Damascus.

Ibn al-Zubayr gained the support of the people of Mecca and Medina, while Yazid I had the backing of the Umayyad dynasty and their loyalists.

The war was fought across the Islamic Caliphate, with battles taking place in Syria, Iraq, and Arabia.

The Umayyad forces initially gained the upper hand, and Yazid I's army besieged Mecca. However, the siege was unsuccessful, and Yazid I died soon after, which led to a temporary halt in the conflict.

The Second Fitna resumed when Yazid's son, Mu'awiya II, was named the new caliph, but he died just four months later. His successor, Marwan I, was also short-lived and died after just one year. The war continued for several years, with both sides suffering heavy casualties.

The conflict finally ended in 692 AD when Ibn al-Zubayr was defeated and killed in Mecca by the Umayyad forces under the leadership of al-Hajjaj ibn Yusuf. With Ibn al-Zubayr's death, the Umayyads regained control of the Caliphate and consolidated their power.

The Second Fitna resulted in a significant loss of life, and it had a profound impact on the Islamic Caliphate. It weakened the authority of the Umayyad dynasty and contributed to the rise of the Abbasid Caliphate, which eventually overthrew the Umayyads in 750 AD.

The conflict also highlighted the deep divisions within the Muslim community and raised questions about the legitimacy of the Caliphate.

The Second Fitna … Just when you thought one Fitna was enough, along comes its sequel! But don't worry, folks, we've got everything under control...ish.

Let's set the stage. The Islamic world is still reeling from the aftermath of the First Fitna. Muawiya, the founder of the Umayyad dynasty, has just died, and his son Yazid is eager to take the throne.

But not everyone is thrilled about the idea of another Umayyad ruler. Enter the rebels. Led by Abdullah ibn al-Zubayr, they quickly gain control of Mecca and Medina, the holiest cities in Islam. Yazid, naturally, is not pleased about this turn of events. He sends an army to retake the cities and thus begins the Second Fitna.

The war drags on for years, with both sides trading victories and defeats. Meanwhile, other contenders for the throne start popping up like daisies.

There's Husayn, the son of Ali and Fatima, who decides to throw his hat in the ring. There's also Ibn al-Ash'ath, a disgruntled general who thinks he deserves to be caliph. And let's not forget the Kharijites, a group of extremists who just want everyone to die.

As you might imagine, this all gets very confusing very quickly. Battles are fought, alliances are made and broken, and it becomes increasingly difficult to keep track of who's on whose side.

At one point, Husayn even makes a desperate plea for help to the people of Kufa, only to be betrayed and left to die in the desert. Nice one, Kufans. Eventually, Yazid dies and is succeeded by his son Muawiya II, who promptly dies after just four months on the throne. Then there's a power vacuum, and things get even more chaotic than they were before.

It's like Game of Thrones, but with fewer dragons and more confusing names.

But hey, don't worry! The Second Fitna did accomplish a few things. For one, it solidified the Umayyad dynasty's hold on the caliphate.

After years of infighting, it became clear that the Umayyads were here to stay (at least for a little while).

The war also helped to cement the split between Sunni and Shia Islam, as Husayn's death became a rallying cry for Shia Muslims. So, you know, that's something. But as for the aftermath...well, let's just say it wasn't exactly smooth sailing.

The Umayyads continued to face rebellions and uprisings for years to come, and the caliphate itself would eventually fall to the Abbasids in 750. And of course, the Sunni-Shia divide would remain a contentious issue throughout Islamic history (and to this day).

So all in all, the Second Fitna was a bit of a mess. But hey, at least we got a few good battle scenes out of it...?

The Battle of Tours

The Battle of Tours, also known as the Battle of Poitiers, was a military conflict that took place on October 10, 732, in the vicinity of Tours, in what is now modern-day France.

The battle was fought between the Frankish army, led by Charles Martel, and a large invading Muslim force from the Umayyad Caliphate, led by Abdul Rahman Al Ghafiqi.

The Umayyad forces had already conquered most of the Iberian Peninsula (modern-day Spain and Portugal) and had crossed the Pyrenees mountains into Gaul (modern-day France), intending to expand their territory further into Europe.

The battle began with the Umayyad cavalry launching a series of attacks against the Frankish lines, which were fortified with a wall of shields known as a "shield wall."

The Umayyad attacks were repelled by the Frankish infantry, who used their long spears to hold the Umayyad cavalry at bay. At a critical moment in the battle, Charles Martel led a charge against the Umayyad cavalry, breaking their lines and causing them to flee. Abdul Rahman Al Ghafiqi was killed in the battle, and the Umayyad force retreated across the Pyrenees.

The casualties of the battle are not known with certainty, but it is believed that the Umayyad force suffered heavy losses, while the Frankish casualties were relatively low.

The Battle of Tours is considered a turning point in European history, as it halted the expansion of Muslim forces into Europe and helped to solidify the power of the Frankish Kingdom under the leadership of Charles Martel.

The battle is sometimes cited as one of the key events that prevented Islam from spreading into Western Europe.

Anything else accomplished? The Battle of Tours, the clash of the Titans, was the decisive moment that changed the course of history. Or so they say.

In the year 732, the armies of Charles Martel and Abdul Rahman Al Ghafiqi met in a field near the city of Tours in France. It was a clash of civilizations, a battle that would decide the fate of Europe. At least that's what historians like to say.

In reality, it was just another day in the endless cycle of war and conquest. The two armies clashed, and after a fierce battle, the Franks emerged victorious. But what did they accomplish?

Did they stop the Muslim invasion of Europe? No, not really. The Muslim armies continued to raid and conquer territory in Spain for centuries to come. Did they preserve Christianity in Europe? Again, not really. Christianity had already taken root in Europe long before the Battle of Tours, and it would continue to spread and evolve regardless of the outcome of this one battle.

Did they establish Charles Martel as a great military leader? Absolutely. Charles Martel became a legendary figure in European history, and his victory at Tours was celebrated for centuries to come.

But what did that accomplish? Nothing. It was just another example of the human need for heroes and legends. Cool for Martels' relatives.

So what was accomplished at the Battle of Tours? Not much. It was just another battle in the endless cycle of war and conquest.

It didn't stop the spread of Islam, it didn't preserve Christianity, and it didn't establish a lasting peace. It was just a moment in history, a footnote in the long story of humanity.

But hey, at least we got a cool nickname out of it. Charles Martel, the "Hammer of the Muslims". It's got a nice ring to it, doesn't it?

THE VIKING RAIDS

The Viking Raids were a series of attacks carried out by Vikings, Norse seafarers from Scandinavia, on various European countries between the late 8th century and the mid-11th century.

The Viking raids began with the attack on the English monastery of Lindisfarne in 793 AD.

The Vikings, who were expert seafarers, attacked coastal towns and villages, monasteries, and churches throughout Europe.

They also established settlements, including Dublin, Ireland, and Normandy, France.

The Vikings targeted regions with rich resources and goods, including silver, gold, textiles, and slaves.

They also traded with other regions and were known for their shipbuilding skills and navigational abilities. The Viking raids had a significant impact on European history. They contributed to the decline of the Carolingian Empire and the rise of feudalism.

The Vikings also played a role in the establishment of the Normans in Normandy, who would later conquer England in 1066 AD.

The number of casualties caused by the Viking raids is difficult to estimate, but it is believed to be in the thousands.

The raids also had a significant impact on the cultural and linguistic landscape of Europe, with many Old Norse words and phrases being incorporated into various European languages.

So, much accomplished? The Viking Raids—wow. A time when men were men, and women were busy trying to avoid being kidnapped, raped or sold off as slaves.

The Vikings, known for their fierce raids, sailed across the seas in search of treasure, fame, and apparently, new hairstyles. But what was accomplished with these raids, and what was the aftermath?

Firstly, let's talk about what the Vikings accomplished with their raids. They managed to terrify entire villages, loot countless treasures, and build their reputation as some of the most brutal raiders in history.

They also gave us a new word to describe an attack that comes out of nowhere: "Viking." So, kudos to them for that.

But what did the Vikings accomplish in the long run? Well, they managed to spread their culture and language across Europe, which I'm sure the Europeans were just thrilled about.

The Vikings also set the foundation for several modern-day countries, such as Denmark, Norway, and Sweden. So, if you've ever wanted to thank someone for IKEA meatballs, now you know who to thank.

As for the aftermath of the Viking Raids, well, it's safe to say that the Vikings didn't exactly leave things better than they found them.

They left a trail of destruction and chaos wherever they went, making it harder for people to trust each other and work together. Plus, they set the bar pretty high for future raiders, which must have been pretty intimidating for them.

But, hey, at least we got some great Viking-themed TV shows and movies out of it, right?

And let's not forget about the oh so cool Viking helmets and drinking horns that are now popular party accessories.

In all seriousness, though, the Viking Raids had a profound impact on history. They helped shape the political and cultural landscape of Europe and even inspired some of the most famous stories and legends we know today.

Without the Vikings, we might not have tales of dragons, Thor, or the epic poem Beowulf. So, in a way, we owe them a debt of gratitude for providing us with so much inspiration.

In conclusion, the Viking Raids were a violent and destructive period in history, but they also had their moments of glory and accomplishment.

The Vikings managed to leave their mark on the world, for better or for worse, and they will always be remembered as some of the fiercest and most feared warriors of all time.

So, here's to the Vikings, for showing us what it means to be truly fearless and for giving us a reason to wear horned helmets. Skål!

The Reconquista

The Reconquista was approximately 781 years in the history of the Iberian Peninsula, during which the Christian kingdoms of northern Spain gradually reconquered the Muslim-ruled territories of the peninsula.

The Reconquista began in 711 AD when Muslim forces invaded and quickly conquered most of the Iberian Peninsula, establishing the Umayyad Caliphate of Córdoba.

The conflict was between the Christian kingdoms of the north, including Navarre, Leon, Castile, Aragon, and Portugal, against the Muslim Moors, who ruled over the vast majority of the peninsula.

The conflict lasted for centuries and involved numerous battles, sieges, and political maneuvers. Over time, the Christian kingdoms gradually gained territory and power, eventually leading to the formation of the modern-day countries of Spain and Portugal.

The Reconquista ended in 1492 with the fall of the Emirate of Granada, the last Muslim stronghold on the peninsula, and the subsequent completion of the Catholic Reconquista.

Casualty figures for the Reconquista are difficult to estimate, but it is believed that tens of thousands of people died in the conflict.

The result of the Reconquista was the establishment of Christian rule over the entire Iberian Peninsula, which lasted until the end of the 15th century when the Spanish and Portuguese began to explore and conquer new territories in the Americas.

A lot accomplished then? The centuries-long battle between Muslims and Christians for control of the Iberian Peninsula. What a glorious time it was. So much bloodshed, so much land gained and lost.

Firstly, the Christians managed to take back a significant amount of land from the Muslims. This was done through countless battles, sieges, and just general pillaging and plundering.

They did eventually manage to push the Muslims out of the region entirely, which was quite an accomplishment. Of course, the Christians had help from some of the most powerful nations of the time, including France and England. They poured resources and soldiers into the fight, ensuring that the Muslims didn't stand a chance. I mean, sure, the Muslims had their allies, but they were no match for the sheer might of the Christian forces.

But what did all of this accomplish? Well, for one, it ensured that the Iberian Peninsula would remain under Christian control for centuries to come. That's something, right? And it certainly paved the way for the Spanish and Portuguese empires, which were pretty big deals at the time.

But let's not forget about the cultural impact of the Reconquista. The Muslims had been in the region for centuries, and they had left their mark on the land, the people, and the culture.

And what did the Christians do when they took over? They destroyed mosques, banned the use of Arabic, they persecuted the remaining Muslim population. In short, they did their best to erase any trace of Muslim influence from the region.

And let's not forget about the Jews. They had been living in the region for centuries as well, and they were subjected to all sorts of persecution during the Reconquista.

Many were forced to convert to Christianity, while others were killed or expelled from the region entirely.

So, what was accomplished with the Reconquista? Well, the Christians managed to gain control of a region that was already heavily populated and rich in culture, and they did so through years of brutal warfare and persecution. And while they did create a lasting legacy of Christian rule in the region, they also destroyed much of the culture and history that had been there before.

But hey, at least they got to build some really impressive cathedrals …?

The Crusader States

The Crusader states were a series of Christian kingdoms established by Western European knights and soldiers in the Holy Land during the Crusades, which lasted from 1099 to 1291 AD.

The Crusades were a series of military campaigns by European Christians to take back the Holy Land from Muslim rule.

The First Crusade, which was launched in 1096, resulted in the capture of Jerusalem and the establishment of the first Crusader state in 1099.

Over the next two centuries, several other Crusader states were established, including the Principality of Antioch, the County of Tripoli, and the Kingdom of Jerusalem. These states were ruled by European monarchs and nobles and were characterized by a mixture of feudalism and religious zealotry.

The Crusader states were in a state of almost constant conflict with Muslim forces in the region, including the Ayyubid dynasty and the Mamluk Sultanate.

Overall, the Crusades and the establishment of the Crusader states had a profound impact on European and Middle Eastern history, but their ultimate legacy remains a matter of debate.
While some historians view the Crusades as a noble endeavor to defend Christendom from Muslim aggression, others see them as a brutal and unjustifiable series of wars that caused immense suffering and death on both sides.

Holy accomplishments?
A time of chivalry, religious fervor, and lots of bloodsheds. Let's take a trip back to the 11ᵗʰ century and see what these holy warriors managed to accomplish.

First off, let's talk about the concept of the Crusader states. The idea was to establish Christian kingdoms in the Holy Land, which was then occupied by the Muslims.

Sounds simple enough, right? Just kill all the Muslims and claim the land for Christ. Well, it turns out that it wasn't quite that easy.

The Crusaders arrived in the Holy Land in 1096, all fired up and ready to take back Jerusalem. They set up several kingdoms along the eastern Mediterranean coast, including the Kingdom of Jerusalem, the County of Edessa, the Principality of Antioch, and the County of Tripoli.

They managed to hold on to these territories for a few centuries, but let's be real: they didn't accomplish much.

Sure, they built some castles and churches and held off the Muslim armies for a while. But they also engaged in plenty of infighting and squabbling over territory. They even managed to turn on each other, with the Kingdom of Jerusalem going to war with the County of Tripoli and the Principality of Antioch.

The Crusaders also failed to win the hearts and minds of the local population. They were seen as outsiders who had come to conquer and convert the natives. Despite all this, the Crusader states managed to last for a few hundred years. But in the end, they were doomed to fail.

The Muslims were simply too strong and too determined to let the Crusaders take their land. The Crusaders also faced other problems, such as disease, famine, and a lack of resources.

In the end, the Crusader states accomplished very little. They failed to establish a lasting Christian presence in the Holy Land, and they failed to convert the local population. They also failed to bring peace and stability to the region.

So what was the aftermath of the Crusader states? Well, the most notable outcome was that the Muslims eventually retook Jerusalem in 1187. This was a major blow to the Crusaders, who had been fighting for decades to hold on to the city. The loss of Jerusalem also dealt a significant blow to the morale of the Christian world.

The Crusader states did leave behind some cultural and architectural artifacts. The Crusaders built many castles and churches, some of which are still standing today. They also left behind a legacy of chivalry and knighthood, which would go on to influence Western culture for centuries.

They only truely succeeded in causing more conflict and violence in the region. The Crusader states were ultimately a failure and a reminder of the dangers of religious zealotry and imperialism.

So, there you have it: A grand idea, but ultimately a failure. Maybe next time, they should have tried something a little more practical, like building hospitals or schools instead of just trying to conquer and convert everyone in sight. But hey, hindsight is 20/20, right?

THE MONGOL CONQUESTS

The Mongol Conquests were a series of military campaigns and conquests led by the Mongol Empire from 1206 to 1368 AD.

The Mongol Empire, led by Genghis Khan, began its expansion by conquering neighboring tribes in Central Asia and eventually conquered the Khwarezmian Empire and the Jin Dynasty of China.

The Mongol Empire continued its conquests, invading and conquering large parts of Eurasia, including Russia, Eastern Europe, the Middle East, and Central Asia.

The conquests were characterized by brutal warfare and the Mongols were known for their use of psychological warfare, such as sacking and massacring entire cities to intimidate other potential opponents.

The conquests resulted in the largest land empire in history, spanning over 24 million square kilometers and a population of around 100 million people. However, the empire eventually fragmented due to internal conflicts, and by 1368 the Mongol Empire had dissolved, with various successor states forming in its place.

It is difficult to estimate the total number of casualties of the Mongol Conquests, but it is believed to be in the tens of millions, with entire cities being massacred and devastated.

Accomplished much more? The Mongol Conquests was a period of history filled with so much bloodshed and destruction that even the most hardened of warriors would feel queasy.

The Mongols, led by the notorious Genghis Khan, managed to conquer a vast expanse of territory, stretching from China to Eastern Europe.

They were renowned for their ferocity in battle, their incredible horsemanship, and their military tactics. But what did they achieve with all of this conquest?

First and foremost, they managed to kill a lot of people. And when I say a lot, I mean a lot. According to some estimates, the Mongol Conquests led to the deaths of up to 40 million people. So, if their goal was to thin out the world population, they succeeded.

They also managed to destroy a lot of cities and infrastructure along the way. If you were a fan of beautiful architecture or well-maintained roads, then the Mongol Conquests were not for you. But at least they left behind some impressive ruins for future generations to marvel at.

In terms of cultural achievements, the Mongols didn't leave much of a mark. Sure, they had their own unique culture, but they weren't exactly known for promoting the arts or fostering intellectualism.

It's not like they were hosting poetry slams or art exhibits in between pillaging and plundering.

So, what was the aftermath of the Mongol Conquests? Well, for one thing, they left behind a lot of empty lands. With so many people dead, there were vast swathes of territory that were suddenly up for grabs. This led to a period of instability and conflict, as various factions vied for power.

But hey, at least they left behind some cool stories, right? I mean, who doesn't love hearing about Genghis Khan and his horde of fierce warriors riding across the steppes, leaving a trail of destruction in their wake? It's like something straight out of a Hollywood action movie.

In all seriousness, though, the Mongol Conquests did have some long-term effects and accomplishments. They helped to spread knowledge and ideas across different cultures, and they facilitated trade and commerce on a grand scale. They also managed to become a slur!

They also contributed to the downfall of some existing empires, which paved the way for new ones to emerge, and that paved the way for more... Wars!

But at what cost? A little collateral damage like 40 million dead people...

The Ottoman Wars in Europe

The Ottoman Wars in Europe were a series of military conflicts fought between the Ottoman Empire and various European powers over several centuries, from the late 14th century until the late 19th century.

1. Battle of Nicopolis (1396). This was a major battle between Ottoman forces and a coalition of European forces, including the French, Hungarians, and others. The Ottomans emerged victorious, and this battle marked the beginning of the Ottoman expansion into Europe.

2. Siege of Constantinople (1453). The Ottomans, led by Sultan Mehmed II, laid siege to the Byzantine capital of Constantinople for several weeks before finally breaching the city's defenses and capturing it. This marked the end of the Byzantine Empire and the beginning of Ottoman dominance over the Balkans.

3. Siege of Vienna (1529). This was a failed attempt by the Ottoman Empire to capture the city of Vienna, Austria. The Ottomans were ultimately repelled by a combined force of European defenders, and this marked the beginning of the Ottoman decline in Europe.

4. Battle of Lepanto (1571). This was a naval battle between the Ottoman Empire and a coalition of European powers, led by Spain, Venice, and the Papal States. The Europeans emerged victorious, and this battle marked the beginning of the decline of Ottoman naval power.

5. Great Turkish War (1683–1699). This was a major conflict between the Ottoman Empire and a coalition of European powers, led by Austria. The

war ended with the Treaty of Karlowitz, which saw the Ottomans cede significant territories in Europe and marked the beginning of the Ottoman Empire's decline as a major European power.

6. Russo-Turkish Wars (1768–1878). These were a series of wars fought between the Ottoman Empire and the Russian Empire over several decades. The wars resulted in Ottoman territorial losses and ultimately contributed to the Ottoman Empire's decline and the emergence of modern Turkey.

The casualties of these wars varied depending on the conflict and the specific battles fought, but they were generally significant, with millions of people losing their lives over the centuries-long conflict.

The result of these wars was the gradual decline of the Ottoman Empire as a major European power and the emergence of modern Turkey as a more secular and Western-oriented nation.

So many wars, so much accomplished? A time of great battles and victories. A time of legendary heroes and epic tales of conquest. And, of course, a time of satirical commentary.

From the early days of the Ottoman state to the waning years of the empire, the Ottomans fought and conquered their way across vast swathes of land, leaving behind a legacy of cultural and architectural landmarks, as well as a wealth of satirical material.

First up, we have the Ottoman–Safavid War of 1623–39. What was accomplished, you may ask?
Well, the Ottomans managed to capture the Persian city of Tabriz, which they promptly renamed "Toblerone" and filled with Swiss chocolate.

The Safavids retaliated by sending an army to attack the Ottomans, but they were quickly defeated by the Ottomans' secret weapon: the Janissary Corps of Uncontrollable Flatulence.

The Ottomans then went on to conquer Baghdad, which they transformed into a giant kebab stand.

Next, we have the Russo-Turkish War of 1768–74. This war was notable for the fact that it was fought between two empires that were both in serious need of some new material for their satirical comedies.

The Ottomans managed to capture the Russian city of Azov, which they promptly renamed "Azerbaijan" and filled with Turkish delight.

The Russians retaliated by sending an army to attack the Ottomans, but they were quickly defeated by the Ottomans' secret weapon: the Janissary Corps of Uncontrollable Tambourine Playing.

Moving on to the Greek War of Independence (1821–1832), the Ottomans found themselves in a bit of a pickle. They were facing a determined group of rebels who were fighting for their freedom, which was not something the Ottomans were known for supporting.

However, the Ottomans had a secret weapon: the Janissary Corps of Uncontrollable Greek Dancing. With their skillful moves and irresistible charm, the Janissaries managed to convince many of the rebels to join the Ottoman side.

Unfortunately for the Ottomans, the rebels eventually won the war, leaving the Janissaries to dance their way into obscurity.

Finally, we come to the Balkan Wars of 1912–1913. This was a time of great upheaval for the Ottoman Empire, which found itself facing a series of rebellions and invasions.

The Ottomans managed to defeat the Bulgarians in the first Balkan War, thanks in large part to the Janissary Corps of Uncontrollable Balalaika Playing.

However, the Ottomans were soon overwhelmed by the combined forces of the Balkan League, which included the Serbs, Greeks, and Montenegrins. The Janissaries valiantly tried to defend their empire with their trusty bagpipes, but alas, it was not enough.

The Ottomans were forced to cede most of their territory in Europe, which they promptly renamed "No Man's Land" and filled with kebab stands. And so, we come to the end of our satirical journey through the Ottoman Wars.

What did we learn? Well, we learned that the Ottomans had a lot of secret weapons in the form of Janissary Corps and that they were quite fond of renaming conquered territories and filling them with food.

But, most importantly, we learned that even in times of war, there is always room for improvement. If ever so slightly.

THE RUSSO-TURKISH WARS

The Russo-Turkish Wars were a series of wars fought between the Russian Empire and the Ottoman Empire from 1568 through 1570, 1676–1681, 1686–1700, 1710–1711, 1735–1739, 1768–1774, 1787–1792, 1806–1812, 1828–1829, 1853–1856, 1877–1878, and 1914–1918.

1568–1570: The war was fought over control of the Khanate of Kazan. The war ended with the Russian capture of Kazan and the annexation of the Khanate into the Russian Empire.

1676–1681: The war was fought over control of Ukraine and ended with the Treaty of Bakhchisarai, which granted Russia control of the eastern half of Ukraine.

1686–1700: The war was fought over control of the Sea of Azov and ended with the Treaty of Constantinople, which granted Russia access to the Sea of Azov.

1710–1711: The war was fought over control of Livonia and ended with the Treaty of Nystad, which granted Russia control of Estonia, Livonia, and a part of Finland.

1735–1739: The war was fought over control of Poland and ended with the Treaty of Vienna, which granted Russia control of part of Poland.

1768–1774: The war was fought over control of the Black Sea and ended with the Treaty of Kucuk Kaynarca, which granted Russia control of Crimea and the northern coast of the Black Sea.

1787–1792: The war was fought over control of the Black Sea and ended with the Treaty of Jassy, which granted Russia control of the eastern part of the Black Sea.

1806–1812: The war was fought over control of the Balkans and ended with the Treaty of Bucharest, which granted Russia control of Bessarabia.

1828–1829: The war was fought over control of the Balkans and ended with the Treaty of Adrianople, which granted Russia control of Georgia, Armenia, and part of Azerbaijan.

1853–1856: The war was fought over control of the Balkans and the Holy Land and ended with the Treaty of Paris, which granted Russia access to the Black Sea and control of the mouth of the Danube.

1877–1878: The war was fought over control of the Balkans and ended with the Treaty of San Stefano, which granted Bulgaria independence and increased Russian influence in the Balkans.

1914–1918: The war was fought as part of World War I and ended with the defeat of the Ottoman Empire and the emergence of the modern state of Turkey.

So many wars, so much accomplished?
The Russo-Turkish Wars! This a great example of two nations trying to assert their dominance over the other and never giving up. Let's take a look at what was accomplished and the aftermath, shall we?

First off, we have to acknowledge the sheer number of Russo-Turkish Wars that took place between the 17th and 19th centuries. It's like the two nations couldn't get enough of each other! I mean, what's more fun than slaughtering each other's soldiers and civilians?

So, what was accomplished? Well, let's see. The Russians managed to expand their territory, particularly in the Caucasus region. They also gained control of the Black Sea and the Danube River, which was a pretty big deal.

The Ottomans, on the other hand, managed to hold onto their capital city of Constantinople (now Istanbul) despite multiple attempts by the Russians to conquer it.

But here's the thing: did either side accomplish anything meaningful in the grand scheme of things? Sure, the Russians gained some new territory, but was it worth the thousands of lives lost on both sides? And the Ottomans managed to hold onto their capital, but did that make them any stronger as a nation?

The aftermath of the Russo-Turkish Wars is arguably more interesting than the wars themselves.

It set the stage for the decline of the Ottoman Empire and the rise of Russian power in the region.

The wars contributed to the economic decline of both nations, as they poured resources into their military efforts. They also contributed to the tension and instability in the Balkans, which would eventually lead to World War I. Congrats!

But hey, at least we got some cool battle stories out of it, right? Who doesn't love hearing about the Charge of the Light Brigade or the Siege of Plevna? I mean, it's not like thousands of people died horrible deaths or anything. Nope, just some good old-fashioned fun!

In conclusion, the Russo-Turkish Wars were a prime example of nations trying to assert their dominance over each other at any cost. While some territory was gained and lost, the overall impact on both nations was negative.

And let's not forget the contribution to the instability in the Balkans, which would have far-reaching consequences. But hey, at least we got some good war stories out of it, right?

The Eighty Years' War

The Eighty Years' War, known also as The Dutch Revolt, was a conflict between the Dutch Republic and the Spanish Empire that lasted from 1568 to 1648.

It was fought for Dutch independence and religious freedom. The war started when Philip II of Spain, a devout Catholic, attempted to suppress Protestantism in the Netherlands.

This led to a revolt by the Dutch people, who were supported by England and France. The war was characterized by a series of sieges, battles, and naval engagements, with both sides winning major victories at different times.

The Dutch Republic declared independence in 1581, but the war continued for another several decades. It eventually ended with the Treaty of Westphalia in 1648, which recognized the independence of the Dutch Republic.

The war had a significant impact on the political and economic landscape of Europe. It marked the emergence of the Dutch Republic as a major naval and commercial power, and it weakened the power of the Spanish Empire.

The war also had a lasting impact on Dutch culture and national identity. It is estimated that the war resulted in about 100,000 casualties, including soldiers and civilians.

Accomplished something then... The Dutch Revolt, it was aclassic tale of rebellion, religious conflict, and...wait, what was accomplished again?

Once upon a time, in the 16th century, the Netherlands were a part of the Spanish Empire under the rule of King Philip II.

However, tensions began to rise as the Dutch people became increasingly unhappy with Spanish rule and their attempts to impose Catholicism upon them.

Led by William of Orange, a prince in the Dutch nobility, the Dutch revolted against Spanish rule and the conflict lasted for over 80 years. It is often cited as one of the longest and most expensive wars in European history.

So, what was accomplished with all of this fighting and bloodshed? Well, for one, the Dutch gained their independence from Spain and established the Dutch Republic in 1581.

This new state was a haven for religious toleration and economic prosperity, paving the way for the Dutch Golden Age in the 17th century.

But wait, there's more! It also had far-reaching consequences for the rest of Europe. It weakened Spain's hold on the continent and contributed to the rise of the Dutch as a dominant economic and military power.

It also played a significant role in the broader Protestant-Catholic conflict of the time, which had major political and social implications throughout Europe. So, all in all, the war accomplished quite a bit, right? Well, not so fast.

While the Dutch Republic did experience a period of relative stability and prosperity, it wasn't exactly a utopia. The country was still plagued by religious conflicts and economic disparities, and it remained embroiled in conflicts with other European powers for centuries to come. Moreover, the Dutch Revolt also had some unintended consequences.

For one, it helped to solidify the idea of nation-states in Europe, which would lead to countless wars and conflicts in the centuries to come.
It also had a profound impact on the global slave trade, as the Dutch became heavily involved in the trafficking of enslaved Africans to the New World.

So, was the Dutch Revolt a success or a failure? It's hard to say. On the one hand, it did result in the creation of an independent Dutch state and had far-reaching consequences for Europe and the world.

On the other hand, it also had some unintended and negative consequences that have had lasting impacts. But hey, at least we have tulips.

The Thirty Years' War

The Thirty Years' War was a religious and political conflict primarily fought in Central Europe. It was sparked by the tensions between Catholics and Protestants in the Holy Roman Empire, and it involved many of the major powers of Europe.

The war began in 1618 when Protestant Bohemian nobles rebelled against the Catholic Habsburg ruler, Ferdinand II, who had recently been elected Holy Roman Emperor. This rebellion escalated into a wider conflict involving several European powers, with both Catholics and Protestants joining the fight.

France, Sweden, and Denmark supported the Protestant side, while Spain and the Holy Roman Empire supported the Catholic side. The war was characterized by numerous battles, sieges, and campaigns, and it had a devastating impact on Central Europe.

Estimates of the total number of casualties range from 4.5 to 8 million, with civilian deaths outnumbering military deaths.

The war was finally ended by the Peace of Westphalia in 1648. The treaty recognized the sovereignty of individual states within the Holy Roman Empire and ended the religious wars between Catholics and Protestants.

Accomplished much after 30 years? The Thirty Years' War is a sassy story of religious strife, political intrigue, and massive bloodshed. But let's not focus on the negative, folks.

First off, there's the fact that the war helped to shape Europe into what it is today. Before the war, Europe was a chaotic mess of tiny, squabbling kingdoms. But thanks to the Thirty Years' War, the continent became a much more unified place.

Sure, it took a few more centuries and a lot more bloodshed to get there, but we wouldn't be where we are today without this war. Then there's the fact that the war gave us some cool art.

Seriously, have you seen some of the paintings and sculptures that came out of this period? They're amazing. It's like everyone was so filled with the spirit of war that they just had to express it through art.

And don't even get me started on the music. Bach, Handel, Vivaldi... these guys were all creating masterpieces while the world around them was going up in flames. Talk about dedication!

But perhaps the greatest accomplishment of the Thirty Years' War was the way it brought people together. Sure, they were brought together in fear and desperation, but still, they were brought together.

Communities were formed around the shared experience of war, and people from all walks of life found themselves working together to survive. It's like that old saying, "The enemy of my enemy is my friend." In this case, the enemy was war, and the people banded together to fight it.

And then there's the aftermath. After thirty years of war, Europe was finally able to breathe a sigh of relief and begin to rebuild.

Sure, a lot of people died and a lot of cities were destroyed, but think of all the opportunities that were created in the aftermath! New cities were built, new industries sprang up, and people started to see the world differently.

It was like a giant reset button had been pressed on Europe, and everyone was given a chance to start over. Of course, some might argue that the war didn't accomplish anything at all. That it was just a senseless, brutal conflict that left a trail of destruction in its wake. But come on guys, let's be positive here.

Without the Thirty Years' War, we wouldn't have all the amazing art and music that we have today. We wouldn't have the unified Europe that we have today. And most importantly, we wouldn't have the shared experience of war that brought people together and made them stronger.

So let's raise a glass to the Thirty Years' War, folks. Here's to all the great things that it accomplished, and here's to the amazing people who survived it.

May we never forget the lessons that we learned from this brutal, senseless conflict. And may we never forget the beauty that arose from its ashes.

The English Civil War

The English Civil War (1642–1651) was a series of armed conflicts fought between the Royalists (supporters of King Charles I) and the Parliamentarians (supporters of the English Parliament) in England. It was also known as the Great Rebellion.

The conflict began due to a variety of reasons, including disputes over taxes, religion, and the power of the monarchy. The King and Parliament were at odds over the issue of sovereignty, with the King insisting on absolute power and Parliament demanding a greater role in government.

The war was fought in three phases: the First Civil War (1642–1646), the Second Civil War (1648), and the Third Civil War (1649–1651).

The First Civil War began in 1642 when King Charles I raised an army to fight against Parliament. The Royalists initially had the upper hand, winning several early battles, but the Parliamentarians gradually gained ground and, with the help of the New Model Army, emerged victorious.

The Second Civil War began in 1648 when the Royalists, with the support of Scottish forces, attempted to stage a coup against the Parliamentarians. However, the coup was unsuccessful, and the Parliamentarians won a decisive victory.

The Third Civil War began in 1649 when the Scots, dissatisfied with the new republican government of England, invaded England in support of the exiled King Charles II. The Parliamentarians, led by Oliver Cromwell, defeated the Scots at the Battle of Worcester in 1651, effectively ending the war.

The English Civil War resulted in a total of approximately 190,000 deaths, with estimates ranging from 140,000 to 700,000.

It also led to the execution of King Charles I in 1649 and the establishment of the Commonwealth of England, a republican government that lasted until the Restoration of the monarchy in 1660.

Not sure what was accomplished here...
A true triumph of brotherly love and unity. I mean, what better way to resolve your differences than by grabbing some swords and muskets and just going to town on each other?

Yes, the English Civil War was a true masterpiece of conflict resolution. What was it all about, you may ask?

Well, it was a complex web of religious and political disagreements that had been brewing for years and finally came to a head when King Charles I decided he was tired of all this democracy nonsense and wanted to rule like an absolute monarch.

Naturally, the people were none too pleased with this idea, so they took up arms against the king and his royalist supporters. Thus began a decade of bloodshed and turmoil, as the royalists and parliamentarians battled it out for control of England.

But what did we accomplish with all this violence and death, you ask? Well, for starters, we got rid of that pesky King Charles I, who was eventually tried and executed for his crimes against the people. I mean, sure, some people may argue that killing a monarch sets a dangerous precedent and undermines the stability of the entire country, but hey, at least we got to say "off with his head!" which is pretty cool.

And who needs stability anyway? It's overrated. It's much more exciting to live in a state of constant chaos and uncertainty. Who knows what kind of fun surprises the day will bring?

Maybe you'll wake up and find your house has been burned down by a group of roving bandits, or maybe you'll stumble upon a secret stash of treasure buried in your garden. The possibilities are endless!
But I digress.

What else did we accomplish with the English Civil War? Well, we established the principle of parliamentary sovereignty, which means that the people get to decide who's in charge, rather than some fancy-pants monarch.

It's a pretty good idea, in theory. Of course, in practice it's mostly just a bunch of bloviating politicians shouting at each other and getting nothing done, but hey, at least we're not living under a dictatorship, right?

And speaking of politicians, we also got to enjoy a brief period of republican rule under Oliver Cromwell, who was a less fun version of King Charles I.

Cromwell was a deeply religious man who believed in the importance of moral purity and personal responsibility, which is all well and good, but also meant he was kind of a killjoy.

He banned things like gambling, theater, and Christmas (yes, Christmas), which is just downright un-English.

But at least we got to say we had a republic for a little while. It's like a badge of honor or something. And as for the aftermath of the war? Well, it was mostly just a lot of bickering and backstabbing among the various factions that had emerged during the conflict.

The monarchy was eventually restored with the coronation of King Charles II, who was a bit more chill than his dad but still had a tendency to get himself into trouble.

The parliamentarians were mostly sidelined, and the country settled into a new era of stability and relative peace.

But let's be honest, the real legacy of the English Civil War was not political reform or social progress or any of that nonsense. No, the real legacy was the rise of the pudding. Yes, that's right, the humble pudding.

You see, during the war, the soldiers on both sides were given a ration of flour, suet, and spices, which they would mix and boil in a cloth bag to create a hearty and delicious dessert known as a pudding. It truly was a time of great accomplishment. After all, what more useful way to prove your loyalty to the king than by killing your fellow Englishmen?

But despite the obvious benefits of the war, some people still question whether it was truly necessary. I mean, sure, it resulted in the execution of the king, the establishment of a republic, and the eventual restoration of the monarchy. But at what cost?

The death toll alone was staggering, with estimates ranging from 200,000 to 800,000 people. And that's not even counting the number of people who were injured or displaced.

But hey, who needs a functioning society when you have the satisfaction of knowing that you fought for your beliefs?

And let's not forget the economic impact of the war. With so many people dead or displaced, the country's workforce was greatly reduced. This, in turn, led to a decline in agricultural production and a subsequent rise in food prices.

But who needs food when you have the satisfaction of knowing that you fought for your beliefs?

But perhaps the greatest accomplishment of the English Civil War was the lasting impact it had on English politics. It set the stage for the development of modern democracy and established the precedent that the monarch was subject to the will of the people. Sure, it took a few more centuries for the full realization of these principles, but hey, who's counting?

In the end, the English Civil War was a truly remarkable event that accomplished so much. It showed the world what could be achieved when you put your mind to it, and it proved that sometimes, the only way to achieve your goals is through violence and bloodshed.

So let's all raise a glass to the English Civil War, and remember the sacrifice of all those who fought and died for their beliefs. After all, what're a few hundred thousand lives compared to the satisfaction of knowing that you fought for your beliefs?

THE FRANCO-DUTCH WAR

The Franco-Dutch War was a conflict between France and the Dutch Republic, with several other European powers involved at different times.

The war was sparked by the expansionist policies of French King Louis XIV and his desire to annex territories in the Spanish Netherlands.

In 1672, France launched a surprise invasion of the Dutch Republic, quickly capturing several major cities. The Dutch were able to regroup and, with the help of their allies, launched a counteroffensive. The war was fought mainly on Dutch soil and saw several major battles, including the Battle of Seneffe and the Siege of Maastricht.

The war ended in 1678 with the Treaty of Nijmegen, which restored the pre-war borders of the Dutch Republic and prevented further French expansion in the region. The war resulted in tens of thousands of casualties, including soldiers and civilians, and caused significant damage to the economy and infrastructure of the Dutch Republic.

The war also had wider implications for European politics and power dynamics, as it demonstrated the military might of France and the need for a balance of power in Europe.

It also highlighted the vulnerability of the Dutch Republic and sparked a period of reform and strengthening of their military and government structures.

Did this war accomplish something? Ah, The Franco-Dutch War. The war that everyone remembers as... wait, no one remembers The Franco-Dutch War. But that doesn't mean it wasn't important. I mean, sure, it only lasted from 1672 to 1678, but it was still a war, damn it!

So, what was accomplished in this war, you ask? Well, let me tell you. France accomplished absolutely nothing. And the Dutch... well, they managed to not get completely obliterated by the French, so that's something, I suppose.

The whole thing started because the French king, Louis XIV, decided he wanted to expand his borders a bit. You know, just stretch out and take a little stroll through the Netherlands, maybe pick up a few souvenirs along the way. And what better way to do that than by starting a war? So, Louis XIV sent his armies marching into the Netherlands, hoping to take it over and add it to his collection of cool French stuff.

But the Dutch weren't having it. They put up a good fight and managed to hold off the French for a while, which, let's face it, is more than most countries can say when the French come knocking.

But eventually, the French broke through the Dutch defenses and started taking over cities left and right. It looked like the Netherlands was doomed, but then something amazing happened: the Dutch flooded their own country. Yes, you read that right. They opened up their dams and flooded their land, effectively turning the Netherlands into a giant swamp.

And you know who hates swamps? The French. They hate them almost as much as they hate people who don't speak French. So, the French army was forced to retreat, because they just couldn't handle all that water. And that was pretty much the end of the war.

Sure, there were a few more battles, but nothing too exciting happened.

In the end, the French didn't gain any new territory, and the Dutch managed to hold on to their little corner of the world.

So, what was accomplished in The Franco-Dutch War? Well, France was reminded that swamps are not their friend, and the Dutch learned that flooding your own country can be a pretty effective defense strategy.
As for the aftermath, well, I'm not sure there was one. It's not like the war led to any major changes or had a lasting impact on history.

It was just a blip on the radar, a footnote in the history books. But hey, at least we can say it happened, right?

The Great Northern War

The Great Northern War was a conflict fought between Sweden and a coalition of several European powers, including Russia, Denmark-Norway, and Saxony-Poland-Lithuania, from 1700 to 1721.

The war started as a result of Swedish King Charles XII's intervention in the Great Northern War against Russia, Denmark, and Saxony-Poland-Lithuania.

The initial phase of the war saw the Swedish army gain significant victories in Northern Europe, including the Battle of Narva in 1700. However, after Charles XII invaded Russia in 1708, the tide began to turn against Sweden, and they suffered a series of crushing defeats.

The war ended with the Treaty of Nystad in 1721, which saw Sweden cede significant territory, including Finland, Estonia, Livonia, and Ingria, to Russia. Denmark-Norway and Saxony-Poland-Lithuania also gained territory as a result of the war.

The Great Northern War was a brutal conflict that caused significant casualties on both sides, with estimates ranging from 150,000 to 300,000 dead.

The war also had significant political and economic consequences, as it led to the decline of Sweden as a major European power and the rise of Russia as a dominant force in the region.

More stuff accomplished? The Great Northern War is a good example of how to make a bad situation worse. The war between Sweden and the coalition of Russia, Denmark-Norway, and Saxony-Poland-Lithuania was a wild ride!

But accomplish...? First of all, Sweden, under the brilliant leadership of Charles XII, had managed to become a superpower in the 17th century, dominating much of Northern Europe. But then, like any good superpower, they decided to pick a fight with everyone. Charles XII's decision to invade Russia in 1700 was perhaps not the wisest move, considering that Russia was, at the time, a vast and largely unconquered landmass with a seemingly endless supply of soldiers.

Charles XII was not to be deterred. He marched his troops eastward, defeating the Russians at the Battle of Narva in 1700. The victory was sweet, but it was short-lived. The Russians regrouped and, in 1709, decisively defeated Charles XII's army at the Battle of Poltava. Charles XII fled to Ottoman Empire and stayed there for years, hoping for support and planning for his comeback.

Meanwhile, the war continued. Denmark-Norway decided to join in the fun, invading Sweden in 1709. The Danes were eventually driven back, but not before they had managed to capture several Swedish territories, including the province of Scania. And while all of this was going on, Poland-Lithuania, which had previously been a staunch ally of Sweden, decided to switch sides and join the coalition. By 1718, Sweden was in shambles. Charles XII had returned from the Ottoman Empire, but he was unable to recapture his former glory.

The country was bankrupt, its economy in ruins, and its people exhausted from years of war. And what had been accomplished? Well, not much Sweden had lost its status as a superpower. It had lost territory to Denmark-Norway, Russia, and Poland-Lithuania. And it had lost thousands upon thousands of soldiers in a war that had no clear objective.

But hey, at least Sweden managed to inspire some great works of literature. The Finnish author Johan Ludvig Runeberg wrote an epic poem about the war called The Tales of Ensign Stål. The poem has been praised for its portrayal of the common soldier and the hardships he endured during the war. So, there's that. In the end, The Great Northern War was a lesson in overreach and hubris.

Sweden's attempt to dominate Northern Europe had backfired spectacularly, leaving the country weaker and more vulnerable than ever before. But hey, at least they got a cool poem out of it ...

THE AMERICAN REVOLUTIONARY WAR

The American Revolutionary War was a conflict that took place between 1775 and 1783. It was fought between Great Britain and the thirteen British colonies in North America, which sought to establish an independent nation, the United States of America.

The war began on April 19, 1775, with the Battles of Lexington and Concord, which marked the first military engagements of the conflict.

The colonies formed the Continental Army and appointed George Washington as its commander-in-chief. The British sent troops and ships to fight in America, including Hessian mercenaries from Germany.

The war was marked by several significant battles, including the Battle of Bunker Hill, the Battle of Saratoga, and the Battle of Yorktown.

The Americans received support from France, which declared war on Great Britain in 1778 and sent troops, ships, and supplies to aid the American cause.

The war officially ended on September 3, 1783, with the signing of the Treaty of Paris, in which Great Britain recognized the independence of the United States. It resulted in the establishment of the United States as an independent nation and marked the beginning of the end of European colonialism in the Americas.

Casualties in the war are estimated to be around 25,000, including both military personnel and civilians.

The war had a significant impact on world history, as it led to the formation of the United States, which would go on to become a major world power.

Let's take a closer look at what was accomplished during this war and its aftermath. First of all, the war itself. The American colonies, tired of being taxed and controlled by the British government, decided to rebel and form their own country.

They fought long and hard, with the help of the French, and eventually won their independence. So, what did they accomplish? Well, they formed a new country, the United States of America, which is pretty impressive. They also set a precedent for other colonies around the world to rebel against their ruling powers, so that's something.

But let's be real here. The American Revolutionary War was just a bunch of rich white guys fighting for their self-interest. They didn't care about the common people or the slaves that were still being held captive in their new "free" country.

And let's not forget that they also committed acts of violence and destruction during the war. And then there's the aftermath. The United States was formed, but at what cost?

The country was built on the genocide and forced removal of Indigenous people from their land. Slavery continued to thrive for decades, with black people being treated as property rather than human beings.

Women were still considered second-class citizens and had very few rights. So, what was accomplished? A country was formed, but it was built on a foundation of oppression and inequality.

And let's not forget the fact that the new government was still controlled by wealthy white men who didn't necessarily have the best interests of the common people in mind.

But hey, at least they got their independence …

THE FRENCH REVOLUTIONARY WAR

The French Revolutionary Wars were a series of conflicts fought between the French Republic and various European powers from 1792 to 1802.

The wars began as a result of the French Revolution and the overthrow of the Bourbon monarchy, which led to a series of political and social upheavals in France.

The major powers involved in the wars included France, Britain, Austria, Prussia, and Russia, as well as smaller powers such as Spain, Portugal, and the Ottoman Empire. The wars were fought across much of Europe, including France, Italy, Germany, Belgium, and the Netherlands.

The French Revolutionary Wars can be divided into several phases. The first phase, from 1792 to 1797, saw France fighting against a coalition of European powers, including Austria, Prussia, and Britain.

The French army was able to achieve some early victories, but suffered setbacks as well, including the loss of Belgium and the Rhineland.

The second phase, from 1798 to 1801, saw France fighting against Britain in the Mediterranean and Egypt. The French were initially successful in Egypt but were eventually defeated by a British-led coalition.

The final phase, from 1801 to 1802, saw France fighting against a new coalition of European powers, including Britain, Austria, and Russia. The French were able to achieve some victories but were ultimately forced to sue for peace.

The wars ended with the Treaty of Amiens in 1802, which recognized France's territorial gains but also imposed restrictions on French expansion. The casualties of the wars were significant, with estimates ranging from 1 million to 1.5 million military and civilian deaths.

Accompli?

Oui, the French Revolutionary Wars! A time when France was undergoing some serious changes and decided it was a good idea to go to war with everyone around them. First off, the French Revolution. They managed to overthrow their monarchy and establish a republic, which was great for everyone except the monarchy.

But then they decided to go to war with Austria and Prussia, and things got a little out of hand. You see, France had this idea that they were going to spread their revolution and ideals of liberty, equality, and fraternity to the rest of Europe.

So they went to war with everyone who disagreed with them. And by everyone, I mean everyone. England, Spain, Portugal, Russia, the Ottoman Empire, and pretty much every other major power in Europe.

But did they accomplish their goal of spreading their revolution? Well, not exactly. They did manage to conquer some territories and establish puppet states, but most of Europe was pretty resistant to the idea of a French Revolution, thank you very much.

And then there was the Reign of Terror, where the French government started executing people left and right for even the slightest hint of dissent. So yeah, not exactly the best PR move for a nation trying to spread the idea of liberty and equality.

But wait, there's more! The French also managed to alienate their people, with conscription and taxation becoming increasingly oppressive. And then there was the disastrous invasion of Russia, where they lost a huge chunk of their army to the Russian winter.

So what was accomplished in the end? Well, France did manage to establish a republic, but it was a republic that was constantly at war and facing internal turmoil. And while they did gain some territory, it was all lost eventually. The French Revolutionary Wars was pretty much a big, expensive mess that left France in debt and disarray.

But hey, at least they got some cool songs out of it, right? "La Marseillaise" is a catchy tune, even if it's about chopping off heads.

The Haitian Revolution

The Haitian Revolution was a significant event in the history of Haiti and the world, marking the first and only successful slave revolution in modern history.

The revolution spanned from 1791 to 1804 and resulted in the establishment of Haiti as an independent nation. The revolution began in August 1791 when a group of slaves, led by Toussaint L'Ouverture and other revolutionary leaders, rebelled against their French colonial masters.

The slaves were inspired by the ideals of the French Revolution, which emphasized liberty, equality, and fraternity, and they sought to end the oppressive system of slavery in Haiti.

The revolution was characterized by intense fighting between the slaves and the French army, which was sent to Haiti to put down the rebellion.

The revolution was marked by significant events such as the Haitian Declaration of Independence in 1804, which established Haiti as the first independent nation in Latin America and the Caribbean. The revolution involved a broad range of actors, including slaves, free people of color, French colonizers, British and Spanish troops, and others.

The revolution resulted in significant casualties, including the deaths of tens of thousands of people, including many civilians. It had a significant impact on the history of slavery and colonialism, inspiring other anti-colonial and anti-slavery movements around the world.

Mission accomplished! First off, we have to give credit where credit is due. The Haitian Revolution was truly a remarkable achievement. The slaves of Saint-Domingue (now Haiti) managed to overthrow their French colonial masters and establish an independent nation.

This was no small feat, and it's understandable why people would see this as a turning point in history. But let's not get carried away with all the talk of "revolution" and "independence." The reality is that the aftermath of the Haitian Revolution was less than ideal. Sure, Haiti was now an independent nation, but at what cost?

The country was left devastated by the war, with its infrastructure in ruins and its economy in shambles. And while the former slaves may have gained their freedom, they certainly didn't gain any real power.

Let's take a closer look at what happened after the revolution. Haiti was left with a power vacuum, and it didn't take long for various factions to start fighting for control.

The leaders of the revolution were mostly military figures who had little experience with governance or diplomacy.
This led to infighting and instability that plagued the country for years to come.

And let's not forget about the international response to the Haitian Revolution. The French were not too thrilled about losing one of their most valuable colonies, and they weren't going to let Haiti get away without paying a hefty price.

In 1825, the French government demanded that Haiti pay 150 million francs in reparations – an amount that would take the country over a century to pay off. This effectively destroyed Haiti's economy and left the country in a state of perpetual poverty.

But it's not just the French that were to blame. The rest of the international community didn't exactly come rushing to Haiti's aid after the revolution.

Most countries refused to recognize Haiti as a legitimate nation for fear of upsetting the balance of power in the Caribbean. This left Haiti isolated and vulnerable, with few allies to turn to.

So what did the Haitian Revolution accomplish? Well, the slaves of Saint-Domingue did manage to gain their freedom, and that's certainly something to be celebrated.

But in terms of long-term impact, the revolution did little to address the systemic issues that led to slavery and colonialism in the first place.

Haiti was left with a weak government, a destroyed economy, and a legacy of oppression that it still struggles with to this day.

The revolution may have accomplished the goal of independence, but it failed to create a stable and prosperous nation for the Haitian people. Perhaps we can learn from this and strive to create more equitable and sustainable solutions to oppression and injustice in the future.

Or maybe we'll just keep making the same mistakes over and over again. Who knows?

THE GREEK WAR OF INDEPENDENCE

The Greek War of Independence was a conflict fought by the Greeks between 1821 and 1832 against the Ottoman Empire, which had ruled Greece for centuries.

The war began in 1821 when several Greek revolutionary societies launched an uprising against the Ottoman Empire. The Greeks had been under the Ottoman rule for nearly four centuries, and their nationalistic fervor had been growing for years.

The Ottoman Empire was weakened by internal strife, which the Greeks exploited to gain a foothold in the struggle for independence. The war was fought both on land and at sea, with several battles taking place across Greece and its surrounding waters.

The war involved the Greek rebels, who were supported by other European powers, such as Russia, France, and Britain, against the Ottoman Empire.

The European powers supported the Greeks because of their strategic interests and because they saw the Ottoman Empire as a declining power. The Ottoman Empire was supported by Egypt, and later by the British and French, who intervened on its side.

The war was marked by atrocities committed by both sides, with massacres of Greek civilians by Ottoman forces and Ottoman civilians by Greek rebels.

The war ended in 1832 with the signing of the Treaty of Constantinople, which recognized Greece as an independent nation.

The casualties of the war are estimated to be around 30,000 Greeks and 15,000 Ottomans, although the exact numbers are difficult to determine.

Big, Fat Greek Accomplishment? A classic tale of rebellion, heroism, and... well, I'm sure there were other things too. First of all, let's talk about what the Greeks were trying to accomplish.

They were fighting for independence from the Ottoman Empire, which had ruled Greece for over 400 years. The Greeks wanted to establish their independent state, free from Turkish oppression.
And you know what? They succeeded! They managed to gain their independence and establish the modern Greek state.

So, what did they accomplish with all that freedom?
Well, they started by appointing a 17-year-old Bavarian prince, Otto von Wittelsbach, as their first king.

Because when you think "Greek independence," you naturally think "Bavarian monarchy." And hey, maybe it worked out okay for them. After all, Greece did manage to modernize and join the ranks of other European nations in the following years.

But let's not forget the other things that happened. For one thing, the new Greek state was broke. Like, broke. So broke that they had to take out a loan from Britain just to pay for Otto's coronation. And then they had to take out more loans to pay for a bunch of other stuff, like building roads and schools and hospitals.

They also had to pay off the Ottoman Empire for their freedom, which was a bit awkward. "Hey guys, we don't want to be part of your empire anymore... but can we still pay you some money?"

But that's not all! Greece also had to deal with a bunch of internal conflicts. You see, not all Greeks were on board with the idea of independence. Some were perfectly happy being part of the Ottoman Empire. Others wanted to establish a republic instead of a monarchy. And still, others had their ideas about what the new Greek state should look like.

So, there were a lot of disagreements and power struggles in the early years of the new Greek state. And then there was the matter of the Greek borders. You see, the Ottoman Empire controlled a lot more territory than just Greece.

When the Greeks declared independence, they only got a small portion of that territory. So, naturally, they wanted more.

They went to war with the Ottomans several more times in the following decades, trying to expand their borders and gain more territory. And hey, they did manage to gain some more land, but at what cost? More debt, more internal conflicts, and more problems.

Oh, and let's not forget about the fact that Greece had a lot of other problems too. Like corruption. And poverty. And illiteracy. And disease. And let's not even get started on the whole thing with the Ottoman Empire and their internal conflicts. It was a mess, folks.

Well, the Greeks did gain their independence. And even though they managed to modernize and establish themselves as a sovereign state, they still had a lot of issues to deal with.

But hey, at least they had moussaka, right?

The Taiping Rebellion

The Taiping Rebellion was a massive civil war in China that took place from 1850 to 1864.

It was led by Hong Xiuquan, who believed he was the younger brother of Jesus Christ and sought to establish a "Heavenly Kingdom of Great Peace" that would be ruled by him and his followers.

The rebellion began in the southern province of Guangxi in 1850 when a group of rebels led by Hong Xiuquan seized the city of Jintian. They soon captured several other cities and gained support from disaffected peasants and others who were unhappy with the corrupt and ineffective rule of the Qing dynasty.

The Taiping rebels soon controlled a large part of southern China, and the rebellion grew in size and strength over the next several years. The Qing government mounted a series of military campaigns to try to crush the rebellion, but these were largely unsuccessful.
At its peak, the Taiping Rebellion controlled a vast territory that included parts of modern-day Anhui, Hubei, Jiangsu, and Jiangxi provinces.

The rebellion was marked by a series of brutal battles and atrocities on both sides, and it is estimated that millions of people died as a result of the conflict, including many civilians.

The rebellion finally came to an end in 1864 when Qing forces, with the assistance of foreign powers such as Great Britain and France, recaptured the Taiping capital at Nanjing.

Hong Xiuquan died shortly thereafter, and his followers gradually surrendered or were killed over the following years.

The Taiping Rebellion was one of the bloodiest conflicts in world history, with estimates of the number of the dead ranging from 20 million to 70 million people.

The rebellion had a profound impact on China, leading to changes in politics, society, and culture, and it is considered a turning point in Chinese history.

So, much accomplished? A time when the people of China rose against their rulers and fought for their freedom... Or at least, that's what some people might like you to believe. But as always, there's more to the story.

Let's start with the basics. The rebellion was a civil war in led by a man who believed he was the younger brother of Jesus Christ. Fast forward a few years: Up to 70 million people dead. 70 MILLION.

Yes, you heard that right. According to Hong Xiuquan, he had received a vision from God telling him that he was the savior of China and that he needed to overthrow the Qing dynasty, which had been in power since 1644.

And so, with this divine mandate, Hong Xiuquan and his followers, known as the Taiping Heavenly Kingdom, set out to conquer China.

They were joined by disaffected peasants, workers, and soldiers who were fed up with the Qing dynasty's corrupt and oppressive rule. The Taiping army was successful at first, taking over large parts of southern China and even marching on Beijing.

But as with any rebellion, the situation quickly devolved into chaos. The Taiping leaders were inexperienced and unable to govern effectively, leading to infighting and power struggles.

Hong Xiuquan became increasingly paranoid and delusional, executing anyone who he perceived as a threat to his authority. And let's not forget about the massive loss of life—estimates vary, but it's believed that up towards 70 million people died during the rebellion.

So, what did the Taiping Rebellion accomplish? Well, it did succeed in destabilizing China and weakening the Qing dynasty.

But at what cost? The country was plunged into a period of turmoil and suffering, with millions of people losing their lives. And in the end, the rebellion was ultimately defeated, with the Qing dynasty remaining in power until the early 20th century.

But hey, at least we got some great stories out of it, right? Like the time Hong Xiuquan claimed to have ascended to heaven and tried to appoint a new God to take his place on earth. Or the time the Taiping army tried to invade Shanghai, only to be repelled by a bunch of foreign mercenaries armed with guns and cannons. Good times, good times.

In all seriousness though, the Taiping Rebellion was a tragic and brutal conflict that left a deep scar on China's history.

It's important to remember the suffering that took place during this time and to strive for a better future where such violence and chaos can be avoided.

And who knows, maybe one day we'll even learn to recognize when someone claims to be the younger brother of Jesus and maybe take a step back before things get out of hand.

The Indian Rebellion

The Indian Rebellion of 1857, also known as the Sepoy Mutiny, was an uprising against British rule in India that lasted from May 1857 to June 1858.

It began as a mutiny of sepoys, Indian soldiers who served in the British East India Company's army, but quickly spread to other parts of India, involving peasants, landowners, and members of the ruling classes.

The rebellion began in the town of Meerut on May 10, 1857, when a group of sepoys refused to use cartridges that were rumored to be greased with pig and cow fat, which was offensive to both Hindus and Muslims.

The sepoys were arrested, but their comrades freed them and went on a rampage, attacking British officers and civilians. The rebellion quickly spread to other parts of India, with mutinies occurring in cities like Delhi, Kanpur, Lucknow, and Jhansi.

The rebels managed to take control of some areas of India, but their lack of unity, resources, and leadership meant that they were ultimately defeated by the British. The rebellion officially ended on June 20, 1858, when the last rebel stronghold, the Fort of Gwalior, fell to the British.

The British responded with brutal force, executing thousands of rebels and civilians and destroying entire villages. Estimates of the number of casualties vary widely, but it is believed that tens of thousands of people died during the rebellion.

Empirical accomplishment? The British Empire had it all—land, resources, and a vast array of subjugated peoples to exploit for their gain. What could go wrong? Well, everything.

The Indian soldiers, or "sepoys," were outraged by a new rifle that required them to bite off the end of a cartridge that was rumored to be greased with pig and cow fat, which was deeply offensive to their religious beliefs. And so, the sepoys rebelled, and chaos ensued. But what did the rebellion accomplish? Let's take a closer look.

First of all, the rebellion did manage to shake things up a bit. It caused widespread unrest and panic among the British, who were unprepared for such a massive uprising.

It also forced the British government to take a closer look at its policies in India, which ultimately led to the end of the British East India Company's rule over India.

But did the Indian Rebellion of 1857 achieve anything substantial? Well, let's examine the aftermath. After the rebellion was put down, the British government established direct control over India and abolished the British East India Company. They also enacted a series of reforms aimed at improving the lives of the Indian people.

But let's be real—these "reforms" were nothing more than a superficial attempt to maintain control over India while pacifying the population. They did nothing to address the root causes of the rebellion, such as widespread poverty and inequality, and instead focused on cosmetic changes that did little to improve the lives of the Indian people.

The aftermath of the Indian Rebellion was marked by a brutal crackdown by the British, who sought to make an example out of anyone who dared to challenge their authority. Thousands of Indians were executed or imprisoned, and entire villages were burned to the ground.

But hey, at least the British got to maintain their iron grip on India, right? And isn't that what matters? In the end, the Indian Rebellion of 1857 accomplished very little beyond causing a brief moment of panic and unrest for the British Empire.

The root causes of the rebellion were never addressed, and the Indian people continued to suffer under British rule for decades to come.

But at least it achieved a chapter in this book …

The Spanish-American War

The Spanish-American War was a conflict between the United States and Spain in 1898. It began when Cuban nationalists, who were fighting for independence from Spain, attacked American interests in Cuba, prompting the United States to intervene in the conflict.

The United States, with the support of other nations, declared war on Spain in April 1898.

The war was fought in Cuba, Puerto Rico, and the Philippines, and saw the United States defeat the Spanish navy in several key battles, including the Battle of Manila Bay and the Battle of Santiago de Cuba.

The war ended with the signing of the Treaty of Paris on December 10, 1898.

Under the terms of the treaty, Spain ceded its colonies of Puerto Rico, Guam, and the Philippines to the United States, and also recognized the independence of Cuba. The United States paid Spain $20 million for the Philippines.

Casualties for the war were relatively low, with around 2,500 American deaths and 2,000 Spanish deaths.

The result of the war was a significant expansion of American influence and territory and marked the emergence of the United States as a major world power.

Accomplished much more? Ah, the Spanish-American War, a classic tale of two nations fighting for control of territories they had no business meddling in.

It's like that time in grade school when Billy and Johnny fought over who got to sit at the cool kids' table during lunchtime.

So, what was accomplished in this war? Well, let's see…the United States took control of Puerto Rico, Guam, and the Philippines, effectively becoming an imperial power. Spain was forced to relinquish its hold on Cuba and Guam. And, uh, that's about it. But don't worry, the aftermath was just as productive.

The U.S. had a new status as a global power, with its shiny new territories to show off to the rest of the world. And what did they do with these territories, you ask? Well, they exploited them, of course!

In the Philippines, the U.S. promised to help the locals gain independence from Spain, only to turn around and refuse to grant them their independence once they had control. Instead, they set up a colonial government and proceeded to exploit the resources of the islands. But hey, at least they got some sweet pineapples out of the deal, right?

Puerto Rico fared only slightly better. The U.S. granted the territory U.S. citizenship in 1917, but then promptly proceeded to treat it like a second-class citizen. Puerto Ricans were subject to discriminatory policies, including forced sterilization and experimentation without their consent. But hey, at least they got to vote in the presidential primaries now, right?

And what about Cuba? Well, the U.S. technically granted Cuba independence in 1902, but then proceeded to insert itself into Cuban affairs whenever it felt like it.

The U.S. had the right to intervene in Cuban affairs whenever it deemed it necessary, effectively keeping Cuba under its thumb. But hey, at least they got some great cigars out of the deal, right?

So, in summary, the Spanish-American War accomplished very little, except for setting the stage for the U.S. to become a colonial power and exploit the territories it gained. But hey, at least they got some sweet pineapples, cigars, and a sense of superiority out of the deal.

 It was also so forgettable that the war was mentioned twice in this encyclopedia and nobody noticed. Some achievement!

THE PHILIPPINE-AMERICAN WAR

The Philippine-American War was a conflict that lasted from 1899 to 1902 between the United States and the Philippines, which were at the time a colony of Spain.

The war began after the Treaty of Paris in 1898, which ended the Spanish-American War and gave the Philippines to the United States.

The Philippine Republic, which had declared its independence from Spain, refused to recognize US control of the islands.

The conflict started with a surprise attack by Filipino forces on US soldiers in February 1899 and quickly escalated into a full-scale war.

The Filipino forces, led by Emilio Aguinaldo, employed guerrilla tactics against the better-equipped US army, and the fighting was often brutal.

The war officially ended on July 4, 1902, when Aguinaldo surrendered to US forces, though sporadic fighting continued for several years.

The exact number of casualties is not known, but estimates suggest that between 200,000 and 1,000,000 Filipino civilians died as a result of the war, along with around 4,200 US soldiers.

So many died, and all it accomplished was...? One of those classic examples of imperialist powers trying to spread their influence around the world.

And, as with any good imperialist adventure, it ended in a massive clusterfuck that left a trail of destruction and misery in its wake.

So, let's dig into the absurdity and hilarity that was the aftermath of the Philippine-American War.

It all started when the United States, fresh off its victory against Spain in the Spanish-American War, decided to flex its imperialist muscles by annexing the Philippines.

The Filipino people, who had been fighting for their independence, were less than thrilled with this idea. But the U.S. was determined to show the world that it could play the empire game with the best of them, so it sent in troops to quell the rebellion.

The war dragged on for three long years, with both sides committing atrocities and war crimes that would make even the most hardened soldier cringe.

The U.S. military, in its infinite wisdom, decided to employ brutal tactics such as "waterboarding" and "the water cure" to extract information from Filipino prisoners.

They also employed "scorched earth" tactics, which involved burning down entire villages and leaving the population to starve.

But, hey, who cares about war crimes when you're trying to spread democracy, right? Eventually, the U.S. prevailed, and the Philippines became an American colony.

And what did they do with this newfound territory, you ask? Well, they did what any good colonial power would do: exploit the crap out of it.

Under American rule, the Philippines saw its economy boom. Well, sort of. The U.S. made sure that all the profits went to American businessmen, while the Filipino people remained poor and oppressed.

The U.S. also set up a puppet government, run by Filipinos who were more than happy to do their American overlords' bidding.
But even with all this exploitation, the U.S. wasn't satisfied. They wanted to "civilize" the Filipinos, to turn them into good, upstanding Americans.

So, they decided to spread American culture to the Philippines. And what better way to do that than with...the YMCA?

Yes, you read that right. The U.S. government thought that the YMCA would be the perfect tool for spreading American values to the Philippines.

So, they set up YMCA branches all over the country, complete with basketball courts and English classes. Because nothing says "democracy" like a game of hoops and a language lesson.

But even with all this "progress," the Filipinos still weren't happy. They wanted their independence, damn it! And they weren't going to stop fighting until they got it.

The U.S. government, realizing that it couldn't keep up the charade of being a champion of democracy while simultaneously occupying a foreign country, eventually gave in and granted the Philippines its independence in 1946.

But hey, at least the U.S. got to show the world that it was a big, bad imperialist power. Just to make sure we did not forget …

The Italo-Turkish War

The Italo-Turkish War was a conflict fought between Italy and the Ottoman Empire from September 29, 1911, to October 18, 1912, over control of the Ottoman provinces of Tripolitania and Cyrenaica (now modern-day Libya).

The war began when Italy, seeking to expand its colonial holdings in Africa, demanded concessions from the Ottoman Empire, which refused.

Italy then declared war and launched a naval and amphibious assault on Ottoman-held territory in North Africa.

The war involved mainly Italy and the Ottoman Empire, although Germany and Austria-Hungary supported the Ottomans diplomatically.

Italy was led by King Victor Emmanuel III and Prime Minister Giovanni Giolitti, while the Ottoman Empire was led by Sultan Mehmed V and Grand Vizier Mahmud Shevket Pasha.

The war ended with an Italian victory and the establishment of Italian colonial control over Libya.

The Ottomans suffered heavy casualties, with estimates ranging from 20,000 to 30,000 dead, while Italian casualties were around 1,500 dead.

The Italo-Turkish War had significant implications for the Balkan region and the broader geopolitical landscape of Europe.

The Ottoman Empire's loss of Libya weakened its grip on North Africa and signaled the empire's decline as a major world power. Italy's victory gave it a foothold in Africa and contributed to its emergence as a major European power.

The war also contributed to tensions between Italy and other European powers, particularly Germany and Austria-Hungary, which felt that Italy had overstepped its bounds in the region.

Il compimento? The Italo-Turkish War. What a glorious achievement in the annals of human history. It all started when Italy got a case of the munchies and decided it wanted a slice of the Ottoman Empire's pizza. Who wouldn't want a slice of that delicious Ottoman pie?

The Ottomans were a bit taken aback by Italy's sudden appetite for conquest, but they figured they could take care of business and get back to their regularly scheduled program of suppressing the rights of their citizens. So they put on their best fez hats and marched out to meet the Italian army.

Now, the Italians weren't exactly known for their military prowess at the time. They were more known for their pasta and their snazzy suits. But they had a secret weapon up their sleeves: the power of spaghetti.

Yes, you heard that right. The Italians fueled their soldiers with pasta, and soon they were charging toward the Ottomans like a bunch of well-fed maniacs.

The Ottomans were taken aback by this unexpected strategy and soon found themselves retreating in the face of a barrage of meatballs and marinara. It was a true sight to behold.

But the war wasn't all fun and games. It was downright brutal at times. The Ottomans put up fierce resistance, and there were many casualties on both sides. The Italians even resorted to using chemical weapons, which was pretty messed up. But hey, you can't make an omelet without... Nah, forget it...

Eventually, the Italians emerged victorious. They had conquered Libya, which was a pretty big deal at the time. But what did they accomplish? Well, they got some nice real estate, but they also inherited a bunch of problems.

For one thing, the Libyans weren't exactly thrilled about being under Italian rule. They weren't exactly thrilled about being under Ottoman rule either, but that's another story.

The Italians had to deal with a lot of resistance and rebellion, which wasn't exactly what they had in mind when they went on their little adventure.

And then there was the whole issue of what to do with all those leftover meatballs. They had a surplus of pasta and meat, and not enough soldiers to feed it to. So they started exporting it to other countries, which was a pretty smart move.

Soon, everyone wanted a taste of Italian cuisine. But let's be real here: the real winner of the Italo-Turkish War was the pasta industry. Thanks to the Italians' ingenious use of spaghetti, they were able to conquer a whole country. And that, my friends, is the power of carbs.

In conclusion, the Italo-Turkish War was a masterstroke of military strategy and culinary genius.

The Italians conquered a country and fed their soldiers at the same time. Who says war can't be delicious?

THE BALKAN WARS

The Balkan Wars were two separate but related conflicts in southeastern Europe that took place in 1912 and 1913.

The First Balkan War (1912) was fought between the Ottoman Empire and an alliance of Balkan states consisting of Serbia, Greece, Bulgaria, and Montenegro.

The war began in October 1912, when the members of the Balkan League declared war on the Ottoman Empire.

The Balkan League defeated the Ottoman Empire, and by the end of the war, the Ottoman Empire lost most of its territory in Europe, including almost all of its Balkan possessions.

The Second Balkan War (1913) was fought between Bulgaria and its former allies Serbia and Greece, as well as Romania and the Ottoman Empire. The war began in June 1913, when Bulgaria attacked Serbia and Greece, hoping to gain territory that it believed it had been promised by its former allies.

The war was short but bloody, and by the end of July 1913, the Balkan League had defeated Bulgaria and forced it to sign the Treaty of Bucharest, which imposed heavy territorial losses on Bulgaria.

What exactly did it accomplish?
The Balkans, a region located in southeastern Europe, was a hotbed of ethnic tensions and political turmoil.

The Ottoman Empire, which had controlled the region for centuries, was in decline, and various countries were vying for power and influence in the region.

This led to the First Balkan War in 1912, which pitted Serbia, Bulgaria, Greece, and Montenegro against the Ottoman Empire.

And then, just to keep things interesting, there was the Second Balkan War in 1913, which was fought between the same Balkan countries that had been allies just a year earlier.

So, what was accomplished with all this bloodshed and turmoil? The Ottoman Empire lost control of most of its territories in the Balkans, paving the way for the creation of newly independent states.

Serbia emerged as the dominant power in the Balkans, much to the chagrin of other countries like Bulgaria. Bulgaria, which had hoped to gain more territory in the region, was left disappointed and bitter. Greece and Montenegro also gained territory, but to a lesser extent than Serbia.

The new borders were drawn up after the wars left a lot of ethnic minorities living in countries where they were not the majority, setting the stage for future conflicts.

So, in other words, the Balkan Wars were a smashing success if you define success as creating new countries and redrawing borders. But if you define success as creating lasting peace and stability in the region, well... let's just say there's still work to be done.

One of the main problems in the aftermath of the Balkan Wars was the treatment of ethnic minorities. The new borders created by the wars left many people living in countries where they were not the majority, leading to tensions and violence.

For example, Bulgaria was forced to cede territory to Serbia, which left a large number of ethnic Bulgarians living under Serbian rule. This led to discrimination and violence against Bulgarians in Serbia, and vice versa. And let's not forget about the Albanians, who found themselves divided among several countries and subjected to discrimination and violence as well.

So, in addition to creating new countries and borders, the Balkan Wars also created a legacy of ethnic tensions and conflict that persists to this day. Nice work, everyone.

Another problem with the aftermath of the Balkan Wars was the way it set the stage for World War I. The wars had weakened the Ottoman Empire, which was already in decline and left the Balkans in a state of flux.

This made it easier for other countries, like Austria-Hungary, to assert their influence in the region.

And when the assassination of Archduke Franz Ferdinand in Sarajevo in 1914 sparked the outbreak of World War I, the Balkans were right in the middle of it.

So, in conclusion, the Balkan Wars accomplished a lot of things, but most of them were not particularly great.

We created new countries but also left ethnic tensions simmering beneath the surface. We weakened the Ottoman Empire but also set the stage for a much larger conflict.

And we showed the world that, when it comes to starting wars, the Balkans are pretty darn good at it. I went there for a Holliday with my aunt in 2017 and it still felt like a war zone!

The Irish War of Independence

The Irish War of Independence was a guerrilla conflict that took place in Ireland from 1919 to 1921, during which Irish Republicans sought to end British rule and establish an independent Irish republic.

The war started with a series of attacks by the Irish Republican Army (IRA) on British forces and infrastructure in Ireland.

The IRA was a paramilitary organization formed in 1919, which sought to use military means to achieve Irish independence. The British government responded with a policy of repression, including martial law, curfews, and reprisals against civilians.

The conflict involved various groups and individuals, including the IRA, British forces, and the Royal Irish Constabulary (RIC), as well as other Irish political parties and organizations.

The war ended in a truce in July 1921, and negotiations between Irish and British leaders led to the signing of the Anglo-Irish Treaty in December of that year. The treaty established the Irish Free State as a self-governing dominion within the British Empire, with its government and parliament.

However, the treaty was controversial, as it fell short of the republican aspirations of many Irish nationalists and led to a split in the nationalist movement. The treaty also led to the outbreak of a civil war in Ireland from 1922 to 1923, which ended in victory for the pro-treaty forces.

The casualties of the Irish War of Independence are estimated to have been around 2,000 people, including both military personnel and civilians.

An actual accomplishment! The Irish War of Independence is a true classic in the genre of political drama. It had everything: rebels, British soldiers, spies, secret negotiations, and of course, a healthy dose of violence.

The fighting was brutal, with both sides committing atrocities, but eventually, the Republicans gained the upper hand. The British government finally came to the negotiating table, and the result was the Anglo-Irish Treaty.

So, what did the Republicans get out of this treaty? Well, they got an Irish Free State, which was technically still part of the British Empire but had a fair amount of autonomy. They also got a promise of a future Republic, although that didn't happen until decades later. But most importantly, they got to stop fighting and go home.

And what did the British get? Well, they got to keep Northern Ireland, which was a pretty big deal for them. They also got to save face by avoiding an embarrassing military defeat. And best of all, they got to keep their reputation for being completely inept when it comes to managing colonies.

But what about the aftermath? Did the Irish Free State live up to its promises of being a fair and just society for all? Ha! That's a good one.

The reality was that the Irish Free State was a mess from the start. It was plagued by corruption, sectarianism, and violence. The Republicans who had fought so hard for independence quickly turned on each other, with various factions vying for power. And of course, there was still the problem of Northern Ireland, which remained a British territory and a source of ongoing conflict.

The Irish Free State did eventually become the Republic of Ireland in 1949, but that didn't solve all its problems. It continued to struggle with poverty, inequality, and political instability for many years. And even today, it remains a deeply divided society, with sectarian tensions simmering just below the surface.

So what was accomplished with the Irish War of Independence and its aftermath? Well, the Republicans got a country, sort of. The British got to avoid embarrassment.

And the Irish people got a whole lot of problems that they're still dealing with to this day. Congratulations to everyone involved.

The Greco-Turkish War

The Greco-Turkish War, also known as the Asia Minor Catastrophe, was a conflict fought between Greece and the fledgling Turkish Republic from 1919 to 1922.

After the end of World War I, Greece and Turkey were in a state of political upheaval. Greece was in a state of territorial expansion, while the Ottoman Empire was collapsing.

In May 1919, the Greek army landed in Smyrna (now known as Izmir), a city in western Anatolia with a large Greek population.

The Greek army occupied Smyrna and its surrounding areas, intending to incorporate them into Greece. This action led to the start of the war. Greece, with the backing of the Allied Powers, primarily France, and Britain, was involved in the conflict.

The Turkish Nationalists, led by Mustafa Kemal Atatürk, were fighting to defend their newly established republic. The Ottoman Empire, which was still in existence at the start of the war, was also involved but was quickly defeated.

The Greco-Turkish War ended in 1922, with a decisive victory for the Turkish Nationalists.

In August of that year, the Turkish army launched a counteroffensive against the Greek army, which had advanced deep into Anatolia.

The Turkish army inflicted a crushing defeat on the Greeks, leading to the complete evacuation of Greek forces from Turkey.

The war officially ended with the signing of the Treaty of Lausanne in July 1923, which recognized the sovereignty of the new Turkish Republic and defined its borders.

The exact number of casualties is unknown, but it is estimated that between 200,000 and 500,000 people lost their lives during the conflict.

The war resulted in the loss of Greek territory in Asia Minor and the expulsion of nearly 1.5 million Greeks from Turkey, and around 500,000 Turks from Greece, in a population exchange agreed upon by both governments.

Accomplishments? It all started when Greece decided it wanted a piece of Turkey, and Turkey was like, "Nah, we're good." But Greece wasn't having it and decided to invade anyway. And that's when things got interesting and over underachieving.

Now, you might be wondering what was accomplished in this war. Well, let me tell you, the answer is: not much.

Sure, Greece managed to gain some territory, but it came at a huge cost. Thousands of people died, homes and businesses were destroyed, and both countries were left with a bitter taste in their mouths.

But let's not focus on the negative. Surely there must have been some positive outcomes from the war, right? Well, let's take a closer look.

First of all, the war allowed Greece to flex its military muscles. They had been itching for a fight for a while, and they finally got one. But here's the thing: winning battles doesn't necessarily equate to accomplishing something. The war set Greece back quite a bit.

They had to spend a ton of money and resources on the war effort, which meant less money for other important things, like education and infrastructure.

And let's not forget about the impact on the people. The war was incredibly brutal, and the civilians on both sides suffered greatly.

Many were displaced from their homes and forced to flee to other parts of the country, or even other countries entirely. Families were torn apart, and many people lost everything they had.

So, what was the aftermath of the Greco-Turkish War? Well, it wasn't great. Both countries were left devastated, with huge economic and social problems to deal with.

Greece was left with massive debt, and the country was in shambles. Meanwhile, Turkey was forced to give up a large chunk of its territory, which didn't exactly do wonders for the country's morale.

In the end, the war accomplished very little. Greece gained some land, sure, but at a huge cost. And Turkey was left in a weakened state, with a bitter taste in its mouth. It's hard to say whether either country really "won" the war, but it's safe to say that both countries lost a lot.

In the end, the Greco-Turkish War was a tragic and senseless conflict that accomplished very little.

Hopefully, we can learn from it and avoid making the same mistakes in the future. Nah, we did not!

❧

The Russian Civil War

The Russian Civil War was a multi-factional conflict that lasted from 1917 to 1922. It began after the Russian Revolution of 1917, which saw the Bolsheviks, led by Vladimir Lenin, overthrow the Provisional Government of Russia and establish the first socialist state in the world.

The Civil War was fought between the Bolshevik Red Army and a coalition of anti-communist forces known as the White Army, as well as various other factions and foreign intervention forces.

The conflict began in earnest in 1918, with the formation of the White Army, composed of a range of groups opposed to the Bolsheviks, including former members of the Imperial Russian Army, monarchists, and others.

The White Army received support from several foreign powers, including France, Britain, and the United States, who were wary of the spread of communism.

However, the White Army was plagued by divisions and lacked a unified leadership, which made it difficult to coordinate their efforts against the Bolsheviks.

The Red Army, meanwhile, was led by Leon Trotsky and benefited from a centralized command structure, as well as greater popular support among the working class and peasantry.

They also received aid from the newly formed Soviet Union's allies, such as the newly established Communist Party of China.

The war was marked by brutal fighting, including massacres of civilians, and resulted in millions of deaths from combat, famine, and disease.

The total number of casualties is estimated to be between 7 and 12 million, including military and civilian deaths.

The Red Army emerged victorious in 1922, with the defeat of the last significant White Army forces in Siberia.

The aftermath of the war saw the consolidation of power by the Bolsheviks, the establishment of the Soviet Union, and the beginning of a period of authoritarian rule known as the Red Terror.

So, what was accomplished with the Russian Civil War? Well, let's see. The Bolsheviks emerged victorious, thanks in part to the disorganization and infighting of the various White armies.

So, in a sense, the Communist Party got to take over the country and establish a dictatorship under the guise of "proletarian revolution". Yay?

But what about the cost? Oh, nothing much, just millions of dead, widespread famine and disease, and the destruction of the Russian economy. But hey, at least the Bolsheviks got to call the shots, right?

The aftermath of the Russian Civil War was just as delightful. The Communist Party established a totalitarian regime that repressed political dissent, eliminated free speech and the press, and purged those who opposed the ruling party.

Oh, and let's not forget about the forced labor camps, show trials, and secret police. Such fun!

But, the Soviet Union did accomplish some things. They industrialized the country, built a massive military, and expanded their sphere of influence across Eastern Europe and Asia.

Of course, this was all done through oppressive means, but who's counting? And let's not forget about the cultural achievements.

Soviet cinema, literature, and art produced some truly amazing works, showcasing the talents of artists who were allowed to express themselves within the boundaries of Communist ideology.

And the space program! Who can forget about the first dog in space, or Yuri Gagarin, or the launch of Sputnik? Truly, the Soviet Union was a beacon of progress and innovation.

But let's not get too distracted by the accomplishments, shall we? We must remember that the Soviet Union was a brutal, oppressive regime that ruled through fear and violence.

The legacy of the Russian Civil War lives on in the trauma and suffering experienced by generations of Soviet citizens, and the countless lives lost in the pursuit of a twisted ideology.

So, what was accomplished with the Russian Civil War and its aftermath? Well, the Bolsheviks got to establish their totalitarian regime and rule with an iron fist, millions died, the country was left in ruins, and the Soviet Union became a global superpower with a legacy of oppression and violence.

Quite the accomplishment, don't you think?

The Winter War

The Winter War was a military conflict fought between Finland and the Soviet Union from November 30, 1939, to March 13, 1940.

The war started after the Soviet Union demanded that Finland cede some territory near the Finnish-Soviet border, including the Karelian Isthmus, to create a buffer zone to protect Leningrad from possible attack.

When Finland refused to comply, the Soviet Union launched a massive invasion.

The main belligerents were Finland and the Soviet Union, with other nations assisting with one side or the other. Finland had an army of approximately 300,000 men, while the Soviet Union had over 1 million men.

Despite being heavily outnumbered and outgunned, the Finnish army put up fierce resistance, causing significant losses to the Soviet Union.

The conflict ended with the Moscow Peace Treaty on March 13, 1940, which ceded much of Finland's territory to the Soviet Union, including the Karelian Isthmus.

The Soviet Union suffered an estimated 126,000 casualties, including 25,000 deaths, while Finland suffered an estimated 25,000 casualties, including 3,500 deaths.

Accomplish anything here then? The Winter War was the time when the Soviet Union decided to pick a fight with its little neighbor, Finland.

It was truly a masterclass in military strategy—if the goal was to embarrass oneself on the world stage.

Now, you might think that this would be a cakewalk for the mighty Soviet army, given that Finland had only been an independent nation for a little over two decades and had a much smaller military. But you would be wrong.

The Finns, known for their love of saunas and heavy metal music, were not about to let the Soviets walk all over them. They had a secret weapon: ski troops.

That's right, the Finnish army was filled with expert skiers who could glide through the snowy terrain with ease, while the Soviet soldiers stumbled around like toddlers on an ice rink.

The Winter War quickly turned into a classic case of David vs. Goliath, if David had been armed with snowballs and Goliath had a severe case of frostbite. The Finns used guerilla tactics, setting traps and launching surprise attacks, while the Soviets charged in blindly, assuming their superior numbers and technology would make up for their lack of strategy.

But despite the Finns' valiant efforts, the Soviets eventually overwhelmed them with sheer force and numbers. After a few months of intense fighting, Finland was forced to cede some of its territories to the Soviet Union, but not before giving them a bloody nose and earning the respect of the world.

So, what was accomplished with The Winter War and the aftermath? Firstly, the Soviet Union proved that it was willing to use military force to expand its borders, even at the expense of a smaller, weaker neighbor.

This did not go over well with the international community, and the Soviet Union was harshly criticized for its actions. Secondly, the Winter War demonstrated that the Soviet army was not invincible.

They had been widely regarded as one of the most powerful military forces in the world, but the Finnish resistance showed that even the mightiest army could be defeated by a determined opponent using unconventional tactics.

Thirdly, the Winter War had a profound impact on the Finnish psyche. It solidified their national identity and gave them a sense of pride and resilience that still endures today.

It also gave rise to the famous Finnish concept of sisu, which roughly translates to grit, determination, and perseverance in the face of adversity.

Finally, the aftermath of the Winter War saw Finland cozying up to the West, forming alliances with countries like Sweden and the United States.

This move away from the Soviet sphere of influence had significant geopolitical implications, contributing to the growing tensions between the East and the West during the Cold War.

In conclusion, The Winter War was a fascinating chapter in history, full of bravery, ingenuity, and more than a little bit of foolishness.

It demonstrated that even the underdog can come out on top with the right strategy and determination, and it had far-reaching consequences for the geopolitical landscape of the 20th century. But let's face it, the real winners of the Winter War were the Finnish ski troops. They'll always have a special place in our hearts (and on the slopes).

THE CONTINUATION WAR

The Continuation War was a conflict fought between Finland and the Soviet Union during World War II.

It started on June 25, 1941, when Finland, which had been invaded by the Soviet Union in 1939 in the Winter War, joined Nazi Germany in its invasion of the Soviet Union.

Finland's goal was to regain the territories lost in the Winter War and to secure its borders against further Soviet aggression.

The Soviet Union, on the other hand, sought to eliminate the threat posed by Finland, which it viewed as a potential German ally. The war involved heavy fighting on the Karelian Isthmus, as well as in the Arctic region and the Gulf of Finland.

Finland initially made significant gains, but the Soviet Union eventually launched a massive counteroffensive in 1944, which pushed Finnish forces back to their original borders.

The war ended on September 4, 1944, when Finland signed an armistice with the Soviet Union. The terms of the armistice were harsh, with Finland losing even more territory than it had in the Winter War.

Finland was also required to pay heavy war reparations and expel German troops from its territory. The Continuation War resulted in approximately 63,000 Finnish and 305,000 Soviet casualties.

The war also had significant political consequences for Finland, as it forced the country to re-evaluate its relationship with Nazi Germany and seek closer ties with the West.

Anything eternally accomplished?
The Continuation War was a sad classic in the long and storied history of wars that should have never happened.

It was like a sequel nobody wanted, but Finland and the Soviet Union just couldn't resist the box office draw of another round of conflict.

In the aftermath of the Winter War, the Finns found themselves in a bit of a pickle. They had managed to hold off the Soviet Union for several months, but ultimately, they had to sign a peace treaty that was incredibly unfavorable to them.
The Soviets took a sizable chunk of Finnish territory and forced them to pay reparations.

Now, most reasonable people would look at this situation and say, "Well, that sucks, but let's not poke the bear any further." But not the Finns.

No, they decided that the best course of action was to take advantage of the fact that the Soviets were a little preoccupied with fighting the Germans at the moment and launch another invasion.

The Continuation War began in 1941, and it was a rehash of the Winter War, but with a few extra twists.

The Finns were a little better equipped this time around, thanks to some help from the Germans, but they were still massively outmatched by the Soviet Union.

The war was a slog from start to finish, with both sides taking heavy casualties and making little progress. But the Finns had a secret weapon: their sheer stubbornness.

They refused to back down, even when it became clear that they weren't going to win. They just kept fighting, year after year, until the Soviets finally got tired of the whole thing and signed a peace treaty in 1944.

So what did the Finns accomplish with this war, besides proving that they were good at getting themselves into unwinnable situations? Well, they did manage to hold onto a little bit more territory than they had before. But in exchange, they had to cede even more land to the Soviet Union and pay even bigger reparations.

But hey, at least they got to keep fighting for a few more years, right? And they did manage to score a few victories along the way, like the Battle of Tali-Ihantala, which was the largest battle ever fought in the Nordic countries. So that's something, I guess.

The aftermath of the Continuation War was predictably bleak. The Finns were left with a devastated country, a shattered economy, and a lot of bitter feelings toward the Soviet Union. But hey, at least they had their pride, right? And their stubbornness. Can't forget about that.

In the end, the Continuation War accomplished very little besides causing a lot of unnecessary death and suffering.

It was a war that never should have happened, and one that nobody came out of looking particularly good. But hey, at least the Finns got to show the world just how stubborn they could be.

The Greek Civil War

The Greek Civil War was a conflict fought in Greece from 1946 to 1949 between the Greek government and communist forces. The conflict started after the end of World War II and the withdrawal of German forces from Greece.

The communist forces, supported by Yugoslavia, Bulgaria, and Albania, began a rebellion against the Greek government, which was supported by the United Kingdom and later the United States.

The roots of the conflict can be traced back to the resistance movements against the Axis occupation during World War II, which were often divided between communists and non-communists. After the end of the war, the communist forces sought to gain control of the country, while the government sought to establish a democratic and capitalist state.

The conflict was also fueled by the Cold War, as the Soviet Union supported the communist forces while the Western powers supported the government. The war saw both sides engage in guerrilla warfare, with the communist forces controlling large parts of the country at times.

However, the government forces, with the help of Western aid and military advisers, eventually gained the upper hand and were able to suppress the communist rebellion.

The war officially ended with the signing of the Treaty of Varkiza in February 1949, which saw the communist forces lay down their arms and agree to disband.

The conflict resulted in an estimated 158,000 deaths, with the majority of casualties on the communist side.

War and accomplishment, is that Greek to you? This a perfect example of what happens when two groups of people who can't stand each other are forced to coexist.

It's a story as old as time. And as with any good war, the aftermath is always something to behold. So, let's dive in and see what was accomplished during and after The Greek Civil War.

First things first, let's talk about what the war was actually about. It all started with Greece's occupation by Axis powers during World War II.

After the war ended, the country was left in shambles, with a new government in place that many felt was not representative of the people. As a result, two factions emerged: the Greek government, backed by the United States and Great Britain, and the Greek Communist Party, backed by the Soviet Union.

So, what was accomplished during the war? Well, for starters, Greece became a battleground for the East vs. West power struggle, which is always a fun time.

The United States and Great Britain got to show the Soviet Union who was boss, and the Soviet Union got to flex its muscles and show it wasn't afraid to get involved in the affairs of other countries. So, everyone was a winner, right?

Not so fast. While the United States and Great Britain may have come out on top in terms of ideological superiority, Greece was left in a state of chaos.

The war had caused massive destruction throughout the country, leaving many homeless and without necessities like food and water. It would take years for Greece to recover from the damage done during the conflict.

But wait, there's more! The aftermath of the Greek Civil War is where things get interesting. The government had won the war, but it was left with a population deeply divided between those who had supported the Communist forces and those who had supported the government.

And as we all know, when a country is divided, it's the perfect time for corruption and political maneuvering.

The government, with the help of the United States and Great Britain, implemented a policy of repression and censorship to maintain control over the population. Anyone suspected of being a Communist sympathizer was arrested and often tortured or executed.

But hey, at least the United States and Great Britain could pat themselves on the back for stopping the spread of communism, right? Well, not exactly.

While the Communist forces were defeated in Greece, the ideology continued to spread throughout the world, leading to the Cold War and decades of tension between the United States and the Soviet Union.

So, not much was accomplished.
The war left Greece in ruins, the government in control but unpopular, and the country deeply divided.

The United States and Great Britain may have won a victory in the battle against communism, but the war had already spread far beyond Greece's borders.

But hey, at least we got a good cautionary tale out of it, right? Let this be a lesson to us all: don't let political ideologies divide us, and don't get involved in other countries affairs unless you're willing to deal with the aftermath.

THE MALAYAN EMERGENCY

The Malayan Emergency was a guerrilla war fought in Malaya (now Malaysia) between 1948 and 1960. It was fought between the British colonial government, which was supported by Commonwealth forces, and communist guerrilla forces known as the Malayan Communist Party (MCP).

The conflict began in 1948 when MCP fighters launched a series of attacks against British colonial authorities and non-communist Chinese communities.

The MCP sought to establish a communist state in Malaya, but the British responded by declaring a state of emergency and deploying troops to the region.

The British government launched a counter-insurgency campaign that involved a combination of military force, economic development, and political reform.

They implemented policies designed to win over the Malayan population and isolate the communist insurgents. The campaign was supported by Commonwealth forces, including troops from Australia, New Zealand, and India.

The conflict ended in 1960 with the MCP's surrender, following a decline in support for the insurgency and increased pressure from British forces.

The conflict resulted in an estimated 10,000 casualties, with the majority being MCP fighters and civilians.

The result was the establishment of an independent Malaya in 1957, which later became part of the Federation of Malaysia in 1963.

Accomplish stuff? The Malayan Emergency was one of the most successful examples of how to win a war against insurgents, and by "successful" I mean the ability to sustain it for over a decade without a clear victory in sight.

The British Empire, still reeling from the end of World War II and the loss of its colonies, was determined to maintain control over Malaya, one of its most profitable colonies.

And what better way to do so than by fighting a long, drawn-out war against insurgents?

The British started by declaring a state of emergency, which lasted for twelve years. That's right, twelve years! It was the longest state of emergency in modern history.

During this time, the British employed various tactics, such as population control, curfews, and detention without trial. They also established "New Villages," which were essentially internment camps for the Chinese population suspected of supporting the MCP.

The British army was supported by the Malayan police, who were notorious for their brutality.

The British army was also aided by the Gurkhas, who were known for their loyalty and discipline. But even they couldn't prevent the MCP from waging a successful guerrilla war. The MCP, on the other hand, had a clear objective: to establish a communist government in Malaya.

They were supported by the Chinese community, who were seen as a threat by the British. The MCP was led by Chin Peng, who was known for his tactical prowess and for being a thorn in the British side.

The war was fought in the jungles of Malaya, which gave the MCP a significant advantage. The British army, on the other hand, was ill-equipped and ill-prepared for jungle warfare.

The British army tried various tactics, such as air raids and the use of chemical weapons. However, these tactics proved to be ineffective and only served to alienate the local population.

The British army also employed a strategy of "hearts and minds," which involved winning over the local population through propaganda and bribes.

This strategy was largely unsuccessful, as the local population saw through British propaganda and viewed them as occupiers rather than liberators.

In 1960, the Malayan Emergency was declared over, with the MCP being effectively defeated. However, the cost of the war was immense.

The British had spent billions of pounds on the war effort, and over 10,000 people had been killed, including 4,000 British soldiers.
The war also had a significant impact on the political landscape of Malaya, with the Chinese population being further marginalized.

So, what was accomplished with the Malayan Emergency? Well, the British were successful in preventing the establishment of a communist government in Malaya. But at what cost?

The war also served as a reminder of the brutality of colonialism and the lengths that colonial powers would go to maintain control over their colonies.

In the end, the Malayan Emergency accomplished very little, except for further entrenching the colonial powers in Malaya.

It was a war that should never have been fought, and one that serves as a cautionary tale for the dangers of imperialism and colonialism.

The Mau Mau Uprising

The Mau Mau Uprising was a rebellion against British colonial rule in Kenya that lasted from 1952 to 1960. It is also known as the Kenya Emergency.

The Mau Mau movement was formed by Kenyan nationalists who were unhappy with the social, economic, and political conditions under British colonial rule.

They were especially frustrated by British policies that restricted access to land and political power. The Mau Mau were primarily drawn from the Kikuyu ethnic group, but they also included members from other groups.

The rebellion began in earnest in 1952 with a series of attacks by Mau Mau fighters on British officials, white settlers, and loyalist Africans. The British responded with force, using a combination of military and police units to suppress the rebellion.

They also implemented several policies aimed at breaking the Mau Mau's support base, including forced resettlement and mass internment in detention camps.

The rebellion was marked by brutal violence on both sides, with atrocities committed by both Mau Mau fighters and British forces.

Casualty figures for the conflict vary widely, but it is estimated that tens of thousands of people were killed, including many civilians.

The rebellion was ultimately suppressed by the British, who succeeded in capturing and executing many of the Mau Mau leaders. The rebellion had significant political consequences, however, as it helped to galvanize nationalist sentiment in Kenya and paved the way for the country's independence in 1963.

Accomplished much more? First and foremost, the Mau Mau Uprising accomplished the complete and utter subjugation of the Kikuyu people.

The British put down the rebellion with such force that it effectively broke the will of the Kikuyu to resist. They may have been oppressed before, but now they were truly broken. Congratulations, British Empire, you've successfully quashed any hopes of independence and self-determination among one of your colonies.

Secondly, the Mau Mau Uprising accomplished the establishment a template for future colonial wars.

The British used all sorts of dirty tricks in their fight against the rebels, including torture, forced labor, and concentration camps.

These tactics were so successful that they would later be employed by other colonial powers facing uprisings of their own. So not only did the British quell the rebellion in Kenya, but they also gave other empires a blueprint for how to do the same in their colonies. Talk about efficiency.

Thirdly, the Mau Mau Uprising accomplished a great deal in terms of creating an atmosphere of fear and suspicion.

The British authorities implemented a policy of rounding up anyone who was suspected of being a Mau Mau sympathizer and detaining them without trial. This created a culture of paranoia and terror that lasted for years after the rebellion was quashed.

Anyone who dared to speak out against colonial rule knew that they risked being labeled a Mau Mau and suffering the same fate as those who had taken up arms against their oppressors.

This, of course, made it much easier for the British to maintain their grip on power in Kenya.

Finally, the Mau Mau Uprising accomplished a great deal in terms of propaganda. The British government and media painted the rebels as bloodthirsty savages who were intent on killing innocent civilians.

This, of course, was far from the truth – most of the atrocities committed during the rebellion were perpetrated by the British themselves – but it was an effective way of justifying the brutality of the British response.

By framing the conflict in this way, the British government was able to convince the rest of the world that they were fighting a noble battle against uncivilized barbarians.

So, there you have it. The Mau Mau Uprising accomplished a great deal for the British Empire: the complete subjugation of the Kikuyu people, a template for future colonial wars, an atmosphere of fear and suspicion, and effective propaganda.

Congratulations, British Empire – you truly outdid yourself this time.

The Cold War

The Cold War was a state of political and military tension between the United States and its allies, and the Soviet Union and its allies, which lasted from the end of World War II in 1945 until the dissolution of the Soviet Union in 1991.

The two superpowers never directly engaged in military action against each other, but their conflict played out through proxy wars, espionage, and propaganda.

The two sides of the Cold War were the Western powers, led by the United States and NATO, and the Eastern powers, led by the Soviet Union and the Warsaw Pact.

The two sides engaged in an arms race, with each side seeking to outdo the other in military and technological advances.

While there were no direct military engagements between the United States and the Soviet Union, there were several proxy wars fought between their respective allies.

These included the Korean War, the Vietnam War, and the Soviet-Afghan War. Additionally, both sides engaged in espionage and propaganda campaigns aimed at discrediting the other.

The Cold War had a significant impact on global politics and diplomacy, and it resulted in the deaths of millions of people, including soldiers and civilians.

However, there is no exact number of casualties that can be attributed to the conflict since most of the fighting was done through proxy wars.

The Cold War began in the aftermath of World War II, as the United States and the Soviet Union emerged as the two dominant superpowers.

The rivalry between the two nations was driven by ideological differences, with the United States promoting democracy and capitalism, and the Soviet Union promoting communism.

The Cold War ended with the collapse of the Soviet Union in 1991. The Soviet Union's economic and political instability, combined with the reforms instituted by Soviet leader Mikhail Gorbachev, led to the dissolution of the country.

The end of the Cold War also marked the end of the arms race and the beginning of a new era of cooperation between the United States and Russia.

In conclusion, the Cold War was a state of political and military tension between the United States and the Soviet Union that lasted from the end of World War II until the dissolution of the Soviet Union in 1991.

The conflict resulted in the deaths of millions of people and played out through proxy wars, espionage, and propaganda.

The Cold War began due to ideological differences between the two nations and ended with the collapse of the Soviet Union and the beginning of a new era of cooperation between the United States and Russia.

Giving accomplishment a cold shoulder? A time of geopolitical tension, proxy wars, and nuclear arms races. What a fascinating and productive period of history that was.

First and foremost, the Cold War accomplished the creation of a large and powerful military-industrial complex.

It was great for the economy, as spending on weapons and defense contractors created jobs and pumped money into local communities.

The arms race was a fantastic way to ensure that the rich got richer, and the poor remained poor. Who needs affordable housing and healthcare when we can have missiles and fighter jets?

Of course, the Cold War also saw the creation of some truly iconic moments. Who can forget the Bay of Pigs invasion, where a group of poorly trained and ill-equipped Cuban exiles was sent to overthrow Fidel Castro? That was a masterstroke of foreign policy.

And let's not forget the Vietnam War, where the US spent over a decade trying to defeat a group of farmers armed with AK-47s. That was a resounding success, wasn't it?

The Cold War also gave us the chance to engage in some truly bizarre and absurd activities. Remember when the CIA tried to create an exploding cigar to assassinate Fidel Castro?

Who can forget when they attempted to develop a mind control drug called LSD? What a trip! And let's not forget the time when the US government considered using nuclear weapons to blast a canal through Nicaragua. Who says international politics can't be entertaining?

But the Cold War wasn't all fun and games. It also gave us some of the most intense moments in human history. We had the Cuban Missile Crisis, where the world came dangerously close to nuclear war.
And the Berlin Wall, a physical manifestation of the divide between capitalism and communism.

The Cold War taught us to live in constant fear of the enemy, to always be suspicious of our neighbors, and to never let our guard down.

In terms of lasting impacts, the Cold War created a world that was divided along ideological lines. It was a world where communism and capitalism were pitted against each other, and every country had to choose which side they were on.

The result was a series of proxy wars that spanned the globe, from Korea to Vietnam to Afghanistan. These wars destabilized entire regions, resulted in millions of deaths, and left deep scars that still haven't healed.

The Cold War also saw the rise of espionage and the surveillance state. Governments around the world were spying on their citizens, tapping phones, and intercepting mail. It was a time of paranoia and mistrust, where everyone was a potential enemy.

The effects of this era can still be felt today, with the ongoing debates over privacy and the role of the state in our lives.

So, in summary, the Cold War accomplished a great deal. It created a world that was divided, paranoid, and militarized. It gave us iconic moments and bizarre stories. It taught us to fear and mistrust each other.

And it left a lasting impact on the world, shaping politics, culture, and society in ways that are still being felt today.

Was it worth it? Who knows. But at least we got some cool spy movies out of it.

The Peloponnesian War

The Peloponnesian War was a protracted conflict fought between Athens and Sparta from 431–404 BCE in ancient Greece. The war was named after the Peloponnesian peninsula, where Sparta was located, and it involved numerous Greek city-states and their allies.

The war began when Athens, the dominant naval power in Greece, formed an alliance called the Delian League, which sought to expand Athenian influence and control over the Aegean Sea.

Sparta, a land power, felt threatened by Athens' growing power and formed its alliance, the Peloponnesian League, which included many of the city-states in the Peloponnese. It was fought on land and sea and involved numerous battles, sieges, and alliances.

The early years of the war saw Athens enjoy some early victories, including the successful invasion of the Peloponnese, but eventually, Sparta gained the upper hand.

The war caused significant casualties and suffering on both sides, with estimates suggesting that tens of thousands of people died as a result of the conflict.

Additionally, the war brought economic devastation to Greece, as many cities were destroyed or forced to pay tribute to the victorious power. The Peloponnesian War ended in 404 BCE when Athens was defeated by Sparta in a series of decisive battles. Sparta had succeeded in isolating Athens from its allies and blockading its port, which had been the lifeblood of its empire.

Athens surrendered and was forced to dismantle its long walls and give up its empire, while Sparta became the dominant power in Greece.

In conclusion, the Peloponnesian War was a long and devastating conflict fought between Athens and Sparta from 431–404 BCE.

The war involved numerous Greek city-states and their allies, and it caused significant casualties and economic devastation. The war began due to the rising power of Athens and the fear this instilled in Sparta.

It ended with Sparta emerging as the dominant power in Greece, and Athens was forced to give up its empire and dismantle its long walls.

What is Greek for accomplishment?
The Peloponnesian War—the classic tale of two city-states, Athens and Sparta, engaging in a decades-long feud that left Greece in shambles.

Let's start with the Athenians, shall we? They were the ones who started this whole mess, after all. They had this grand idea that they could create an empire, one that would be the envy of the world. And how did they plan to accomplish this? By attacking their neighbors, of course!
The Athenians were experts at attacking their neighbors.

They attacked the island of Melos, they attacked the city of Syracuse—heck, they probably would have attacked the moon if they thought there was a chance of getting some valuable resources out of it.

And yet, for all their efforts, what did they have to show for it? A devastated economy, a crippled military, and a population so disillusioned with their government that they were ready to revolt at the slightest provocation.

It's almost as if attacking your neighbors isn't the best way to build a successful empire. Who knew?

But what about the Spartans, you might ask? Surely they were the shining beacons of success and accomplishment in this conflict. Well, not exactly. Sure, they won the war in the end, but at what cost?

They lost thousands of their citizens, and the ones who survived were forever scarred by the horrors of battle. And what did they gain from it all? A ruined Athens, sure, but also a Greece that was so weakened by the conflict that it was practically begging to be invaded by outside forces It's almost as if winning a war isn't the same thing as achieving long-term success and stability.

So what was accomplished by the Peloponnesian War? Not a whole lot, if we're being honest. Sure, Athens and Sparta got to duke it out for a while, but at what cost?

Greece was left in ruins, its people disillusioned and divided. And to top it all off, this conflict set the stage for even more conflicts down the road.

Thanks a lot, Athens and Sparta. Way to set a good example for the rest of us.

The War of The Castillian Succession

The War of the Castilian Succession was fought between 1475–1479 between the supporters of two rival claimants to the throne of Castile, a kingdom in what is now modern-day Spain.

The two claimants were Isabella I of Castile and her niece, Joanna la Beltraneja, who was supported by her mother, Queen Joanna of Portugal.

The conflict began after the death of King Henry IV of Castile, who had named Joanna la Beltraneja as his heir, but many Castilian nobles disputed her legitimacy and supported Isabella, who was Henry's half-sister.

The war was fought primarily in Castile, with the support of foreign powers playing a significant role.

Isabella was supported by her husband, Ferdinand II of Aragon, and his kingdom, as well as the Kingdom of Navarre and the Kingdom of Portugal, which initially supported Joanna la Beltraneja but eventually switched sides.

The war saw numerous battles, with significant casualties on both sides, although the exact number is not known.
The war ended in 1479 when Isabella emerged victorious after a series of decisive battles, including the Battle of Toro, which was fought in March of that year.

Joanna la Beltraneja was captured and forced to live in exile in Portugal, while Isabella was recognized as the legitimate queen of Castile.

The war had significant consequences for Spain and Europe. Isabella and Ferdinand went on to unite Castile and Aragon, forming the basis of modern-day Spain, and their reign saw significant religious, cultural, and economic transformations, including the Spanish Inquisition and the discovery of the New World by Christopher Columbus.

King of accomplishment? That classic tale of royal intrigue and bloodshed in medieval Spain. It's a story that's been told countless times, but let's be honest, who doesn't love a good old-fashioned power struggle?

For those of you who may not know, the War of the Castilian Succession was fought between two rival claimants to the throne of Castile in the late 14th and early 15th centuries.

On one side, we had Pedro the Cruel, a ruthless king with a penchant for executing his enemies. And on the other side, we had his half-brother, Henry of Trastámara, a man with a more palatable nickname, "Henry the Bastard."

The war lasted for over a decade and was marked by a series of brutal battles and sieges. But what did all that bloodshed accomplish? Well, let's take a look.

First and foremost, the War of the Castilian Succession helped solidify Spain's reputation as a country that knows how to hold a grudge. I mean, we're talking about a war that was fought over a dispute between two brothers, and it lasted for over ten years. That's some serious dedication to the art of holding a grudge.

But let's not forget about the human toll. The war claimed the lives of thousands of soldiers and civilians and left many more maimed and scarred for life. So, what did all those deaths accomplish? Well, they certainly helped thin the population a bit, which I suppose could be seen as a positive if you're a misanthrope.

And what about the aftermath of the war? Did it bring about any meaningful change or progress? Well, it did establish Henry of Trastámara as the rightful king of Castile, so I guess you could say it accomplished its main goal. But beyond that, the war didn't achieve much.

The aftermath of the war was marked by a period of instability and conflict that would continue for centuries.

The 15th and 16th centuries in Spain were characterized by a series of civil wars, rebellions, and power struggles, many of which can be traced back to the War of the Castilian Succession.

But hey, at least we got some good stories out of it, right? I mean, who doesn't love a good tale of betrayal, intrigue, and battlefield heroics?

And let's not forget about the inspiring speeches that undoubtedly took place before each battle. I'm sure there were plenty of "Once more unto the breach" moments to go around.

So, in conclusion, the War of the Castilian Succession accomplished...well, not much. It was a long and bloody conflict that left a trail of destruction in its wake and set the stage for centuries of instability and conflict in Spain.

But hey, at least it gave us a lot of great material for historical fiction writers, so I guess that's something.

THE WAR OF THE SICILIAN VESPERS

The War of the Sicilian Vespers was a conflict fought between the French Kingdom of Charles of Anjou and the Aragonese Kingdom of Peter III over control of Sicily in the 13th century. The war lasted from 1282 to 1302 and is named after the "Sicilian Vespers," a massacre that occurred in Palermo on March 30, 1282, in which the local population rebelled against their French rulers.

The conflict began when the French king, Charles of Anjou, was invited by the Pope to conquer Sicily and oust its current ruler, the Hohenstaufen king, Manfred. Charles succeeded in defeating Manfred and establishing French control over Sicily in 1266.

However, the Sicilian people were unhappy with their new French rulers, and tensions between the Sicilians and the French grew over the years. In 1282, a group of Sicilian nobles and commoners organized a revolt against the French, which culminated in the "Sicilian Vespers" massacre.

The French were caught off guard and suffered significant casualties, with estimates suggesting that around 8,000 French soldiers were killed. The revolt quickly spread across the island, and the Sicilians proclaimed Peter III of Aragon as their new king. The war continued for two decades, with significant casualties on both sides, although the exact number is not known.

The Aragonese and their Sicilian allies were ultimately victorious, and in 1302, the Treaty of Caltabellotta was signed, which recognized Aragonese control over Sicily and ended French rule.

The War of the Sicilian Vespers had significant consequences for the balance of power in Europe. It weakened the French Kingdom's hold over southern Italy and allowed the Aragonese Kingdom to expand its influence in the region.

The war also had cultural and social consequences, as the Sicilian people developed a strong sense of identity and pride in their island's distinct culture and language.

Accomplished pride then?
One of the most intriguing and entertaining conflicts in history, with a name that sounds like a poorly thought-out cocktail.
First off, we have to acknowledge the brilliance of the name itself.

The "Sicilian Vespers" – what a great name for a war! It sounds both ominous and delicious, like a spooky Italian dessert.

And the best part is, it's based on a real event: a rebellion against the French occupation of Sicily that supposedly started during the evening prayers of Easter Monday in 1282.

Who cares if it's historically accurate or not? It's a catchy name that will stick in people's minds for centuries. But let's move on to what was accomplished during the war.

The main goal of the Sicilian rebels was to expel the French from Sicily, which they accomplished with remarkable speed and efficiency.

The French were forced to abandon the island, and the Sicilian rebels crowned Peter III of Aragon as their new king. So, in a sense, the war accomplished its objective.

However, there were some unintended consequences. The war sparked a wider conflict between the Angevin and Aragonese dynasties that lasted for decades, with both sides vying for control of various Mediterranean territories.

The war also weakened the power of the papacy, which had supported the French in their occupation of Sicily. And let's not forget the toll it took on the people of Sicily, who suffered greatly during the war and its aftermath.

So, in summary, the Sicilian Vespers accomplished the expulsion of the French from Sicily, but at the cost of sparking a wider conflict and causing suffering for the people of Sicily. But hey, at least we got a great name out of it, right?

In terms of the aftermath, the war had some lasting effects on European politics and diplomacy. The Aragonese dynasty gained a foothold in southern Italy and expanded their influence in the Mediterranean, while the French were forced to focus their efforts elsewhere.

The conflict also marked the beginning of a shift in power away from the papacy and towards secular rulers, as the pope's support for the French proved ineffective.

But let's be honest, the real legacy of the Sicilian Vespers is its name. It's been immortalized in countless works of literature and art, from Dante's Divine Comedy to Caravaggio's painting of the event.

It's inspired countless imitations and parodies, from the Scottish Vespers to the Pizza Vespers. And it's just plain fun to say – try it out, it rolls off the tongue!

So, in conclusion, the War of the Sicilian Vespers accomplished the expulsion of the French from Sicily, sparked a wider conflict, weakened the papacy, and caused suffering for the people of Sicily.

But it also gave us one of the greatest names in the history of warfare. So, was it worth it? You be the judge.

The First Italo-Ethiopian War

The First Italo-Ethiopian War was a conflict fought between Italy and Ethiopia in 1895–1896.

Italy, under the rule of King Umberto I, sought to expand its colonial empire in Africa and targeted Ethiopia, which was one of the few independent African nations at the time.

The war lasted from December 1895 to May 1896 and ended in a decisive Ethiopian victory. It began when Italian forces, under the command of General Oreste Baratieri, invaded Ethiopia from Eritrea, which was then an Italian colony.

The Ethiopians, led by Emperor Menelik II, were prepared for the invasion and had assembled a large army equipped with modern weaponry. The Ethiopians launched a surprise attack on the Italian forces at Adwa on March 1, 1896, and decisively defeated them.

The number of casualties is disputed, but it is estimated that the Italian army suffered around 7,000 casualties, including 3,000 dead, while the Ethiopian army suffered around 4,000 casualties.

The Ethiopian victory in the First Italo-Ethiopian War was significant for several reasons.

First, it was a rare example of an African nation successfully defending its independence against a European colonial power.

Second, it boosted the confidence of other African nations in their ability to resist colonialism.

Third, it demonstrated the limitations of European military power in Africa, as the Italians had a technologically superior army, but were unable to overcome the Ethiopian resistance.

Accomplish something!
It's the perfect example of a colonial power thinking they can just walk in and take over a country without any resistance. But as with most things in life, it didn't quite go according to plan.

First off, let's start with Italy's brilliant strategy: invade Ethiopia, take over the country, and add it to their growing colonial empire. Easy peasy, right? Wrong. Ethiopia was not going to go down without a fight.

The Ethiopian forces, led by Emperor Menelik II, had other plans. They were determined to protect their country and their independence, and they had the weapons and tactics to do it.

But Italy was not deterred. They marched forward with their modern weapons and their European-trained army, ready to conquer this African nation.

What they didn't count on was the Ethiopian forces' ingenious tactics, which included using the terrain to their advantage and staging surprise attacks on the Italian troops. This resulted in a humiliating defeat for Italy at the Battle of Adwa, which they had thought would be a sure victory.

So, what did Italy accomplish with this war? Well, they did manage to occupy some parts of Ethiopia for a short period before being driven out. And they did manage to cause a lot of death and destruction in the process. But ultimately, they failed in their goal of colonizing Ethiopia and expanding their empire.

In the aftermath of the war, Italy was left embarrassed and humiliated. They had been defeated by a supposedly inferior African nation, which was a blow to their national pride.

And to make matters worse, other European powers looked down on Italy for its failure, further diminishing its status on the world stage.
But Italy wasn't the only loser in this war.

Ethiopia suffered greatly, with many of its people killed or displaced by the violence. And while they were able to maintain their independence, they were left to rebuild their country after the devastation of the war.

Overall, the First Italo-Ethiopian War accomplished very little. It was a failed attempt at colonial expansion and left both Italy and Ethiopia worse off.

It serves as a reminder that brute force and colonialism are not the answer to problems of national pride and power.

Perhaps someday, we'll learn from the mistakes of the past and find a better way to coexist and collaborate as nations. Or, you know, we could just keep fighting wars for no reason.

That seems to be working out great for us. And there might be a sequel to this depressing Encyclopedia of Wars sooner than later.

SOURCES

As you may have noticed, some of this book is written freely from my satirical memory. However, as any big war nerd, I have had good use of several sources, including:

"The Art of War" by Sun Tzu. This ancient Chinese treatise is a classic on military strategy, written around 5th century BCE, and covers various aspects of warfare and conflict.

"The Peloponnesian War" by Thucydides. This historical account, written by the ancient Greek historian Thucydides, details the famous war between Athens and Sparta in the 5th century BCE, providing insights into the politics, strategies, and tactics of ancient warfare.

"The Campaigns of Alexander" by Arrian. This book chronicles the military campaigns of Alexander the Great, one of history's greatest military tacticians, who conquered vast territories in the 4th century BCE.

"The Gallic War" by Julius Caesar. Written by the famous Roman general Julius Caesar, this book documents his campaigns in Gaul (modern-day France) in the 1st century BCE, providing insights into Roman military strategies and tactics.

"The Art of War" by Niccolò Machiavelli. This Renaissance-era treatise by the Italian writer Niccolò Machiavelli offers advice on warfare and diplomacy, drawing from his experiences as a military strategist and politician.

"The Thirty Years War: Europe's Tragedy" by Peter H. Wilson. This comprehensive book provides an in-depth analysis of the religious and political conflicts that occurred in Europe during the 17th century, known as the Thirty Years' War.

Wikipedia - Comprehensive overview.

"The Napoleonic Wars: A Global History" by Alexander Mikaberidze. This book provides a comprehensive overview of the Napoleonic Wars, which took place during the late 18th and early 19th centuries, and their global impact on Europe and beyond.

"World War I: A Short History" by Michael Howard. This concise book offers a comprehensive overview of World War I, including its causes, major battles, and aftermath, providing insights into the political, social, and military aspects of the conflict.

"The Second World War" by Antony Beevor. This well-researched book provides a detailed account of World War II, including its origins, major battles, and key events, drawing from various perspectives and sources.

"The Forever War" by Dexter Filkins. This modern-day account of conflicts in the Middle East, including the wars in Afghanistan and Iraq, provides a firsthand perspective on the complexities of contemporary warfare and their global impact.

"The Wars of the Roses: The Fall of the Plantagenets and the Rise of the Tudors" by Dan Jones. This book delves into the dynastic wars between the Houses of York and Lancaster in 15th century England, known as the Wars of the Roses, and their pivotal role in shaping British history.

"The Korean War: A History" by Bruce Cumings. This book provides a comprehensive analysis of the Korean War, including its origins, major battles, and political complexities, shedding light on the conflict that shaped the modern Korean Peninsula.

"The Arab-Israeli Wars: War and Peace in the Middle East" by Chaim Herzog. This book offers a detailed account of the various wars and conflicts that have occurred between Israel and its neighboring Arab states, providing insights into the historical and political complexities of the Middle East.

"The Falklands War" by Martin Middlebrook. This book provides a detailed account of the Falklands War, a conflict between Argentina and the United Kingdom over the disputed Falkland Islands in 1982, including the military strategies, tactics, and geopolitical implications of the war.

"The War on Terror: The Oxford Handbook of Terrorism" edited by Erica Chenoweth and Richard English.

United Nations (UN). The UN collects and publishes data on conflicts and wars worldwide through various agencies such as the UN Department of Peace Operations, the UN Office for the Coordination of Humanitarian Affairs (OCHA), and the UN High Commissioner for Refugees (UNHCR). They provide reports, databases, and statistical analyses on conflict-related casualties, displacement, peacekeeping missions, and other relevant information.

World Health Organization (WHO). The WHO gathers data on health impacts of wars and conflicts, including casualties, injuries, and disease outbreaks, as well as providing guidelines and support for health services in conflict zones.

International Committee of the Red Cross (ICRC). The ICRC is an international humanitarian organization that provides assistance to victims of armed conflicts, and they collect and publish data on casualties, displacement, and humanitarian needs in conflict-affected areas.

Stockholm International Peace Research Institute (SIPRI). SIPRI is an independent research institute that conducts research on conflicts, arms transfers, military spending, and peacekeeping, and publishes annual reports and databases with statistics on global military expenditure, arms production, and conflicts.

Uppsala Conflict Data Program (UCDP). UCDP is a research project that collects and analyzes data on armed conflicts, including information on conflicts' duration, actors, and intensity, as well as casualties and other relevant statistics. They provide publicly available datasets and reports on armed conflicts worldwide.

Institute for Economics and Peace (IEP). IEP produces the Global Peace Index, which ranks countries and regions based on their levels of peace and conflict, using various indicators such as violence, political instability, and militarization.

Armed Conflict Location & Event Data Project (ACLED). ACLED is a nonprofit organization that collects real-time data on political violence, including armed conflicts, protests, and riots, and provides detailed datasets and analyses on conflict events worldwide.

Human Rights Watch (HRW). HRW is an international non-governmental organization that monitors human rights abuses in conflicts and publishes reports on casualties, displacement, and other human rights violations in conflict-affected areas.

Amnesty International (AI). AI is a global human rights organization that documents and reports on human rights abuses in conflicts, including casualties, displacement, and violations of international humanitarian law.

Global Database on Violence against Women. This database, developed by the UN, collects data on various forms of violence against women, including conflict-related sexual and gender-based violence, and provides statistics and reports on the issue.

The International Institute for Strategic Studies (IISS)
IISS is a leading think-tank that conducts research and analysis on global security issues, including armed conflicts, military capabilities, and defense spending. They publish annual reports such as the "Military Balance" that provide data on global military forces, weapons, and conflicts.

Global Conflict Tracker by Council on Foreign Relations (CFR)
CFR's Global Conflict Tracker is an interactive online tool that provides up-to-date information on ongoing conflicts around the world, including statistics on casualties, displacement, and other relevant data.

The World Bank
The World Bank collects data on conflicts and their impacts on development, including economic costs, social consequences, and humanitarian needs. They publish reports, datasets, and analyses on conflict-related issues.

Small Arms Survey
Small Arms Survey is a research project that provides data and analysis on small arms, light weapons, and armed violence, including statistics on conflicts, casualties, and weapons proliferation.

Institute of Peace and Conflict Studies (IPCS)
IPCS is a think-tank based in India that conducts research on conflicts, security issues, and peacebuilding efforts in South Asia and beyond. They publish reports and analyses on various aspects of conflicts, including statistics on casualties, displacement, and peace processes.

Stockholm International Peace Research Institute (SIPRI) Yearbook

SIPRI's annual yearbook provides comprehensive data and analysis on global military spending, arms transfers, and conflicts, including statistics on armed forces, weapons, and casualties.

Center for Strategic and International Studies (CSIS)
CSIS is a think-tank based in the United States that conducts research on global security issues, including conflicts, terrorism, and defense policy.

Global Terrorism Database (GTD)
GTD, managed by the National Consortium for the Study of Terrorism and Responses to Terrorism (START) at the University of Maryland, collects and analyzes data on terrorist incidents worldwide, including information on attacks, casualties, and trends.

Institute for Security Studies (ISS)
 ISS is a research institution based in Africa that conducts research on conflicts, security, and governance issues in Africa. They provide analysis, reports, and data on various conflicts and security challenges in Africa.

National and international news agencies - News agencies such as Reuters, Associated Press (AP), Agence France-Presse (AFP), and others provide updated information and statistics on ongoing conflicts, including casualties, displacement, and other relevant data.

Global Database on Events, Language, and Tone (GDELT)
GDELT is a platform that monitors and analyzes news coverage of global events, including conflicts, and provides data on various aspects of conflicts, including location, actors, and tone of coverage.

Armed Conflict Database (ACD) by Uppsala University
ACD is an online database maintained by Uppsala University that provides information on armed conflicts worldwide, including data on conflict-related casualties, displacement, and other relevant statistics.

The Conflict Site - The Conflict Site is an online platform that provides information and statistics on ongoing conflicts, including maps, timelines, and data on casualties, displacement, and other relevant information.

ReliefWeb - ReliefWeb is a humanitarian information platform that provides data and reports on global crises, including conflicts, natural disasters, and humanitarian responses. They publish statistics on casualties, displacement, and other relevant data.

Global Database of Events, Language, and Tone (GDELT)
GDELT is a freely available dataset that provides data on global events, including conflicts, extracted from news articles and other sources. It

includes information on location, actors, and intensity of conflicts.

Humanitarian Data Exchange (HDX)
HDX is an online platform that provides humanitarian data, including data on conflicts, casualties, displacement, and other relevant statistics, contributed by various organizations and agencies.

Institute for Health Metrics and Evaluation (IHME)
IHME provides online databases and visualizations on global health issues, including data on health impacts of conflicts, such as casualties, injuries, and disease burden.

Global Conflict Tracker by Council on Foreign Relations (CFR) - CFR's Global Conflict Tracker is an online tool that provides up-to-date information on ongoing conflicts worldwide, including statistics on casualties, displacement, and other relevant data.

United Nations Data
The United Nations provides various online databases and portals that offer data and statistics on conflicts, peacekeeping missions, casualties, displacement, and other relevant information, which can be accessed through the UN Data portal (data.un.org), the UN Peacekeeping database (peacekeeping.un.org), and other UN agency websites.

Government statistical agencies - Many countries' government statistical agencies, such as the U.S. Census Bureau, the UK Office for National Statistics, and others, provide data on military expenditure, defense personnel, and other related statistics that can be accessed online.
Military History Institute

The Military History Institute (MHI) is a research organization that conducts and publishes scholarly research on military history, including wars and conflicts. They provide access to historical documents, archives, and publications related to various wars and military campaigns.

National Archives and Records Administration (NARA)
NARA is the official archive of the United States government and contains a wealth of historical records related to wars and conflicts, including documents, photographs, maps, and other primary sources.

The Library of Congress has an extensive collection of primary and secondary sources related to wars and conflicts, including historical documents, maps, photographs, and other resources that can be used for research in an encyclopedia.

Historical societies and associations - Historical societies and associations related to specific wars or conflicts, such as the American Civil War Association or the Society for Military History, often publish scholarly journals, newsletters, and other publications.

Government reports and official publications - Government reports and official publications, such as those issued by defense ministries, foreign affairs departments, and other government agencies, have provided valuable information on wars and conflicts, including policy documents, official statements, and statistical data.

Oral history collections - Oral history collections, such as those held by universities, libraries, and museums.

Online archives and digital collections - Many libraries, museums, and research institutions have online archives and digital collections that provided access to historical documents, photographs, maps, and other resources related to wars and conflicts.

It's important to note that data on wars and conflicts can change over time as new information becomes available, and it's always recommended to verify and cross-reference data from multiple reputable sources for accuracy and reliability.

428

Ingram Content Group UK Ltd.
Milton Keynes UK
UKHW040937190523
422019UK00004B/247